THE WORK OF REFORM

THE WORK OF REFORM

LITERATURE AND POLITICAL ECOLOGY FROM LANGLAND TO SPENSER

WILLIAM RHODES

CORNELL UNIVERSITY PRESS
Ithaca and London

Copyright © 2025 by William Rhodes

All rights reserved. Except for brief quotations in a review, this book, or parts thereof, must not be reproduced in any form without permission in writing from the publisher. For information, address Cornell University Press, Sage House, 512 East State Street, Ithaca, New York 14850. Visit our website at cornellpress.cornell.edu.

First published 2025 by Cornell University Press

Librarians: A CIP catalog record for this book is available from the Library of Congress.

ISBN 9781501783241 (hardcover)
ISBN 9781501783258 (paperback)
ISBN 9781501783272 (epub)
ISBN 9781501783265 (pdf)

For Adrian and Marcelo

Contents

Acknowledgments ix

Introduction: Political Ecology and Literary History from Langland to Spenser ... 1

1. Manorial Political Ecology and Passus 6 of *Piers Plowman* ... 22

2. Ecologies of Antifraternalism in *Pierce the Ploughman's Crede* ... 48

3. The Drone and the Sovereign: Labor and Consumption in *Mum and the Sothsegger* ... 68

4. The Political Ecology of Primitive Accumulation in English Reformation Literature ... 91

5. Why Colin Clout Came to Ireland: The *Piers Plowman* Tradition and Spenser's Late Pastorals ... 130

6. Colonial Political Ecology and *A View of the Present State of Ireland* ... 155

Conclusion: Liberatory Dreams and Colonialist Visions ... 170

Notes 179
Bibliography 211
Index 227

Acknowledgments

Of the many exciting things about finishing a book, finally being able to thank the people who made it possible might be the best of all. I was fortunate to work on this project at three institutions full of supportive mentors and colleagues. At the University of Virginia, Elizabeth Fowler, Bruce Holsinger, and John Parker nurtured the earliest version of this project and have remained intellectual inspirations ever since. My time in Virginia was deeply enriched by the community I found in the Graduate Medieval Colloquium, especially during my codirectorship with Rachel Geer. The University of Pittsburgh Humanities Center, under the leadership of Jonathan Arac, was a fantastic place to begin writing this book. I'm grateful to Hannah Johnson, Ryan McDermott, and Jennifer Waldron of the English Department at Pitt for making crucial comments on early phases of the manuscript. In Pittsburgh, I became friends with Danielle St. Hilaire, whose skill as a reader helped me figure out the right shape for the book. Ben Parris became a fast friend shortly after his arrival at the University of Pittsburgh, and his erudition and encouragement lifted me through some of the most challenging phases of writing.

My colleagues in the English Department at the University of Iowa have been exemplary in their support of junior scholars. Eric Gidal, Blaine Greteman, Adam Hooks, and Jon Wilcox each read parts of the manuscript with admirable attention. Their administrative acumen, along with that of Claire Fox and Loren Glass, created a collegial environment in which to finish this book. I'm grateful for the friendly encouragement of my colleagues at Iowa, especially Hannah Bonner, Jen Buckley, Tara Bynum, Eric Ensley, David Gooblar, Ashley Howard, Sarah Minor, Tommy Mira y Lopez, Bennett Sims, Harry Stecopoulos, Travis Vogan, and Stephen Voyce. Elizabeth Rodriguez Fielder has been a great coparent and colleague. Finally, Kathy Lavezzo read every word of the manuscript and has my deepest gratitude for her guidance from the moment I arrived at Iowa.

ACKNOWLEDGMENTS

I'm especially grateful to the University of Iowa's Obermann Center for Advanced Studies, under the leadership of Teresa Mangum, for organizing the BookEnds Workshop. The outside readers for that occasion, Lisa H. Cooper and Katherine C. Little, offered invaluable insights at a crucial stage of the revision of the manuscript. At the beginning of this project, the support of the Medieval Academy of America's Schallek Fellowship gave me a formative year to research and write. The Midwest Middle English Reading Group has been a wonderful place to try ideas and discuss inspiring works in progress, and I'm very grateful to Julie Chamberlin, Ian Cornelius, Julie Orlemanski, Arthur Russell, Tom Sawyer, and Liza Strakhov for their work in building this community. Coworking sessions at various Iowa City coffee shops with Ben Hassmann and Eric Vázquez carried me through the final stages of revising the manuscript.

Throughout the long process of writing this book, I've been sustained by the intellectual friendships I've made along the way. I had the good luck to present alongside Russ Leo at the first conference I ever attended, and he was later generous enough to read drafts of an article that informed chapters 5 and 6 of this book. My first New Chaucer Society Conference gave me the chance to meet Rebecca Davis, who encouraged me to submit my work on *Piers Plowman* to *Yearbook of Langland Studies* in an exemplary gesture of scholarly welcome. Also at this conference I first met Alexis Becker, whose scholarship and companionship have been ongoing sources of inspiration. Conversations with Alastair Bennett, Taylor Cowdery, Harry Cushman, Megan Cook, Daniel Davies, Jennifer Jahner, R. D. Perry, Kellie Robertson, Myra Seaman, Fiona Somerset, Karl Steel, Zach Stone, Spencer Strub, Kathleen Tonry, and Eric Weiskott sparked helpful questions, lifted my spirits, and kept the work going. Shannon Gayk offered generous guidance at key phases of this project, especially as I worked on the book proposal.

Among early modernists, I'm grateful to Namratha Rao, Steve Mentz, and Tamsin Badcoe for organizing panels and conferences that provided key venues to think through Spenser's relationship to earlier English literature and to Ireland. Richard McCabe offered generous feedback on the last two chapters of the book, and conversations with Matthew Harrison, David Hadbawnik, Thomas Herron, Lowell Duckert, Natalie Suzelis, and Tiffany Jo Werth sharpened my thinking over the years about early modern poetry, Tudor Ireland, ecology, and economics.

Puck Fletcher did a fantastic job helping me finalize the manuscript. I'm exceedingly grateful to Mahinder Kingra at Cornell University Press for his support of this project. The anonymous reviewers he found offered careful, incisive feedback that improved the book immensely. All the errors that remain are my own.

And finally, to my parents, Dee and Mac Rhodes, I owe endless thanks for introducing me early to the joys and consolations of books.

Portions of chapter 1 were previously published in W. Rhodes, "Medieval Political Ecology: Labor and Agency on the Half Acre," *Yearbook of Langland Studies* 28 (2014): 105–31. Portions of chapters 5 and 6 were previously published in W. Rhodes, "Why Colin Clout Came Back: English Reformation Literature and Edmund Spenser's Late Work," *ELH* 84, no. 3 (2017): 503–27.

This book was made possible with generous support from the University of Iowa's Office of the Vice President for Research and College of Liberal Arts and Sciences.

THE WORK OF REFORM

Introduction

Political Ecology and Literary History from Langland to Spenser

Events of the fourteenth through the sixteenth centuries in England carry the historiographical burden of inaugurating an epochal shift from the medieval to the modern in political, religious, and literary arenas.[1] More recently, these narratives of transition have been given an explicitly environmental dimension, as changing climate patterns and infectious diseases across Eurasia interacted with commercial and geopolitical tensions to inaugurate what one scholar calls the "great transition," from which England was by no means immune.[2] Yet powerful narratives of continuity have knit together these centuries as well, from accounts of the shared "Renaissance" ambitions of Geoffrey Chaucer and Edmund Spenser to those of the persistent ideals of religious reformers.[3] This combination of ongoing connection and apparent rupture likewise defines the economic and ecological history of the period, as the plague pandemic, the Reformation, and the rise of colonialism punctuate accounts of a continuous period in which the manorial system of rents and services owed to aristocratic landlords persisted while production for markets and wage labor grew. This book focuses on one strand of the literary history of this period—namely, the influence of William Langland's late fourteenth-century poem *Piers Plowman* on the work of Edmund Spenser—as it intersects with the development and change of the agrarian manor from postplague England to Elizabethan Ireland. It seeks to understand how writers imagined drastic social reform by picturing interventions in the fundamental relationship between agrarian land and labor. It builds on the sense of transition that has defined the historiography of the period while stressing the continuities in literary, economic, and environmental history that join Langland's England at the close of the fourteenth century to Spenser's Ireland at the close of the sixteenth.

A host of scholars have shown the centrality of Langland's poem to the formation of Spenser's retrospectively innovative poetics.[4] How does this literary historical narrative interact with the other narratives of political, ecological, and economic transformation that span the fourteenth to the sixteenth centuries? More specifically, how did the particular concern with agrarian land and labor that defines the *Piers Plowman* tradition relate to changes in the economy and ecology of the manorial estate from the outbreak of the bubonic plague through the English Reformation and the Tudor colonization of Ireland, of which Spenser was a primary theorist and undertaker? This book traces how poets in the *Piers Plowman* tradition constructed figures of social transformation in ways that shaped Spenser's early colonial hopes to extend a version of the English manorial economy to Elizabethan Ireland.

The path between Langland and Spenser winds through the influence of *Piers Plowman* on attempts in the following two centuries to imagine the total reform of the church and the kingdom. The endurance of Langland's agrarian allegory, I argue, stems from his attempt to make the manor farm into a kind of microcosm for the social whole in ways that emphasize the interplay of power and nature. Estate management texts, as we will see, theorize the quotidian process of disciplining land and labor in ways that clarify why agrarian toil enabled poetic visions of a remade world. Spenser's Irish career brings out the continuities between the managerial perspective of earlier estate management texts and colonial projects like the Munster plantation that parallel Spenser's poetic engagement with the *Piers Plowman* tradition in his late pastorals. In this introduction, I lay out the scope of these literary archives, justify my broad definition of the *Piers Plowman* tradition, and explain the context and purpose of estate management texts. But before taking up these traditions in greater detail, I consider the implications of this book's periodization of literary and economic history and define some key theoretical terms for its investigation of the interaction of land, labor, and power in agrarian writing from the fourteenth through the sixteenth centuries.

Political Ecology and So-Called Primitive Accumulation: Economic Power, Sovereignty, and Biopolitics

The basic methodological assumption of this book is that the environments constructed in late medieval and early modern literature are the products of deep thought about the historical interaction of human labor with ecological conditions and political structures. My approach to the texts in this book is fundamentally concerned with the way humans have affected their environments through contingent political relations that organize how people work, consume, and distribute what they make, both responding to and shaping ecological relations in the process. One name for this approach to the historical transformation of ecosystems is "political ecology." The term "political ecology" captures both the etymological weight of ecology as the study (*logos*) of the household relations (*oikos*) that make up the manor and the sense that these relations must be managed in ways that support a particular vision of how a polity ought to be composed.[5] In using this term, I draw from a broad theoretical lineage that owes as much to geographers, environmental historians, and scholars of medieval and early modern literature as to the influential work of Bruno Latour and Jane Bennett.[6] In fact, the latter theorists' rejection of the critical frameworks of historical materialism and the analysis of power relations limits their use in a study that traces the colonial implications of the manorial work ethic.[7] By contrast, my approach to political ecology seeks to bring to light the constitutive relationship of the land to the functioning of economic, biopolitical, and sovereign power.

These three overlapping categories of power bring together Marxist and Foucauldian idioms that are not usually seen as compatible, especially because each relies on incongruent periodization narratives that fall somewhat later than the chronological span covered in this book. Nevertheless, this book furthers Richard Halpern's contention that "the histories of discipline and capital might supplement each other."[8] It does so by situating this rapprochement between Michel Foucault and Karl Marx in the fields of the manorial estate rather than in Halpern's humanist classroom. This book finds the complementarity of the history of primitive accumulation and biopolitics in the congruence of the mode of manorial production and Foucault's inclusion in biopolitics' "last domain" of "the direct effects of the geographical, climatic, or hydrographic environment.... And also the problem of the environment to the extent that it is not a natural environment, that it has been created by the population and therefore has effects on that population."⁹ Poets in the *Piers Plowman* tradition, like the writers of manuals on estate management, recognize how the political hierarchy of the manorial estate exerts control over land and labor in ways that reveal the ecological dimension of Marx's and Foucault's theories of economic power, sovereignty, and biopolitics. Marx's account of how the political power of landlords changed the environment in ways that allowed them to exert economic power over workers, as we will see, brings out dynamics that complement Foucault's account of sovereignty and biopolitics. Because the former narrative occurs in the sixteenth century and the latter begins somewhere in the seventeenth, I am using the strongly periodized terms of these two theorists somewhat against themselves to construct another period that is defined by continuities in agrarian ecology and economy from roughly 1300 to 1600—dates which also encompass the *Piers Plowman* tradition's continuous literary investigation of the nature of historical change across the pre- and post-"feudal" and pre- and post-Reformation divides in economic and religious history.

I will briefly consider the political ecology of Marx's account of so-called primitive accumulation before turning to the environmental implications of Foucault's approach to sovereignty and biopolitics. My account of the writing of agrarian land and labor from the fourteenth to the sixteenth centuries traces and complicates a narrative of epochal change developed by Marxist and non-Marxist historians alike.¹⁰ During this period, the system of manorial production on the agrarian estate shaped mercantile activity and regimes of waged labor in a way that belies an absolute rupture between "feudalism" and "capitalism."¹¹ Nevertheless, Marx's narrative of that transition in his chapters on "So-Called Primitive Accumulation" in the first volume of *Capital* establishes a vital conceptual framework for thinking about the combination of land, labor, and power in estate management texts and the *Piers Plowman* tradition. There, Marx sets out to correct conventional accounts of how the essential elements of capitalist production—money to be invested in the production of commodities, and laborers with nothing to sell but their labor power—were first created.

In telling this story, Marx asserts, "[t]he expropriation of the agricultural producer, of the peasant, from the soil is the basis of the whole process," and he concludes that "[o]nly in England" has this process taken "the classic form."¹² As Marx describes the expropriation of the agricultural producer, he locates the growth of "[t]he class of wage-labourers . . . in the latter half of the fourteenth century," before reviewing the 1349 Statute of Laborers as inaugurating a long period of state coercion of labor.[13] The infrastructural complement to this disciplining of waged labor is the movement of land itself into commodity production through enclosure, or the practice of landlords removing agrarian tenants from arable land and blocking access to commons to create pastures for wool-producing sheep.[14]

Marx's account of primitive accumulation offers an approach to historical change that is attuned to the mutual implication of political economy and ecology—how contingent economic conflicts reshape the timeless fact of humanity's relationship to the biosphere. As eco-Marxist theorists have shown, despite Marx's reputation as a Promethean modernizer with no concern for ecological harm, his thought is fundamentally attuned to how the organization of human labor power affects and is affected by the natural world.[15] A key term for this process in Marx's critique of capitalism and its transformation of the labor process is the "metabolic rift," which is John Bellamy Foster's phrase for the disruption of what Marx called "the metabolic interaction [*Stoffwechsel*] between man and nature."[16] The metabolic rift gets a more detailed consideration in chapter 4, but here it clarifies how Marx's account of enclosure is also a description of an incipient ecological crisis that changed the balance of power between laborers and landowners by transforming the population's relationship to the agrarian ecosystem. As Marx argues, once agrarian workers were separated from reliable access to their sustenance, hunger could be counted on to discipline a nascent waged labor force.

Marx's account of how the political power of landlords changed the environment in ways that allowed them to use scarcity to exert economic power over workers brings out dynamics that complement Foucault's account of sovereignty and biopolitics. Marx's wide-angle view of power working through the population's relationship to the land invites more detailed questions about the daily conditions within which people are compelled to earn a living, which Foucault formulated and attempted to answer, albeit of a later historical moment. By attending to techniques of surveillance and discipline at the level of both individual bodily comportment and collective relations to the environment, Foucault narrates the development of power's intervention in the body and its relation to the biosphere in terms of the transition from sovereign power to biopolitics, located some two centuries after the era of so-called primitive accumulation. In Foucault's account of this transition, sovereign power takes the form of the direct application of physical violence to force people to do things; in Foucault's formulation, it is "the right to *take* life or to *let* live."[17] Biopolitics, by contrast, emerges progressively in early modernity, according to Foucault, as power seeks "the administration of bodies and the calculated management of life" through techniques of surveillance and discipline that shape environments to the needs of power and condition "docile bodies" through their "distribution in space."[18] While related to the rise of capitalism in Foucault's account,[19] the rise of biopolitics was distinct: "[T]his was nothing less than the entry of life into history, that is, the entry of phenomena peculiar to the life of the human species into the order of knowledge and power, into the sphere of political techniques."[20] Where Marx emphasizes the ever-present dialectical interplay of general human life processes with the contingent exercise of political and economic power, Foucault alleges the novelty of power's attempt to discipline bodies through their relations to the biosphere.[21] Despite these significant differences in focus, each thinker seeks to grasp how power functions in ways that go beyond force alone.[22] Force remains important for each thinker, and the manifestation of it in the form of sovereign violence likewise remains central to the political ecology of the *Piers Plowman* tradition. But violent coercion is just one path among many that power takes to change how people live and work on the land. Marx's and Foucault's respective conceptualizations of economic power, biopolitics, and sovereignty illuminate the attempts in the *Piers Plowman* tradition to represent forms of power that not only exist in the arm of a sovereign but also dwell in the environment itself and the social relations that shape it.

The *Piers Plowman* Tradition from Langland to Spenser

In seeking to craft holistic visions of society from Langland's postplague England to Spenser's colonial Ireland, poets in the *Piers Plowman* tradition found an essential model in the manorial estate. A manorial estate was made up of discontinuous parcels of land that were cultivated by wage laborers and tenants who paid rents to landlords, while landlords also retained some lands—the demesne—for profitable cultivation. As Langland's imitators adumbrate, any attempt to imagine drastic social and religious reform would have to attend to the ways the manor disciplined human labor and distributed its fruits.

There are both descriptive and normative components of writing about agrarian labor on the manor. A foundational version of the descriptive phase of this mode of thought can be found in passus 1 of *Piers Plowman*, where Holy Church recounts humanity's dependence on "the erthe" and its helpful stores "of wollene, of lynnen, of liflode at nede" or more specifically, "vesture from chele thee to save," "mete at meel," and "drynke whan thow driest."[23] Insofar as humans must work to obtain food, drink, and clothing, this description of humanity's corporeal existence refers to the primal scene of material determination, God's sentence that "*[i]n sudore* and swynke thow shalt thi mete tilie" (B.6.232). But such descriptions of agrarian labor as a way of thinking about humanity's fallen condition raise questions about how that condition should best be endured.

In his *Boke of Husbandry* (1523), the most popular husbandry manual of the sixteenth century, John Fitzherbert takes up the question of what every person is born to do:

> Whervnto is euery man ordeyned. And as Job saythe, Homo nascitur ad laborem, sicut auis ad volandum. That is to saye, a man is ordeined and borne to do labor, as a byrde is ordeyned to flye. And the apostle sayth, Qui non laborat, non manducet: Debet enim in obsequio de laborare, qui de bonis eius vult manducare. That is to saye, he that laboureth not, shulde not eate, and he ought to labour and do goddes warke, that wyl eate of his goodes or gyftes, the whiche is an harde texte after the literall sence.[24]

Fitzherbert finds in the Book of Job and the Epistle of Paul clear authorities for his ambition to describe humanity's fundamental work as agrarian labor. Every person is born to work, and this work ought to be understood at its most basic level as enabling people to eat, as the citation of 2 Thessalonians 3:10 implies: "Qui non laborat, non manducet" ("who does not work let him not eat").

What Fitzherbert puts forward as a descriptive truism immediately introduces a troubling normative dimension, which he registers in his assessment that Paul's injunction is "an harde texte after the literall sence." As Fitzherbert goes on to explain, "For by the lettre the kynge the quene, nor all other lordes spirituall and temporall shulde not eate, without they shoulde labour, the whiche were uncomely, and not conuenyent for suche estates to labour."[25] From what starts as a description of humanity's dependence on work for food, Fitzherbert stumbles upon the problem of what ought to be. Who should labor with their hands and who shouldn't? How can anyone legitimately withdraw from the universal law of toil? Fitzherbert finds that describing agrarian labor provokes uneasy thoughts about hierarchies that divide the burden of labor unevenly.

This movement from the natural to the normative suggests why figures of agrarian labor enable poets from Langland to Spenser to envision a reformed collective life. Such a project involves thinking about the timeless fact of humanity's embeddedness in the biosphere and the timely problems of who should labor and who should eat; of what "lordes spirituall and temporall" should do; and of how the rest of the population should apply its labor to soil, animals, and plants to produce food. The question of what people ought to do as agrarian workers also implies the need for ways to make people toil if they refuse to do so, and this problem brings about the crisis that precipitates the disastrous conclusion of the first major section of *Piers Plowman*.

Piers Plowman survives in what appear to be three distinct versions, called the A-, B-, and C-texts, reflecting decades of revision across roughly the last third of the fourteenth century. The version I will be focusing on is the B-text because it is the one that was edited in 1550 by Robert Crowley, whose work is considered in chapter 4, and it is the version that Spenser would have read, either in Crowley's edition or Owen Rogers's 1561 reprint of Crowley.[26] *Piers Plowman*, in all its versions, is a dream vision made up of sections called passūs (steps) that attempt to navigate the path between daily life and individual and communal salvation. Piers the Plowman first appears in the poem in passus 5 of the B-text as he offers to guide a group of penitents to Truth, but only after they help him plow a half acre of land. This episode, known among critics as the plowing of the half acre, is a pivotal moment that precipitates a crisis that ends the poem's initial vision of communal salvation. Agrarian work at first seems to allegorize the work of attaining salvation, but the scene ends in conflict and famine after a personification named Wastour flouts Piers's demand of work, and Piers responds by calling on Hunger to attack this figure of parasitic idleness. In the wake of this catastrophe, the collective journey to Truth never takes place.[27]

Many of the poem's readers, including its manuscript copyists and early printers, left annotations that attest to their understanding of the poem's relevance to economic problems, and the plowing of the half acre understandably attracted such responses.[28] Sebastian Sobecki has identified a possible link between the plowing of the half acre in the B version and the actions of a Norfolk participant in the rising of 1381.[29] But plenty of early readers did not evince egalitarian sympathies.[30] A sixteenth-century annotator of a C-text manuscript (British Library, Additional MS 35157) comments tendentiously on the plowing of the half acre, "the pore are gluttons in harvest tyme," while Crowley annotates the personification of Hunger in passus 6 with the tellingly instrumental tag, "how begers mai be made to worke."³¹ In these two early modern annotations, we see in miniature a recurring response to the plowing of the half acre as an analysis of how power works through deprivation, where seemingly natural cycles of plenty and dearth intersect with the maintenance of economic stratification.

Interest in the poem's reflections on power and scarcity also accrued around its prophetic passages, especially the one that concludes the plowing of the half acre:

> Whan ye merke the sonne amys and two monkes heddes,
> And a mayde have the maistrie, and multiplied by eighte,
> Thanne shal deeth withdrawe and derthe be justice,
> And Dawe the Dykere deye for hunger.
>
> (B.6.325-28)

This passage was noted as a "prophecie" in a group of C-text manuscripts; was excerpted as a kind of political prophecy in the sixteenth century; and inspired one of the most controversial prophecies of the mid-Tudor period, Thomas Churchyard's alliterative vision *Davy Dycars Dreame* (ca. 1547-1551), which influenced Spenser's approach to ecclesiastical satire in *The Shepheards Calender* (1579).³² In its painful evocation of what it means, both spiritually and materially, to "deye for hunger," the plowing of the half acre provoked readers to think about the eternal implications of their material relations to one another and to the agrarian ecosystem upon which their survival depended.

Some of *Piers Plowman*'s readers extended the effort of connecting this episode to contemporary conflicts by writing poems of their own. Langland almost immediately influenced works that criticized the existing order of the realm in personification allegories that adopted the alliterative style and prophetic ambitions of *Piers Plowman*. These works situate broad complaints about religious and political corruption in relation to specific contradictions within the manorial economy. This can be seen in the antifraternal controversy of *Pierce the Ploughman's Crede* (ca. 1393-1401), the fall of Richard II and rise of Henry IV in *Mum and the Sothsegger* (ca. 1409), the contentious reign of Cardinal Wolsey in John Skelton's *Collyn Clout* (1522), or the aftermath of the dissolution of the monasteries in Robert Crowley's *Philargyrie of Greate Britayne* (1551). Taken together, these texts, among others, establish a Middle English and early modern *Piers Plowman* tradition. At its most narrowly defined, the *Piers Plowman* tradition refers to Middle English alliterative poems from the late fourteenth and early fifteenth centuries that imitate Langland's form and allegorical method, as collected in Helen

Barr's anthology, *The Piers Plowman Tradition*.[33] However, other scholars have defined the corpus more expansively to encompass works written, circulated, and printed through the end of the sixteenth century in a variety of poetic forms or in prose.[34] As will become clear, I rely on an expansive definition of the *Piers Plowman* tradition because it not only registers Langland's persistent influence on early modern literature but also instantiates a continuous mode of thought about how to reorder the economic, ecological, political, and religious forces in the realm.

Piers Plowman continued to resonate with readers who wanted to think through the inseparability of worldly conflicts and spiritual consequences, one of whom was another foundational figure of English poetry, Edmund Spenser. Notwithstanding his self-presentation as the "new Poete," Spenser was deeply influenced by *Piers Plowman* and other works by prominent early and mid-Tudor readers of Langland like Crowley and Skelton, from whom he took the name Colin Clout for his pastoral persona.[35] For all of Spenser's celebration of Chaucer as the "well of English undefiled," his engagements with the *Piers Plowman* tradition are extensive and formative.[36] As A. C. Hamilton puts it, "Langland's poem was the unique Christian poem of epic proportions, and the single 'continued Allegory, or darke conceit,' written in England before his time. . . . Spenser combines Chaucer's literary sophistication with Langland's intense religious spirit, and his affinities are clearly with the latter poet."[37] While Hamilton's judgment of the affinities between Langland and Spenser captures their shared allegorical ambition, Judith Anderson corrects Hamilton's implicit denial of "literary sophistication" to Langland in her comparative study of *Piers Plowman* and *The Faerie Queene*. Anderson describes Spenser's sympathy with Langland's approach to the plowing of the half acre in terms that could apply to all of the poets in this study when she notes "the emphasis on realization, on the present actuality of the historical fact, which brings Langland's treatment of time and of the human will close to Spenser's."[38] As we will see, however, Spenser departs from Langland in the former's positive understanding of hunger as a useful way to realize, in "the present actuality of the historical fact," the hope of controlling another's will. This aspect of *Piers Plowman*—its impact on generations of poets who envisioned drastic changes to the realm through toil enforced by hunger—made the *Piers Plowman* tradition important to Spenser, not just as an ecclesiastical satirist in *The Shepheardes Calender* or as an apocalyptic visionary in *The Faerie Queene* (1590, 1596) but also as a theorist and poet of colonial domination.

A shared use of personification and prophecy ties this expansively defined *Piers Plowman* tradition together. Spenser sought to assert the poet's prophetic capacity to join celestial visions with humanity's embeddedness in economic networks and political hierarchies. In this, he resembles even imitators of Langland he could not have known, like the anonymous writer of *Mum and the Sothsegger*, a work that survives in only a single manuscript and was not printed until 1936. Yet the *Mum*-poet shares with Spenser an ambition to use prosopopoeic visions to connect high political and religious controversies about the nature of royal authority to the primal fact of humanity's dependence on the earth. A prophetic mode of all-encompassing description and correction defines the *Piers Plowman* tradition throughout. Langland's dreamer surveying "A fair feeld ful of folk" (B.Prologue.17) shapes the errant visionaries of the *Crede*- and *Mum*-poets and Skelton's wandering critic, Collyn Clout, while Spenser makes his Colin Clout an inspired prophet of the greatness of Gloriana or Cynthia, both personifications of Elizabeth I, in the late Irish pastorals. *Piers Plowman* fragments circulated as prophesy throughout the sixteenth century, and its prophetic passages were a consistent source of interest among its sixteenth-century readers, like Stephen Batman, whose *Travayled Pylgrime* (1569) influenced Spenser's *Faerie Queene* and who added lines from Langland's prophecy at B.6.327 to a manuscript of the A-version of *Piers Plowman*.[39] Prophetic visionaries were manifestly an essential component of the broad *Piers Plowman* tradition, and Langland's poem was received as prophecy in ways that both inspired and discomfited its readers.[40]

Personification likewise continuously reappears in this book as a way for poets to make visible the relations among land, labor, wealth, and power. Crowley's *Philargyrie of Greate Britayne* shows what the experience of editing *Piers Plowman* taught him about the usefulness of personification for analyzing the ecological and economic transformations of the Reformation. In his discovery of the usefulness of Langlandian personification to make visible diffuse political ecological relationships, Crowley resembles the *Mum*-poet, who finds in Langlandian personification a way to connect the ideals of sovereign authority to the source of its power in agrarian land and labor. Personification ties together the topical with the timeless, the individual with the collective, in ways that bring out how power works according to general patterns and in specific historical conflicts.[41] Prophecy, meanwhile, was an influential framework for thinking through political and ecological turmoil in late medieval and early modern literature.[42] Their combination in *Piers*

Plowman creates an enduring poetic mode for grasping the material relations of society as a whole.

Langland might have first seen the potential for this poetic mode of analysis in *Wynnere and Wastoure*, an alliterative dream vision written about 1352 to 1370.[43] The poem begins with a prophetic prologue describing mysterious signs of encroaching disorder:

> When wawes waxen schall wilde / and walles bene doun
> And hares appon herthe-stones / schall hurcle in hire fourme
> And eke boyes of blode / with boste and with pryde
> Schall wedde ladyes in londe / and lede hem at will,
> Then dredfull domesdaye / it draweth neghe aftir.[44]

The poem's opening engagement with the tradition of political prophecy situates the ensuing debate between Wynnere and Wastoure within an implicit apocalyptic framework that sutures political (dis)order to upheavals in the natural world.[45] Once Wynnere and Wastoure begin trading specific charges against each other, the manorial estate becomes the specific site for the threats to natural and political order that the prologue describes. Wynnere chides Wastoure for his extravagant lifestyle of feasting and luxurious consumption that destroys the manor's agrarian productivity (234–45, 270–93). Wastoure retorts that the excessive consumption of food increases scarcity and raises prices in a way that enables Wynnere's achievements in the realm of business:

> If fewlis flye schold forthe / and fongen be neuer
> And wild bestis in þe wodde / wonne al þaire lyue
> And fisches flete in þe flode / and ichone ete oþer
> Ane henne at ane halpeny / by halfe ȝeris ende;
> Schold not a ladde be in londe / a lorde for to serue.
>
> (384–88)

If animals were simply allowed to live without humans eating them, Wastoure explains, food prices would collapse, and the resulting natural abundance would mean that no servants would bother to work for any lord. This chain of reasoning leads to the poem's most pithy statement of cyclical interdependence:

> þis wate þou full wele / witterly þiseluen,
> Whoso wele schal wyn / a wastour moste he fynde
> For if it greues one gome / it gladdes anoþer.
>
> (389–91)

Any potential winner must find a waster, and grief in one sphere of the economy can redound to one's benefit in another sphere.

This insight about the nature of political economy emerges from the poem's pervasive concern with the relationship between natural abundance and novel forms of wealth and monetary exchange.[46] In Eleanor Johnson's reading, the poem uses the legal form of the trespass trial "to engineer a vision of the interconnectedness of land and monetary wealth."[47] This legal discourse forms a key part of a broader manorial system in which estate management necessitated an ability to perceive the interactions of mercantile activity, money, and the ecology of the estate. If the literature of estate management is one way for medieval writers to think about ecology and economy together, then *Wynnere and Wastoure* shows how personification could do similar intellectual work. The poem clarifies how Langland's use of personification and prophecy shapes the *Piers Plowman* tradition's perception of political ecological relations at moments of conflict over the distribution of resources and labor. These conflicts also defined the discourse of estate management in which the political and economic project of accumulating wealth for investment in cultivation was seen, with special clarity, as a project that required knowing, measuring, and managing ecosystems.

Models of Totality: Estate Management Texts from Walter of Henley to John Fitzherbert

In what follows, I focus primarily on the most widely circulated husbandry manuals and estate management texts in England before the seventeenth century—*Walter of Henley* (ca. 1276–1286) and Fitzherbert's *Boke of Husbandry* and *Surveying* (1523). These texts document the quotidian interactions of agrarian ecology and explain how to measure and quantify them in systems of accounting and surveying. They are literary constructions of an ideal social and ecological whole—the manorial estate—and, as such, they seek to compose material relations imaginatively within a complex, totalizing system. As the treatises think through the interplay of daily labors with enduring social and ecological conditions, they explore the conflicted dynamics of agency and constraint that define the agrarian allegories of Langland and his followers.

Medieval treatises like *Walter of Henley* or the slightly earlier *Seneschaucy* were written as didactic texts for interested landlords and for high officials on a manorial estate, the bailiff and the reeve, who were responsible for accounting for the productive output of the estate's lands and managing the estate's workforce of tenants and hired laborers.[48] *Walter* and *Seneschaucy*, which I deal with in detail in chapter 1, were first written in Anglo-Norman French, but *Walter* later circulated in Welsh, Latin, and English versions, including a fifteenth-century English version printed by Wynken de Worde in about 1510 and a later sixteenth-century translation in manuscript by the antiquary William Lambarde.[49] Fitzherbert's *Husbandry* and *Surveying*, which I consider at greater length in chapter 4, were written in English and were printed in multiple editions until the end of the sixteenth century. *Husbandry*'s twenty editions up to 1598 and *Surveying*'s run of eleven editions indicate their enduring popularity.[50]

Both the thirteenth- and sixteenth-century estate management texts are attuned to the processes of managing land and people to capture profit. Medieval treatises like *Walter of Henley* and *Seneschaucy* were particularly concerned with profitability because they dealt with demesne farming. The demesne was the land that lords cultivated for their own use rather than renting it to tenants. Landlords would invest directly in the infrastructure, labor, and inputs like seed in order to sell the produce for potentially greater revenues than the lord might have received from gathering rent from tenant farmers on the same land. These texts describe the duties of various officers and workers and explain how the quantitative recording of inputs and outputs, management and discipline of workers, and technical knowledge of agrarian and animal husbandry all contribute to the profitable estate.

These aims serve the maintenance of the hierarchy of the estate by making the unpredictable ecological relations of the manor farm into a stable, measurable basis of lordly wealth. Didactic texts on the documentation of a manor's extents, or its productive capacities and revenues, was necessitated by the Statute of Westminster II of 1285, which enabled landlords to bring before law any bailiff or reeve suspected of defrauding them.[51] To prove or refute such a case, both landlords and manorial officials would need careful documentation of a manor's inputs, outputs, and revenues. The *Extenta Manerii* was the official form such documentation had to follow after the statute, and *Walter of Henley*'s inclusion of the form shows that part of the treatise's purpose was to disseminate knowledge of this documentary procedure, which built on earlier practices of surveying an estate's land, rents, and customs.[52] The formalization of these records in the *Extenta Manerii* enabled landlords both to know the productivity of their demesne lands and to judge the competence of their estate managers. It was a form of legally motivated knowledge that empowered landlords to extract surplus from their holdings: "Demesne farming had to show larger returns if it was to be profitable. If this could not be achieved, either the estate was not suitable for intensive farming and ought to be farmed out [i.e., leased to tenants], or its management was at fault."[53] With these conjoined economic and administrative aims, a treatise like *Walter of Henley* demonstrates the practical functioning of a total system, the ecology and economy of the manorial estate, in which the productive energy of the earth is transmuted into marketable produce and monetary wealth.

While *Walter of Henley* saw its peak of copying and circulation in the early fourteenth century, by the time of the mid-century outbreak of bubonic plague, treatises like this had become less relevant. The farming of the lord's demesne (also called the seigneurial demesne) grew less common across the fourteenth century because falling prices for agricultural commodities and rising wages, the result of the twin shocks of the famine of 1315–1322 and the plague of 1349, made hiring laborers for the production of goods for the market less profitable.[54] By the mid-fifteenth century, "the bulk of all landlords were rentiers rather than direct producers."[55] Fitzherbert's complementary books of 1523, *Husbandry* and *Surveying*, reflect this changed situation by addressing, in *Husbandry*, the small landowner or independent leaseholder, who would have been directly involved in producing for profit (the latter to pay rent), and, in *Surveying*, the great rentier landlord and his agents. But this change should not be taken as an index of an absolute rupture between a so-called feudal system and an incipiently modern one. Despite the fact that Fitzherbert's books no longer describe production on the seigneurial demesne that *Walter of Henley* does, *Husbandry* contains farming advice that is similar to that of *Walter of Henley*, and *Surveying* contains a translation of the form of the thirteenth-century *Extenta Manerii*.[56] There is continuity in the aims and methods described in the medieval treatises and Fitzherbert's books, even if the specific manorial unit has shifted from the demesne to the freehold or the aggregated lands of an entire estate. Each text traces the ecological interactions of various agrarian practices, they show how to count and record the results of those interactions in the form of crop yields and revenues, and they describe the disciplining of workers within a hierarchy that ensures that the fruits of their labor are adequately accounted for and rendered to the lord of the manor.

Despite, or perhaps because of, their practical orientation, which was largely isolated from "the main stream of academic development" in the later Middle Ages, estate management texts are useful for seeing how abstract ideals of social holism were grounded in practical questions.[57] Insofar as the ideology of the three estates (the proverbial division of those who work, those who fight, and those who pray) might have offered a general picture of the social whole, the literature of estate management tried to account for how such a unity might be forged on a daily basis.[58] Estate management texts attempt to bring together the entangled lives of plants, animals, and people alongside and within the institutional discourses of law and accounting, thereby giving form to a broader social and literary challenge. How can one represent, for the purposes of instruction and improvement, the manor as a totality: An agrarian ecosystem? A political structure? An economic relationship? How can a text give a sense of ordered priorities to a complex system in which disparate activities and forces are always interacting?

The interdependent system of the manor served as a ready model for bringing an ineffable, holistic abstraction—the universal church, the nation—to the ground level of how society produces and reproduces itself through labor, from Langland's vision of the "fair feeld ful of folk" to Spenser's all-encompassing constructions of Irish political ecology. In this sense, both estate management texts and the *Piers Plowman* tradition can be seen as sites where the concept of totality has tarried in its adventures from the ancient Greeks to the Western Marxists.[59] The discourse of estate management is an earthy, quotidian parallel to another mode of totalizing thought, that of apocalypticism, which had such demonstrable influence on *Piers Plowman*.[60] In its prophetic treatment of manorial land and labor, *Piers Plowman* activates the tension between a descriptive holism that accounts for all relations in an unchanging, naturalized totality and a critical one that seeks a transformed social whole in the unfolding of historical time.

Political Ecology from Estate Management to the English Plantation in Ireland

The ambition to link the quotidian processes of social (re)production on the manorial estate to the reform of society as a whole makes the *Piers Plowman* tradition especially generative for an early colonial thinker like Spenser, who theorized how to extend the disciplinary paradigms of the English agrarian estate to Elizabethan Ireland. The need to map and measure the extents and revenues of the manorial estate establishes both an outlook and a series of documentary procedures that were applied to colonized landscapes in Tudor Ireland.[61] This reflects broader processes in which precolonial modes of organizing and exploiting land and labor indelibly shaped colonial practices. As Jason W. Moore observes, the ecological interventions of a nascent capitalist world system did not emerge from nothing but grew from earlier modes of enlisting the earth to further the exploitation of labor power in the creation of exchange value: "At every turn, land (forests, silver veins, fertile soils) was organized by empires, planters, seigneurs, yeoman farmers, and others as a force of production in servitude to the commodity form—as a mechanism for advancing the productivity of labor. Treating the whole of uncapitalized nature as a force of production, early capitalism was able to remake planetary natures in epochal fashion."[62] As Marx emphasized the continuity between late medieval ecological changes wrought by the wool economy and the advent of agrarian capitalism and colonialism, so theorists from Cedric Robinson to Silvia Federici have elaborated the continuities between so-called feudal modes of class domination and colonialism.[63] This continuity consists not only in the hierarchical worldviews of a dominating class projecting itself to new shores but also in the practices of transforming ecosystems and harnessing their energies for the extraction of profit.

In Ireland, the ecological devastation of the second Desmond rebellion (1579-1583) was followed by the establishment of the Munster plantation. This colonial scheme necessitated surveys that sought to define potentially productive landscapes and to redistribute them as plots to English landowners in a project of intertwined political and ecological transformation.[64] Spenser participates in the construction of this colonial political ecology as a settler in the Munster plantation, where "[d]eaths from famine, disease, and the war were so numerous that the province had become 'uninhabited.' "[65] As we will see, Spenser's plan—outlined in *A View of the Present State of Ireland* (1596)—to interrupt strategically the ability of Irish rebels to get food is not only a military strategy but also a way to discipline a potential labor force that would occupy these depopulated lands once Irish resistance had been quelled. Spenser's vision of colonial conquest found support from the technologies of the English manorial system—surveys, extents, and hierarchical labor management—as well as the literary traditions that speculated about how hunger could further the work of reform. As we will see in chapters 5 and 6, colonial thinkers like John Rastell at the beginning of the sixteenth century and Spenser at the end combine an estate manager's perspective on the land as a source of alienable wealth with the work ethic of the *Piers Plowman* tradition.

What *Piers Plowman* and its ramifications in texts like Skelton's *Collyn Clout* and Crowley's *Philargyrie* offer a colonial poet and theorist like Spenser is an image, however ultimately conflicted and futile it may be, of a renewed social order in which everyone is made to work how they should. Even though Langland rejects labor coerced by the personification of Hunger in passus 6 of *Piers Plowman*, many of his readers would find in this a warrant for imagining that changing the population's relationship to the sources of its subsistence could change every aspect of the community. While this outlook may have an oppositional appeal when directed against lordly prelates or greedy landlords, Spenser's Irish writing brings out the latent coloniality of a narrowed vision of work that only finds a particular kind of agrarian toil superior to all other modes of subsistence.

Plan of the Book

The political hierarchies and managerial technologies of the medieval estate are central to the construction of a political ecology that develops and changes across the late medieval and early modern period. As I argue in chapter 1, these literate technologies for managing land and labor shape the representation of agrarian work in *Piers Plowman*. This has enduring consequences for the subsequent tradition's visions of reform as a process of defining workers against idlers and fruitful fields against wastelands. Comparing the discourse of estate management with the episode of the half acre in passus 6 of *Piers Plowman*, I show how Langland imagines the control and reform of the community by intervening in the ecological relations that agrarian labor makes visible. Estate management texts like *Walter of Henley* describe the interplay of ecological conditions and political hierarchies in the production of profitable agrarian surplus for the landlord. Langland responds to the political ecology of the manorial estate by at first affirming hierarchy and discipline, represented by the unleashing of Hunger on the idle workers. But by the end of the episode, this model of collective salvation based on coercive deprivation both fails to prevent future famine and prevents the group organized around the plowing of the half acre from going on their pilgrimage to Saint Truth.

Despite this failure, passus 6 envisions collective reform in a way that centers the managerial perspective of the manorial overseer in subsequent attempts to imagine religious and political reform. In chapter 2, I turn to *Pierce the Ploughman's Crede*, the earliest exemplar of the post-Langland *Piers Plowman* tradition. The poem focuses its critique of the fraternal orders on their negative effects on agrarian political ecology, translating timeless, biblical condemnations of wandering and idleness into timely conflicts of the late medieval manorial economy. Where *Piers Plowman* tests and then rejects the possibility that the coercive hierarchies of the manor can model the process of general reform, *Pierce the Ploughman's Crede* embraces the idea that enforced labor can found a renewed religious community. In this way, the mobility and idleness attributed to the friars in antifraternal scriptural exegesis can be transformed into a concrete program of fraternal disendowment. In a consequential revision of *Piers Plowman*'s ambivalent reformism, the *Crede* presents not a contradiction between spiritual flourishing and social and economic hierarchy but rather the strict enforcement of the latter as the precondition for the former.

The maintenance of the realm's productive political ecology involves not only ecclesiastical controversies about the consumption of agrarian wealth but also the realm's political leadership, as chapter 3 demonstrates of *Mum and the Sothsegger*. The poem traces the legitimacy of king and parliament to their inextricable relationship to the political ecology of the manor. In an allegorical dream quest, the narrator hopes to find a truth-telling adviser who can help guide the realm when everyone around the king and the nation's leading institutions are followers of Mum, the personification of fearful silence. These are conventional concerns of the advice-to-princes genre, much like *Pierce the Ploughman's Crede* rehearses familiar tropes from antifraternal exegesis. But as in the earlier poem's coordination of antifraternal tropes with specific figures of agrarian land and labor, *Mum and the Sothsegger* likewise situates high political concerns like the king's relations to parliament within the specific structures that mediate the relationship between land and workers in the manorial system. It does so largely in a dream vision of a garden and a beehive managed by a franklin who destroys any parasites that threaten the productive harmony of his freehold. *Mum and the Sothsegger* sees in the surveillance and discipline of the agrarian workforce a means for the renewal of kingly rule by reestablishing the economic and ecological base of royal power. Both the *Crede* and *Mum* exemplify how, within a few decades of *Piers Plowman*'s initial circulation, its allegorical approach to agrarian political ecology enabled poets to move conventional critiques of church and state to solutions based on the violent intervention of the sovereign in the relationship between workers and the land.

The figure of the sovereign who drives parasites from a dysfunctional agrarian political ecology likewise shapes Tudor writers' approach to the economic and ecclesiastical tensions of the early sixteenth century. Chapter 4 situates poetic critiques of church wealth in relation to the most popular estate management texts of the sixteenth century, Fitzherbert's *Husbandry* and *Surveying*. Chapter 4 reads Fitzherbert's two books as attempts to resolve the contradictions between the ecological flourishing of the small leaseholder and the economic imperatives of the great landlord. The totalizing diagnoses of social corruption in texts like Skelton's *Collyn Clout* and Crowley's *Philargyrie of Greate Britayne* survey the effects of this political ecological contradiction vis-à-vis ecclesiastical landownership. Despite the intervening events of England's break with Rome and the dissolution of the monasteries, Crowley, like his predecessors in the 1520s, still describes an exploitative political ecology that requires for its correction a militant sovereign who listens to truth-telling poets. In so doing, Crowley, who edited *Piers Plowman* in 1550, extends the use of personification allegory to an analysis of so-called primitive accumulation that presages Spenser's vision of the interaction of literary authority and colonial reform in Elizabethan Ireland.

Chapters 5 and 6 turn to the colonial ramifications of the *Piers Plowman* tradition, whose sixteenth-century manifestations have usually been seen as strictly insular and confessional in their interests. Chapter 5 considers the reemergence of Colin Clout in Spenser's late pastoral poems. This chapter takes seriously the Skeltonic source of the name in Spenser's construction of Irish political ecology in *Colin Clouts Come Home Againe* (1595) and book 6 of *The Faerie Queene*. Not only does Spenser deploy his pastoral persona to comment directly on the crises of colonial war and its effects on agrarian ecology; he also modifies its literary self-consciousness as he seeks to imagine the poet's efficacy as an agent of colonial reform. Spenser constructs his role as a truthful surveyor of the enterprise of the English plantation in Ireland who can speak to Elizabeth at the imperial center, using his vatic authority to inscribe sovereign power on the landscape in a figural enactment of the transformation of Irish land and labor into sources of extractable wealth.

Chapter 6 situates Spenser's *A View of the Present State of Ireland* in relation to the political ecological thought of the *Piers Plowman* tradition. The totalizing perspective of agrarian reformist writing enables the ambitions of the so-called New English class of planters in Elizabethan Ireland to transform every aspect of Irish social life by transforming the relationship between the population and the earth. The aims of rendering the agrarian ecosystem knowable and manageable through textual mediation in the form of tracts like Spenser's *A View of the Present State of Ireland* reprise in a colonial context the construction of manorial political ecology in the *Piers Plowman* tradition. Spenser finds in the *Piers Plowman* tradition a source not only for his famously eclectic poetic style but also for the incipient colonial ideology that would seek to extend the political ecology of the manorial estate to Tudor Ireland.

This book tracks the *Piers Plowman* tradition to construct a period of literary history that spans the usual dividing line of medieval-modern periodization, situated around 1500. It does so to renew our sense of the political ecology of the epochal transitions theorized by Marx and Foucault, shifting them further back in time and showing how writers from the fourteenth to the sixteenth century made sense of the totalizing interactions of land, labor, and power in the production and distribution of social wealth. Both sovereign violence and disciplinary deprivation prove to be central to these attempts to envision how new regimes of work might remake the world. Such visions, reprised in the context of Spenser's Ireland, reveal the persistence of earlier modes of disciplining land and labor within emergent forms of colonial domination, which parallels the dynamic of continuity and change that marks the literary history of *Piers Plowman*'s afterlives in the sixteenth century and beyond.

Chapter 1

Manorial Political Ecology and Passus 6 of *Piers Plowman*

Two related copies of the B-text of *Piers Plowman* from the first half of the fifteenth century, Oxford, Oriel College, MS 79 (O), and Cambridge, University Library, MS Ll.iv.14 (C²), share several marginal annotations, including a quotation of 2 Thessalonians 3:10 next to a verse early in the prologue.[1] The prologue announces the poem's vast social scope in its account of the dreamer's vision "Of alle manere of men, the meene and the riche, / Werchynge and wandrynge as the world asketh."[2] This includes, of course, people who do not labor virtuously, and it is the last two lines of a passage describing such idlers that the annotators address:

> Ac japeres and jangeleres, Judas children,
> Feynen hem fantasies, and fooles hem maketh,
> And had wit at wille to werken if they sholde.
> That Poul precheth of hem I wol nat preve it here:
> *Qui loquitur turpiloquium* is Luciferes hyne
>
> (B.prologue.35–39)

The annotators associate the reference to Paul's preaching with his second epistle to the Thessalonians, in which he admonishes the

Christians there to follow his example and earn their living through manual labor, as they write in the margins here: "Qui non laborat non manducet" ("who does not work, let him not eat"). The annotation gives the condemnation of jesters and gossips a disciplinary edge by implying that such idlers could be made to labor through hunger. In this, the annotators anticipate the pivotal events of passus 6, in which Piers the Plowman, during his first appearance in the poem, calls upon Hunger to make Wastour and all other idlers go back to work after they have refused to join in the collective plowing of Piers's half acre of land. Like these annotators' commentary on "japeres and jangelers," the plowing of the half acre and the figure of Hunger raise urgent questions about how the need to eat intersects with the use of power. While it is proverbial wisdom that hunger represents general necessity and coercion, should this fact be deployed to make specific people toil?[3] And what might be the spiritual liabilities of using hunger in this way?

This chapter argues that the perspective of estate management literature, represented by *Walter of Henley* and *Seneschaucy*, sharpens our view of the unresolved tension in the episode between the vision of collective salvation modeled on a timeless ideal of social hierarchy and the historical conflicts of actual agrarian production. It does so by revealing the extent to which Piers Plowman himself exists in an ambivalent social role that seems to require the exercise of an authority that he cannot ultimately accept. The conflict that ends the plowing of the half acre shows that the figural attempt to fuse spiritual agency and material necessity in the person of Piers Plowman falters on the structures of labor discipline and surveillance that define the political ecology of the manorial estate.

The plowing occurs when a group of people, after hearing a sermon by Reason exhorting penitence, decide to go on a pilgrimage to Saint Truth. At this point, Piers Plowman, in his first appearance in the poem, describes himself as if he were a worker on Truth's manorial estate, and he offers to guide the penitential community to Truth, provided they first help Piers plow his half acre. But the pilgrimage to Truth never takes place. The plowing of the half acre ends in calamitous failure when Wastour rejects Piers's demands that he resume his labor, and Piers responds by calling forth Hunger.

The pivotal moment in the episode's shift from hopeful possibility to painful conflict arrives when Piers signals that his authoritative role as a guide to Truth and organizer of the workforce will require making exclusionary judgments:

> I shal fynden hem fode that feithfulliche libbeth—
> Save Jakke the Jogelour and Jonette of the Stuwes,
> And Danyel the Dees-pleyere and Denote the Baude,
> And Frere the Faitour, and folk of his ordre,
> And Robyn the Ribadour, for hise rusty wordes.
> Truthe tolde me ones and bad me telle it forther:
> *Deleantur de libro vivencium*—I sholde noght dele with hem,
> For Holy Chirche is hote, of hem no tithe to aske,
> *Quia cum iustis non scribantur.*
>
> (B.6.69–76)

Piers promises to grow food—but only for those that "feithfulliche libbeth." Sinners that play dice, visit brothels, wander as friars, or tell dirty jokes will not get food. They will not be written in the book of life. Like a manorial overseer, Piers does not list these idlers in his register of productive workers. This makes theological sense in terms of the allegorical doubling of the combined activity of plowing and pilgrimage: these named figures personify general vices that do not belong with Truth. But in a socioecological sense, pleasure-seeking idlers do not actually disappear when they are dismissed, as the rest of the plowing of the half acre makes clear. This moment marks the beginning of the end of the episode's optimistic fusion of the manorial hierarchy and collective salvation. Piers's denial of food to this catalog of sinners activates the managerial perspective of estate management literature in a way that presages the crisis of Hunger's appearance. As Piers articulates his disciplinary role in separating good workers from feckless idlers, the poem confronts his ambivalent position between being a worker himself and a manager who instrumentalizes hunger to make people work.

The Political Ecology of Estate Management

While estate management texts predate *Piers Plowman* by several decades, they describe a system for managing the relationship between land and people through the techniques of surveillance and discipline that persisted in the postplague context of the late fourteenth century. The attempts of postplague labor legislation to limit workers' wages and mobility could be seen as an intensification of the surveillance and discipline on the lord's demesne that the estate management treatises describe.[4] The basic juridico-political structures of the manorial estate, like its fundamental means of production such as the field and plow, shape William Langland's agrarian imaginary. As Christopher Dyer notes, Langland appears to have "a specialist knowledge of agriculture and in particular of manorial administration, suggested by references to such technicalities as the assessment of amercements . . . and the auditing of a reeve's accounts."[5] While Langland might not specifically allude to the earlier estate management treatises, these texts nevertheless construct a managerial vision of the manor farm that defined the daily conditions of agrarian labor that Langland depicts in passus 6.

This kind of management of workers is usually associated with later periods and the rise of phenomena like the modern military and the school as sites for what Michel Foucault describes as the panoptic functioning of "hierarchical observation" and "normalizing judgment" in the creation of "the political technology of the body."[6] But the profit-oriented production on the seigneurial demesne, or the land the lord retained for his own use to produce agrarian commodities for the market, necessitated close supervision of both land and people, the interface of which Foucault describes as "biopolitics' last domain."[7] But this interface can also be given a Marxian cast, in which labor and land combine to create commodities whose appropriation is assured by both the political domination of the landlord and the economic coercion of the necessity of working for a wage to survive. Estate management texts capture the interaction of different modes of economic and juridico-political power. These forms of power encompass the sovereign domination of landlords nominally backed up by the sword, the biopolitical power of estate managers to intervene in workers' embodied relation to the environment, and the "silent compulsion" of economic power.[8] In their descriptions of the different tasks of the manor farm, the manuals situate workers and managers at the vexed meeting point of political hierarchy, economic relations, and the nonhuman forces that shape the conditions of agrarian production.

The didactic literature of estate management finds its most widely circulated form in the treatises known as *Walter of Henley*, named for its author, and the shorter *Seneschaucy*, as well the *Rules* of Robert Grosseteste.[9] *Seneschaucy* and *Walter of Henley* were written in French, as were the *Rules* following Grosseteste's Latin version. These texts illuminate the best-documented (but relatively narrow) part of the agrarian economy of late medieval England: that of the seigneurial demesne that was run for the profitable production of agrarian commodities as part of the larger unit of the great agrarian estate.[10] By the standards of the later fourteenth century, after the mortality crises of the famine of 1315–1322 and the plague of 1349, the conditions of the late thirteenth and early fourteenth centuries were favorable for landlords to produce agrarian surplus for profitable sale, thanks to a large population, low wages, and high food prices.[11] Though a minority of total agrarian activity, demesne farming represents such a well-recorded site of medieval agrarian production because it depended on documentation and accounting practices that enabled the surveillance and management of land and labor for the lord's profit. Demesne farms were also worked by laborers who were not exclusively employed on the manorial demesne and who brought their own local expertise to the tasks recommended in the husbandry manuals as they moved across the permeable boundary between the lord's demesne and the surrounding landscapes of peasant agrarian production.[12]

To make the most of the favorable conditions for demesne production, a literate professional class of record keepers trained in law and accounting was needed on the great estates, especially after chapter eleven of the Statute of Westminster II (1285) allowed landlords to imprison fraudulent manorial officers who were found to owe to their lords more than they reported receiving. Bringing such a case to law required the written documentation of an estate's assets so that these could be reviewed by auditors for evidence of the estate's efficient or fraudulent management.[13] The profit motive of demesne farming, as Dorothea Oschinsky observes, required not only the know-how of a working farmer but "refinement in supervision and accounting."[14] The treatises could thus either help a clerk with some legal training to grasp the basics of agrarian husbandry, or they could help an experienced agrarian manager grasp the basics of law and accounting.[15] Ensuring the lord's profits through intensive cultivation of the demesne rather than renting out the demesne land to tenant farmers necessitated knowledge that these texts provided. First, a landowner had to know whether the demesne was taking in more income through direct production than through rents. If it was, then the estate officials had to know how to maintain that superior profitability by keeping costs low and ruthlessly avoiding waste. This aim was helped by techniques of agrarian husbandry to improve the soil, increase yields, and care for livestock.[16]

While the beneficiaries of this practical knowledge would have been manorial officers, the treatises assume and articulate a lordly perspective.

In *Walter of Henley*, the treatise is delivered as if it were an address from a father to a landowning son. Part of the implicit goal of these texts is to interpellate its managerial readers into the perspective and interests of the landowner. Walter achieves this by counseling an imagined heir to order his life spiritually and materially by first knowing the worth of his land.[17] The instrument that will allow such self-knowledge is the *Extenta Manerii*, the written form of the survey of an estate's holdings.[18] To live wisely, according to Walter, is to know as precisely as possible "how muche a man may sowe an acre of all manner of grayne. And howe many cattayle you may keepe upon everye manor" ("de cumben hom purra semer une acre de terre de tutz manere de blez; e cumben destor hom purra aver en chescun maner").[19] While the *Extenta Manerii* might help its imagined reader "live wiselye according to God" ("vivez sagement solum dieux"), Walter lacks Langland's interest in probing the precise nature of the relationship between the state of one's soul and managing a manorial workforce.[20] Instead, *Walter of Henley* goes on to adumbrate how to deploy ecological knowledge about a manor in textual forms that calculate its monetary value for potential use in the legal enforcement of the manorial hierarchy.[21] Knowing how to document the manorial extent allows manorial officers to exert finer control over the manor's operations, avoid errors that might make them liable to charges of fraud, and provide evidence for their defense should they ever need it in court.[22]

According to the *Seneschaucy*, the seneschal, or steward, makes a circuit of the lord's estates two or three times a year to "inquire into rents, services, and customary payments which have been concealed and are being withheld" ("enquerer dez rentes de services e de custumes conceles e sustretes"), a project that requires the steward "to know the law of the country so that he can defend actions outside the lord's estate" ("saver la assise du regne pur foreyne bosoynes defendre").[23] The steward seeks to redress the loss of his lord's profits by means of accounting and legal action, but this project necessarily includes an intimate understanding of the land and labor that the lord owns:

> On his first visit to the manors the steward ought to arrange for all the demesne lands, of each manor, to be measured by lawful men. . . . And thereby he can learn how much wheat, rye, barley, peas, and beans and how much dredge and oats one should rightly sow on each acre; and he can thereby see whether the reeve or the hayward charge more seed than is necessary. . . . And he can also

see how many acres ought to be ploughed by boon and by custom throughout the year and how many acres by paid labour. And if there is any cheating in the sowing, ploughing, or reaping he will quickly see it. And he ought to arrange that all the meadows and several pastures are measured by acres so that he may assess the expenses, and may know . . . how much stock can be kept on several pasture and how much on the common; and what improvements could be made.

(Le seneschal deit a sa premere venue as maners fere mesurer trestuz lez demeynes de checun mander de leale gent. . . . E partaunt poet il saver cumbien de furment, de segle, de orge, de poys e de feves, e cumbyen de dragge e de aveynes lem deit par reison semer en checune acre, e partaunt poet lem veer sy le provost ou le hayward acuntent plus en semence ke le dreit. . . . E ausy poet il veer quantes acres deyvent estre arez par an de priere e de custume, e quantes acres purs deners. E sy ly ad nul treget en la semence ou en la arure ou en le syer legerement le apercevera. E il face mesurer tuz lez prees e tute lez pastures severales par acres, e partant poet lem saver lez custages e . . . cumbien de estor lem poet sustenir de la pasture severale, e cumbien de la commune e quel apruement en seit fet.)[24]

The passage moves from the ecological knowledge to be gained by learning the relationship between land and seed and land and livestock to the political arrangements that enable that knowledge to be turned to monetary gain by calculating tenants' customary obligations. This in turn leads to the legal enforcement that ensures the lord's political and economic power by detecting if any workers have "cheated" in the process of planting and harvest and by knowing "the law of the country" in order to pursue the lord's interests both within and beyond the confines of the estate. In this litany of official duties, *Seneschaucy* exemplifies how estate management literature constructs the manor through the gaze of a mobile observer, a surveyor and judge of both the land and its laborers' productivity. This mobile supervisory perspective not only builds an implicit contrast between the roving manorial official and the sedentary laborer whose mobility is always potentially illicit; it also, as we will see in the following chapters, mirrors the role, so familiar in the *Piers Plowman* tradition, of the wandering social critic.

The treatises imagine the provisional control of ecological unpredictability by fixing workers in place both physically and socially. Soil, for example, requires special understanding before it can be effectively plowed and cultivated, but *Walter of Henley*'s treatment of the labor necessary for mixing marl and manure into the earth encompasses both the flow of energy between waste and food and the surveillance of the workers' efficiency. At first, detailed attention to the qualities of the ground blends with attunement to the temporal rhythms of seasons and days:

> Youre doung which is myngled with earthe lay it upon gravelly ground, if you have any. And I will tell you why. The tyme of summer is whoate and the gravell is whoate also and the dung is hot and when theise three heates doe meete together by theire great heate they vexe and burne, after midsomer, the barlie that groweth in gravell; as yowe may see as you goe along by the fieldes in many places. In the evening the earth which is myngled with the doung cooleth the gravel and nourisheth a certeine deawe and thearby the corne is muche saved.
>
> (Les fens qe sunt medlez ove terre les metez sur terre sablunouse, si vous eez. Pur qey? Ieo vous diray. Le tens destee est chaud, e le sablun chaud, e les fens chaudz; e qant les treis chalines ensemblent par la grant chaline si flestrisent les orges apres la seint Johan qe cressent en sablun, si cum vous poez veer la ou vous alez par paise n plusurs lius. Al vesper la terre, qest medlee ove les fens, refreydit le sablun e norrit une rosee e partant est le blee meuz sauve.)[25]

The intricate interplay of physical properties like heat, dryness, and moisture unites the seemingly disparate elements of rock, soil, manure, air, water, and barley in a process of fluctuation and condensation that ultimately results in grain saved from distress in the cool of evening. This detailed account captures an essential feature of manuals like *Walter of Henley*: the frequent recourse to close observation of the smallest actors and events on the farm, animated by a sensuous attunement to physical processes and the vital relations of matter. But such attunement to the ecology of the farm is of a piece with the more obviously disciplinary motives of these texts. As Walter explains,

> when you shal marle or carry doung have a man whome you may truste which shalbe amongste your carters the first day and shall see that they doe theire woorke well and without loytering. And at the ende of that daye viewe how muche they have done and then lett theim aunsweare you so muche woorke every day after unlesse they can shewe youe some certeine cause of hynderance.

(qant vous devez marler ou fens carier eiez un leal homme, de qi vous affiez, qe seit outre les charetters le premier iour e qe il veit ke eus facent ben lur overayne e sans feyntyse. E a la fyn de la jornee veye cumben eus unt fet, e de tant respoignent a chescune iornee sil ne sachent demustrer certeyne desturbance.)[26]

The bailiff must find a worker he trusts, whose output on the first day will set a benchmark against which subsequent days of marling will be judged. If the amount diminishes, the worker better have "some certeine cause of hynderance." Measurement produces not just more detailed accounts but more occasions to discover fraud. As Walter lays out the measurement of bushels at harvest, he warns, "For in heaped measure theare is great deceipte" ("kar au cumble est grant fraude").[27] The repeated emphasis on viewing, detecting, and forestalling fraud conveys the sense of a roving authority figure who maintains the relations of the manorial estate by moving through them.

The *Seneschaucy* likewise combines its account of the managerial duties of the bailiff with descriptions of ecological relationships that threaten the bailiff's managerial efficiency. Sheep ought to be closely watched by shepherds because "they may eat, unless they are watched well, the film of the autumn fog and the small white snails between the two feasts of Our Lady (15 Aug.–8 Sept.), which will cause them to rot and die" ("si pount eles entre lez deuz festes nostre Dame, par maveise garde, manger la teye de la nyule, e lez petiz blaunche limazons, parunt eles purrirunt e murrunt").[28] The arresting interventions of autumnal miasma and poisonous mollusks vivify these estate management texts with the descriptive charge of nature writing. But moments like this sit in tension with the hierarchical management of the workers who make such interactions visible. Fog and snails might cause losses that could see the bailiff legally punished by his lord, despite the bailiff's lack of direct contact with sheep, herder, and pasture. Likewise, even the emotional state of the shepherd is something a reeve or bailiff must observe and judge, Walter warns, for excessive anger could have undesirable economic consequences: "Looke that your sheaphard be not too testye for thorow anger some of the shepe may be harassed wherof they may die. Looke wheather your sheepe goe feading with the shepheard going amongst theim, for if the sheepe goe shunning him it is no signe that he is gentle unto theim" ("Veez qe votre bercher ne seit pas trop irrous, qar par une ire auqune peot estervilement chacee dunt ele purreyt ester perye. La ou les berbis vunt passantz e le bercher vet entre eus, e les berbis vunt eschiwant dunqe nest pas bon sygne qil seit deboneyre a eus").[29]

Walter of Henley recognizes that the dynamic interactivity of the agrarian ecosystem merges physical processes, social relations, and affective states within and among humans and animals. Whether the subject is soil or sheep, these texts join detailed attention to the lateral physical interactions among various human and nonhuman actors on the estate with the vertically ordered surveillance of the manorial workforce.

The stewards, reeves, and bailiffs of the *Seneschaucy* and *Walter of Henley* represent the point at which the estate, as a working unit of land, animals, and human labor, meets the estate as a political hierarchy. These officers maintain a bifocal perspective on both the physical infrastructure of the manor and the labor regime that maintains it. Surveillance, according to the estate management texts, involves not only the *Extenta Manerii* but also the direct observation and disciplining of potential wasters on the manor to keep labor costs low. In the *Seneschaucy*, for example, not only should the steward seek compensation for damaged equipment or infrastructure "from those who are to blame so that his lord may not suffer any loss" ("de ceus ke sunt encupe issinc ke seon seygnur ne perde"), but he should also "dismiss all servants who are not necessary and all servants who do not work well" ("remuer tuz les serianz nyent besoynables e tuz les servagres ky de ryen ne servent").[30] These sorts of strategies required vigilance. For *Walter of Henley*, "bycause that servauntes customarily doe loyter in their woorke it is necessary to lye in a wayte against theire frawde . . . and if they doe not well that they bee reproved and corrected" ("purceo qe seriantz de custume relynquissent en lur overaigne, il est mester de cuntregweyter lur fraude . . . e sil ne facent ben qil seyent repris e chastiez").[31] Likewise, in the *Seneschaucy*, the reeve "should take care that threshers and winnowers do not take corn and carry it away in their dress, boots, shoes, and pockets or in sacks and bags hidden near the grange" ("prenge garde le provost, ke nul batur, ne nule ventresse ne prengne del ble pur aporter en seyn, ne en huise, ne en soulers, ne en burse pantenere, ne en sak, ne en sakelet musce pres de la grange"), while the dairymaid "ought not to allow under-dairymaids or anyone else to take or carry away milk, butter, or cream whereby the cheese will be less and the dairy will lose" ("ne ele ne deit suffrir ke suzdaye ne autre ne prengent, ne hors porte leit, ne bure, ne creme parunt le furmage seit amenuse e la deyrie enpyre").[32] The suspiciously full pocket of a thresher, the broken plough, or the loitering worker are signs of waste for which supervisors must lie in wait.

Losses can also result from the dreaded propensity of workers not to remain in place—an infraction that might be as minor as temporarily leaving one's post to go for a drink but which carries an implicit tendency toward itinerancy or vagrancy. In the *Seneschaucy*'s managerial outlook, mobility has a fundamental relationship to pleasure seeking, which makes it especially suspect, just as Langland's critique of "japers and jangeleres" in the prologue sits in apposition to "Bidderes and beggeres [that] faste about yede" (B.prologue.40). To guard against this tendency to seek out play instead of work, the *Seneschaucy* rules that recreation can happen only after permission and accountability have been secured: "No shepherd ought to leave his sheep to go to fairs, markets, and wrestling matches or to spend the evening with friends or go to the tavern without asking for leave and putting a good keeper in his place" ("Nul bercher ne deit departir de cez berbiz pur aler a feires, ne a marches, ne a lutes, ne a veiles, ne a la taverne sanz conge demander, ne sanz bon gardein de mettre en son liu").[33] The shepherd must first gain permission to leave lest he become invisible to the overseer. The wayward worker threatens to sunder the link between the physical infrastructure of the estate and its productive use. The ultimate duty of the lord with which the *Seneschaucy* concludes is the dismissal of anyone "he will find making a loss or not making a profit," who "ought to answer for their doings and go away" ("ceuz ky il trovera autres damaganz, e nyent apruanz, respoyngent de lur fez e augent a Deu"). In an attempt to soothe the conscience of readers who fire their underlings, the chapter ends with the assurance that such conduct will lead to wealth and power "without committing sin or wrong against anyone" ("saunz peche fere ne tort a nuly").[34] Piers Plowman, as we will see, is far more worried about the spiritual liabilities of maintaining the manorial hierarchy.

The Statute of Westminster II put manorial officers in a risky spot because now they might be imprisoned for losses that were the result of forces beyond their control. As Oschinsky notes, "They might find themselves in the King's prison for inefficiency even if they had not intentionally defrauded their lords."[35] These manuals bring out the unsettling reality of being responsible for something that might not be controllable. They point to a contradiction between human intentions as they are expressed in institutions like the manorial household and the nonhuman forces that exceed those intentions. These texts construct mechanisms for achieving the "power-knowledge" of the reeve through close surveillance, but they cannot avoid its limits.[36] This perspective on agrarian labor as embedded in a set of ecological determinations and legally enforced responsibilities complicates human agency at the very site where it might otherwise seem to be most straightforwardly operative. Langland shares a similar approach to agrarian land

and labor in the plowing of the half acre in his exploration of the limits of managerial power. As passus 6 attests, in the intricate interactions of agrarian political ecology, the consequences of idleness and waste cannot be made to "go away" as easily as the *Seneschaucy* imagines.

Authority and Ecology on the Half Acre

When Piers Plowman first appears in the poem, the personification of Reason has just preached a sermon that admonishes penitents to "Seketh Seynt Truthe, for he may save yow alle" (B.5.57). In response, "A thousand of men" cry out "To have grace to go to Truthe" (B.5.510-12), but these hopeful seekers almost instantly get lost. At this point, Piers arrives and announces, "I knowe hym [Truth] as kyndely as clerc doth hise bokes" (B.5.538). As Steven Justice observes of this moment, "the folk need Piers Plowman to direct and govern them" because they lack "[their] own principle of order, coherence or purpose."[37] Like the variously unruly workers of the husbandry manuals, they need management. Piers's reference to his clerklike knowledge at once marks a difference between manual and bookish toil and acknowledges their complementarity in a way that aligns Piers with the position of a reeve or bailiff. Scholars have expanded our sense of *Piers Plowman*'s participation in various documentary cultures, encompassing sermons, charters, village bylaws, and the rebel letters of 1381.[38] The literature of estate management likewise illuminates a vital aspect of Langland's agrarian allegory.

As Piers turns from a clerk's books to the labors he performs for Truth, he describes how he has worked for Truth for forty years, doing the range of occupations that a reeve would have been responsible for, even if they might not perform the actual tasks:

> I have ben his folwere al this fourty wynter—
> Bothe ysowen his seed and suwed hise beestes,
> Withinne and withouten waited his profit.
> I dyke and I delve, I do that he hoteth.
> Som tyme I sowe and som tyme I thresshe,
> In taillours craft, in tynkeris craft, what Truthe kan devyse.
> I weve and I wynde and do what Truthe hoteth.
> For though I seye it myself, I serve hym to paye;
> I have myn hire of hym wel and outherwhiles moore.
> He is the presteste paiere that povere men knoweth:
> He withhalt noon hewe his hire that he ne hath it at even.

(B.5.542-52)

One way to understand this résumé is that Piers has, over the course of his forty years of service, done all these jobs, which is why he can now serve in a supervisory capacity during the plowing of the half acre. Another possibility is that Piers changes from a manorial plowman at this point in the episode into an independent peasant later in the episode as we move from this introductory speech to the plowing of the half acre.[39] In either case, Piers here grounds his authority upon a lifetime of agrarian labor in a way that is consistent with the conferral of authority within the manorial hierarchy as described in estate management texts. The *Seneschaucy* specifies that "[t]he reeve ought to be elected and presented by the common assent of the whole township as the best husbandman and farmer and as the most suitable person for looking after the lord's interests" ("Le provost deit ester eslu e presente par commun assentement de tute la ville pur le meillor husebonde, e le meillor gainor, e le meillor aprour dez autres").[40] Piers would be a good candidate for such a role, having spent a lifetime planting Truth's seeds, caring for his livestock, maintaining infrastructure, repairing tools, threshing grain, and even weaving cloth. Piers's abiding experience with horizontal agrarian dynamics authorizes his control over a vertical labor hierarchy. Piers is a loyal overseer, who has "waited [Truth's] profit," fulfilling Walter's axiom that "in making of profite they [bailiffs] ought to thynke that the thing is theire owne but in making expence they should thynke it an other mans" ("e qant a pru fere dussent penser de la chose est lur, e qant a despenses fere qe la chose est autrie").[41] At this point, it seems that Piers not only unites spiritual and manual work but also resolves the tension between the manorial hierarchy and the lateral interaction of land and labor.

Piers's initial status as a guide to Truth is inseparable from a detailed and multifaceted working relationship with the earth. Piers directs them past landmarks including a brook, a ford, a croft, two stumps, and a burgh (hill) labeled with unmistakable moral meanings. In the presence of Piers Plowman, the rural landscape changes from the austere emptiness of the "baches and hilles" (B.5.514) to a recognizable place. As Christopher Dyer points out, these landscape details "resemble (when shorn of their allegorical references) a boundary clause of a piece of land in woodland terrain.... The characteristic features of woodland landscapes were dispersed farms and hamlets, irregular and hedged fields, and a mixture of arable, pasture, and wooded land. The inhabitants included many free tenants and a high proportion of smallholders, who lived on wage earning or crafts. This happens to be the type of country that is found in southwest Worcestershire and adjacent parts of Gloucestershire and Herefordshire, around the Malvern Hills."[42] According to Oschinsky, Gloucestershire and Herefordshire are also where Walter of Henley gained his knowledge about farming.[43] This shared landscape shapes *Walter of Henley*'s depiction of specific agrarian practices, and it likewise lends concreteness to Langland's translation of the pilgrim's abstract goal of seeking Saint Truth into an itinerary across the working landscape of the West Midlands. The ford (a humanmade river crossing), the croft (a small enclosed field), and the tree stumps (from clearing woodland) are all landscape features created by work. Piers's intimate familiarity with the land echoes the duties of surveying that a bailiff or reeve would perform, further underscoring Piers's authority as one of Truth's manorial officials.

Once the trajectory of the episode shifts from pilgrimage to work, Piers's regimentation of the community extends beyond the division of agrarian labor described in the manuals, which remains focused on male commoners, to include women and aristocrats. Piers agrees to guide the pilgrims when his verbal directions fail once they help him plow the half acre, but this conditional offer provokes a lady in the group to wonder, "What shoulde we wommen werche the while?" (B.6.8). This question inaugurates the ambitious social architectonics of this part of the episode, in which the tasks of aristocratic and nonaristocratic women are symmetrically arranged around agrarian production. Piers commands:

> "Somme shul sowe the sak," quod Piers, "for shedyng of the whete;
> And ye lovely ladies with youre longe fyngres,
> That ye have silk and sandel to sowe whan tyme is
> Chesibles for chapeleyns chirches to honoure.
> Wyves and widewes, wolle and flex spynneth:
> Maketh cloth, I counseille yow, and kenneth so youre doughtres.
> The nedy and the naked, nymeth hede how thei liggeth,
> And casteth hem clothes, for so comaundeth Truthe.
> For I shal lenen hem liflode, but if the lond faille,
> As longe as I lyve, for the Lordes love of hevene.
> And alle manere of men that thorugh mete and drynke libbeth,
> Helpeth hym to werche wightliche that wynneth youre foode."
>
> (B.6.9–20)

Piers first institutes a gendered division of labor by detailing the textile-based work that the women will do. He further divides the women along class lines, as "lovely ladies with youre longe fyngres" will embroider church vestments, while "Wyves and widewes" must spin flax and wool.[44] The passage concludes with an imperative to ladies to help "alle manere of men . . . that wynneth youre foode." The command to sew and make cloth is treated as a way to achieve reciprocity with men who produce food. The gendered ideology of feminine dependence on masculine labor, separated as it is from the reality of women's work in the period, makes visible the interaction between agrarian ecology and the practice of charity and education, in which the transformation of flax and wool into cloth for the maintenance of "The nedy and the naked" is also a skill that must be taught to "doughtres" as part of the intergenerational maintenance of the social order. This is a totalizing vision, revolving around the plowland, in which women's work is transformed into a charitable and supportive adjunct to the central activity of (male) agrarian toil, which ensures the reproduction of a workforce that in turn produces the food that women eat.

In a similar configuration of the complementary, "trifunctional" work of the three conventional estates (those who work, pray, and fight), masculine aristocratic violence is also cast as a support for agricultural labor.[45] A knight, at first seized with enthusiasm to learn the plow, ultimately takes up his traditional role as defender of the faith and the common people. He is also charged to hunt, an aristocratic activity that depended on the creation of parklands and often entailed the loss of access to wastes, woods, and pasture for the community in which it was practiced.[46] But Langland chooses here to imagine hunting as having a positive ecological impact on the production of food and to diminish any conflicts or resentment over status it may have caused.[47] At first, Piers's exchange with the knight celebrates the interdependence and reciprocity figured by humanity's relationship to the earth and the estates' relationship to each other:

> "By Seint Poul!" quod Perkyn, "ye profre yow so faire
> That I shal swynke and swete and sowe for us bothe,
> And othere labours do for thi love al my lif tyme,
> In covenaunt that thow kepe Holy Kirke and myselve
> Fro wastours and fro wikked men that this world destruyeth;
> And go hunte hardiliche to hares and to foxes,
> To bores and to bukkes that breken down myne hegges,
> And go affaite thi faucons wilde foweles to kille,
> For swiche cometh to my croft and croppeth my whete."
>
> (B.6.24–32)

The conditions that Piers offers join the defense of traditional religion to the defense of the agrarian landscape. Workers and aristocratic hunters are brought together through their complementary interventions in the rural ecosystem. Piers sees hunting and the implied violence against "wastours" as a facet of agrarian husbandry, in which killing pests and parasites is part of cultivation. (The fifteenth-century *On Husbondrie*, for example, has several recipes and techniques for ridding crops of moles, insects, and other infestations.[48]) The knight's hunt, as Piers understands it, promotes the flourishing of human food by destroying its local animal consumers, which resonates ominously with Piers's demand for protection against "wastours." In this episode, the political and economic status of knighthood is rendered in terms of its effects on a local ecosystem and the population's relationship to its life-sustaining energies. Like the women's charitable textile work, the knight's condition is in part defined by his relations with nonworkers—except that, in the case of the knight, those nonworkers are deserving of punishment rather than charity. In this moment of social schematization, the dividing lines of gender and class appear less fundamental than the division between workers and parasitic "wastours," who are vulnerable to the same violence that the knight metes out to crop-damaging beasts. Piers fashions the role of the knight not only as an ideal complement to the laboring estate but also as its sovereign regulator who destroys "wastours" and "wikked men." This ideal knight resembles the lord described in the *Seneschaucy*'s conclusion who will make sure that any wasters of the manor's profits "go away." Likewise, Piers not only represents himself as part of the laboring estate but also as a managerial adjunct to the landowning class of the military aristocracy who must concern himself with the disciplinary mechanisms that enforce norms of labor and consumption. These include not only the sovereign violence of aristocratic protection but also the intermediary structures of the manorial courts.

Such mediating structures appear in a key moment that subordinates the aristocratic violence of the hunting knight to his bureaucratic function of assessing fines. Piers requests of the knight,

> Loke ye tene no tenaunt but Truthe wole assente;
> And though ye mowe amercy men, lat mercy be taxous
> And meeknesse thi maister, maugree Medes chekes.

(B.6.38–40)

The knight is not just the dispenser of sovereign violence in defense of the faith but is also the enforcer of secular justice, surveying tenants and levying fines ("amercy") in keeping with the structures of discipline upheld by the manorial courts. As Dyer notes, revenues through fines for manorial courts actually increased after the plague, despite the reduced population, as "[l]ords whose income from rents was tending to diminish stepped up pressure on local officials to search out breaches of manorial discipline, such as peasants who allowed their animals to stray on to the demesne land, or who failed to carry out their labour services."[49] This allusion to the legal dimension of the knight's aristocratic status situates him within the political ecology of estate management in a way that exceeds his function as a figure of sovereign enforcement. Piers's injunction envisions an ideal representative of the ruling class, sticking to the law while moderately assessing fines, in a way that was read by at least one possible early reader as a not-so-subtle critique of the actual rapacity of lordly privilege.[50] But as the subsequent episode reveals, and as the literature of estate management attests, even a pointedly idealized figure of lordly authority cannot command the array of ecological, economic, social, and psychological forces that unpredictably combine in the process of cultivation.

The knight's inefficacy and eventual disappearance from the episode is in part a comment on the practical dysfunction of the three-estates model under conditions of wage labor, as David Aers and Andrew Cole observe, but it also suggests the episode's progressive recognition that an authoritatively managed ecosystem cannot be achieved.[51] As Eleanor Johnson says of the knight's failure, "the King's law is incapable of putting a stop to waste by compelling work."[52] In passus 6, Langland begins by imagining a world where worker and knight collaborate to maintain, via their complementary functions, a productive agrarian ecosystem in which inequality is imagined away and even the luxury of hunting is reconfigured as a vital part of this ideal ecosystem.[53] But Piers's mention of the knight's role in legal institutions that are just one of several imperfect means of managing the political ecology of the manorial estate punctures the fantasy of the ecological benefits of the hunt. It shifts the knight's social meaning away from the realm of chivalric violence and toward the political hierarchy of the manor. Langland deflates the chivalric fantasy that violence against animals and humans can support the production of food for the population by turning instead to the bureaucratic and economic power that compels labor on the manor, and which Piers wields with growing levels of discomfort.

Piers's roles, both as a guide on a penitential pilgrimage and as a labor overseer, place on him a conflicting set of demands, embodied in his donning work clothes "in pilgrymes wyse" (B.6.57). The promise to at once feed the commune and judge who should be excluded from it (B.6.69–77) introduces a tension that Langland finds irresolvable, and which explodes when Piers sees Wastour. As the episode builds to its catastrophic conclusion, Piers pauses at his plow to survey the workers: "At heigh prime Piers leet the plough stonde, / To oversen hem hymself; whoso best wroghte" (B.6.112–13). In a detail that underscores Piers's managerial status at this point in the episode, his evaluation of who works well is explicitly tied to his future responsibilities of finding workers for the harvest: whoever works best, "He sholde be hired therafter, whan ervest tyme come" (B.6.114). This not only speaks to Piers's need to maintain a reliable workforce but also hints at the latent disciplinary threat for the workers of not being hired again. Piers quickly finds occasion to exercise such power when he sees a group of people who refuse to work: "Thanne seten somme and songen atte nale / And holpen ere this half acre with 'How trolly lolly!'" (B.6.115–16). Piers is enraged by this display of idleness:

> "Now, by the peril of my soule!" quod Piers al in pure tene,
> "But ye arise the rather and rape yow to werche,
> Shal no greyn that here groweth glade yow at nede,
> And though ye deye for doel, the devel have that recche!"
>
> (B.6.117–20)

In an explosion of extraordinary rhetorical violence, Piers raises the threat of starvation to those who "wasten that men wynnen with travaille and with tene" (B.6.133). In so doing, Langland imagines that it is possible to materialize the spiritual distinction between faithful workers and hedonistic idlers by severing the ties between workers and wasters.

After the drinking idlers appear, Piers continues to try to divide society according to judgments of legitimate and illegitimate idleness based on his managerial observations. In response to "faitours" (B.6.121) who pretend to be injured to justify their lack of work, Piers responds,

> "If it be sooth," quod Piers, "that ye seyn, I shal it soone aspie.
> Ye ben wastours, I woot wel, and Truthe woot the sothe;
> And I am his olde hyne and highte hym to warne
> Whiche thei were in this world hise workmen apeireth."
>
> (B.6.129–32)

CHAPTER 1

Piers again emphasizes his long service to Truth and the surveillance he practices as part of the authority such a position confers. The promise that he will "soone aspie" the potential frauds is only the first step in the exercise of managerial power. It must be followed with an intervention that gives Piers's observations material force, which is obtained not by the ineffectual threats of the knight but by the denial of food:

> "Now, by the peril of my soule!" quod Piers, "I shal apeire yow alle"—
> And houped after Hunger, that herde hym at the firste.
> "Awreke me of thise wastours," quod he, "that this world shendeth!"
> Hunger in haste thoo hente Wastour by the mawe
> And wrong hym so by the wombe that al watrede hise eighen.
> He buffetted the Bretoner aboute the chekes
> That he loked lik a lanterne al his lif after.
>
> (B.6.171–77)

This graphic depiction of bodily suffering is a culmination of the dark side of agrarian ecology that lurked in Piers's negotiation with the knight and with the lady, and in his performance of the reeve-like duties of surveillance and discipline. As Aers says of Hunger's grim illumination of the three-estates model of society, "The social paradigm Langland cherishes, despite its universalizing and religious claims, is revealed in a fresh light: it is dependent on material facts like the perpetuation of a minimal subsistence economy, with a peasant population made obedient through living on the brink of starvation."[54] Such an ever-present threat of starvation, in Britton Harwood's words, acts as "an *internal* force—the Hunger that Piers uses for recruiting labor—[which] moves the landless laborer to exchange labor for wages."[55] The poem thus complicates any simple equation of agrarian labor and spiritual merit by calling attention to the problem of economic power—the compelling necessity to work for food when one lacks independent means of subsistence. After Piers's call for Hunger, collective reciprocity is no longer the basis of general social reproduction; it is now a system of relations among different groups of people and the biosphere that can be strategically manipulated to make people behave according to another's will.

Piers wants Hunger to apply his force selectively to just "thise wastours." But Hunger comes from more sources than just the disciplinary deprivation of idlers. He can appear through events that will have more universal effects. Though Piers's initial plan for the half acre involved the exclusion of sinful wasters like Jakke the Jogelour and Jonette of the Stuwes, Langland does not allow such idlers to be excised so neatly from the world of work. This choice shows how far the half-acre episode goes beyond the perspective of the estate management treatises (and Langland's more strident imitators). Where the treatises counsel the dismissal of workers imagined as lazy and incompetent without further thought, Langland characteristically pushes the question to the limit by not allowing anyone, in the end, to be excluded from the precarious web of the agrarian ecosystem. Piers will have to confront the realities of what will become of (and what to do with) the hungry idler.

The physical beating Hunger gives to Wastour and the Bretoner frightens a mass of nonworkers into taking up their tools of toil:

> Faitours for fere herof flowen into berns
> And flapten on with flailes fro morwe til even,
> That Hunger was noght hardy on hem for to loke
> For a potful of peses that Piers hadde ymaked.
> An heep of heremytes henten hem spades
> And kitten hir copes and courtepies hem made,
> And wenten as werkmen with spades and with shoveles,
> And dolven and dikeden to dryve awey Hunger.
>   Blynde and bedreden were bootned a thousand,
> That seten to begge silver, soone were thei heeled;
> For that was bake for Bayard was boote for many hungry;
> And many a beggere for benes buxum was to swynke,
> And ech a povere man wel apaied to have pesen for his hyre,
> And what Piers preide hem to do as prest as a sperhauk.
> And therof was Piers proud, and putte hem to werke
> And yaf hem mete and money as thei myghte deserve[.]
>
> (B.6.183–98)

With flails, spades, and shovels, false beggars and hermits set themselves to work, and this is, apparently, how Piers expected events to proceed after calling on Hunger. No longer refusing food that would otherwise go to horses, like pea husks and bean cakes, workers meekly take what they "deserve." Piers orders them around, finds his orders carried out "prest as a sperhauk," and "therof was Piers proud." From the "tene" ("anger") of finding his authority flaunted by wasters to the pride of finding his authority unquestioned, Langland is here preparing us for a shift in Piers's relationship to Hunger.

The shift begins when Piers questions Hunger in a way that evinces his discomfort with his newfound dominance and the nature of the material conditions that brought it about.[56] Piers's hesitancy and fear after his invocation of Hunger takes the form of searching questions about the difficulty of reconciling coerced labor with the ideal of charity:

> "Ac I preie thee, er thow passe," quod Piers tho to Hunger,
> "Of beggeris and of bidderis what best be to doone?
> For I woot wel, be thow went, thei wol werche ful ille;
> Meschief it maketh thei be so meke nouthe,
> And for defaute of hire foode this folk is at my wille.
> And it are my blody bretheren, for God boughte us alle.
> Truthe taughte me ones to loven hem ech one
> And to helpen hem of alle thyng, ay as hem nedeth.
> Now wolde I wite of thee, what were the beste,
> And how I myghte amaistren hem and make hem to werche."
>
> (B.6.202–11)

Piers moves rapidly from recognizing his "blody brethren" to desiring to know how to "amaistren hem," bringing the inequity inherent in the practice of charity uncomfortably close to charity's instrumentalization as a disciplinary force. Piers realizes that the wills of the poor are not exactly free but are beholden to *his* "wille" when "defaute of hire foode" effectively destroys their agency. This attempt to instrumentalize need endangers his own ability to avoid sin, as Piers recognizes. He knows even nonworkers are his "blody bretheren," and yet he wants to know how he can exercise "maistrie" over them (one of the sources of Haukyn's penitential anguish in passus 14 is his mastery over others [B.14.328]). After Hunger answers him by counseling charity for both deserving *and* undeserving beggars, Piers is still uneasy and asks "Mighte I synnelees do as thow seist?" (B.6.229).[57] Where *Walter of Henley*, or perhaps even the Piers of an earlier moment in the episode, wants to focus on protecting the productivity of the community, ultimate questions of sin and salvation make such delimited goals now seem potentially untenable to Piers after his recognition of his embodied solidarity with his "blody bretheren."

Piers is apparently struggling with a contradiction between his previous understanding that his duty would involve separating sinful idlers from virtuous workers (where he would not provide food for the former) and Hunger's command to feed "alle manere of men" (B.6.223). Hunger seems to be registering the universality of the need to eat as it runs up against distinctions that determine who should and should not be fed. "[A]lle manere of men" need to eat, but how is this general fact integrated into a system that judges who ought to be fed? As Rebecca Davis notes, this is "an astonishing turn" because Hunger briefly becomes "an unexpected advocate of mercy."[58] But this seemingly merciful outlook is also troublingly out of step with Piers's immersion in the embodied experience of labor within an unequal political and economic system. Hunger's attitude is in keeping with his tendency to give counsel based on moral abstractions rather than the concrete detail that Piers, as Truth's reeve, has spent his life minding. Piers, who has always "waited his [Truth's] profit," wonders whether he can sinlessly give as freely as Hunger suggests because the spiritual and material fruits of his labor are not necessarily his to dispense with as he sees fit but rather are beholden to prior relations of property and service. Piers is attuned to the fundamentally alienable nature of the products of agrarian labor that is assumed in the very structure of estate management. He points to the complex entanglements of the manorial economy, while Hunger voices conventional and imprecise saws about charity and work. Hunger, despite his counsel of charitable giving, still goes on to offer a standard defense of the necessity of work, supported with a digest of biblical quotations, starting with the curse of Genesis. He then jumps from a citation of scriptural authority to an appeal to Kynde Wit, which leads to an elision of the distinction between working manually and working spiritually:

> Kynde Wit wolde that ech a wight wroghte,
> Or in dichynge or in delvynge or travaillynge in preieres
> Contemplatif lif or Actif lif, Crist wolde men wroghte.
>
> (B.6.246-48)

Hunger is speaking at a level of generality that cannot match Piers's enmeshment in the political ecology of the half acre.

Although Piers seems satisfied, praising Hunger's "profitable wordes" (B.6.274), the dialogue continues as Piers returns his attention to the bodily pains of starvation and away from Hunger's moral abstractions about the need to do work, any kind of work. Piers requests medical advice—"lechecraft"—of Hunger because "some of my servants and myself bothe / Of al a wike werche noght, so oure wombe aketh" (B.6.253-55). In this request, Piers shares the feeling of famine's pangs with his hungry servants, effectively contradicting Hunger's blunt use of biblical precepts with an appeal to experience: pain from hunger prevents people from toiling, whether that pain is caused by the hunger itself or, as Hunger assumes, by overeating in order to sate hunger. With this question, Piers reminds Hunger that, timeless precepts aside, getting food to assuage hunger pangs is not as simple as waking up and digging a ditch or saying a prayer. One needs to insinuate oneself into a network of ecological and economic relationships in order to make one's labor a means to obtain "liflode" (livelihood, that is, a means of survival). In other words, the text registers here that a system (political, economic, ecological) precedes the actions of any individual laborer such that their labor can be taken up in both its abstract form as an exchange value (for which the worker receives wages) and in its concrete form as a specific set of tasks for the production of agrarian commodities. Not only does this involve a host of climatic and geographical factors converging favorably so that physical toil results in the growth of food. It also means allying oneself with the kinds of ecological expertise and labor management described in husbandry manuals, which itself necessitates inhabiting, and being recognized as inhabiting, the role of worker or clerk and not waster or fraudster. Neither operation can be performed solely through individual action, and, notwithstanding Hunger's moralizing, his effects on the commune demonstrate the futility of isolating the individual virtues of toil from the ecological and economic contingencies of how people work.

As Hunger's words pull away from specificity, his figural embodiment exposes the brute physicality of suffering and points to the concrete experience of famine. Piers can obtain very little food to give to Hunger because he cannot buy "pulettes," "geese," nor "grys," nor does he have any bacon. Instead, he can offer some fresh cheese, curds, oatcake, and vegetables (B.6.279-85). This, as Robert Worth Frank Jr. observes, describes the foods that people ate in order to bridge the "hungry gap" of the agrarian calendar, and it is not only these foods that help Piers bridge that gap but also "a cart mare / To drawe afeld my donge the while the droghte lasteth" (B.6.286-87).[59] Piers collects and gives to Hunger what "al the povere peple" (B.6.291) gather, and it is a list of mostly vegetables and some fruits, not the fine wheat bread available after harvest. Peapods, beans, apples, onions, cherries, and leafy vegetables round out a catalog of foods whose specificity resists Hunger's understanding of work as an isolable matter of individual flourishing or suffering in either "delvynge" or "travaillynge in preieres," as if these truly were equivalent forms of work. Here, the poetics of the list ground general exhortations about work and hunger in a multitude of foods that bespeak specific labor practices, landscapes, and seasons, heightening the tension between work as an abstract desideratum and work as a physical relation of body to world.⁶⁰

This tension points to the impasse that will define the end of passus 6. The work of ploughing and harvesting has been done: we are told that the people's coarse foods appeased Hunger until "new corn cam to chepyng" ("new corn came to market") (B.6.299), but not even the arrival of new grain can bring about a stable conclusion to the episode. Instead, sated workers become idlers again: "tho wolde Wastour noght werche, but wandren aboute," and "Laborers that have no land to lyve on but hire hands / Deyned noght to dyne aday nyght-olde wortes" (B.6.301, 306–7). The narrator chides these newly emboldened, landless workers for wanting fresh food and higher pay (B.6.309–11) and for traducing conventional norms about the endurance of poverty:

> Ayeins Catons counseil comseth he to jangle:
> *Paupertatis onus pacienter ferre memento.*
> He greveth hym ageyn God and gruccheth ageyn Reson,
> And thane corset he the Kyng and al his Counseil after
> Swiche lawes to loke, laborers to greve.
> Ac whiles Hunger was hir maister, ther wolde noon of hem chide,
> Ne striven ayeins his statut, so sterneliche he loked!
>
> (B.6.313–18)

Instead of accepting their poverty, they identify its political dimension, which the narrator claims would never happen "whiles Hunger was hir maister." At this moment, where "Laborers that have no land to lyve on but hire hands," the need to earn wages combines with the laws of "the Kyng and al his Counseil" to enforce an unequal distribution of toil and its products. The narrator now endorses the mastery that Hunger enables over landless workers that curse their betters and grumble against Reason. Against the backdrop of condemnation of worker discontent, the poem shifts to a prophetic register: there will be a future famine brought about through a storm and flood but that also seems to result from the renewed laxity of the laborers. The narrator warns workers to

> wynneth whil ye mowe,
> For Hunger hiderward hasteth hym faste!
> He shal awake thorugh water, wastours to chaste,
> Er fyve yer be fulfilled swich famyn shal aryse:
> Thorugh flodes and thorugh foule wedres, fruytes shul faille[.]
>
> (B.6.319–23)

Obscure signs (the sun between two monks' heads, a time when "a mayde have the maistrie, and multiplied by eighte") augur the day when "shal deeth wirthdrawe and derthe be justice, / And Dawe the Dykere deye for hunger" (B.6.325-27). The prophetic turn is in keeping with Johnson's reading of Hunger as a version of the *Vastator* (Waster) of the prophetic books of the Bible who punishes evildoers at God's behest.[61] Passus 6 concludes with a seeming endorsement of the naturally coercive powers of scarcity. As the first major part of the poem teeters before its collapse in passus 7, when Piers tears Truth's pardon and renounces worldly toil, the enforced labor of hungry, landless workers appears once again as a necessary corrective to the social disorder ostensibly created by idleness and waste, even if "flodes" and "foule wedres" are identified as the primary cause of this future famine.

In this concluding turn, communal spiritual renewal seems inseparable from the political ecology of the manorial hierarchy, in which voices of authority like Piers, Hunger, or the narrator imagine that ecological precarity can be ameliorated by keeping manual workers in place through managed scarcity. Having once brought up and then retreated from the vision of collective salvation based on enforced labor, the conclusion of the first part of the poem moves from an endorsement of Hunger's disciplinary function to Piers's final rejection of worldly toil. In passus 7, Piers renounces a world of work governed by a necessity that blocks the freedom to "do well" or "do evil" (B.7.112-13), and he instead pursues a form of unworldly *ascesis*. The impasse of the pardon and its tearing launches *Piers Plowman* into a new search for what it is to "do well" (and better and best). This quest, like the vision of collective salvation on the half acre, also ends in failure. The figure of Need in the B-text's concluding passus suggests that the breakdown of the Christian community once again emerges from humanity's embodied lack, its condition of dependence on the biosphere and the labor of others, a universal law of toil that exists in tension with society's other economies of financial and legal personhood because "[N]ede ne hath no lawe, ne nevere shal falle in dette" (B.20.10).[62] The poem's attempt in passus 6 to imagine collective salvation in the figural treatment of manorial labor, the basis of England's political economy, falters because surveillance and discipline through deprivation are the political technologies that manage the human relationship to the earth on the manor. The biophysical strictures of being a hungry worker, and thereby a worker tractable to the will of the bailiff or reeve, undermine the positive vision of reciprocity and charitable concern for others that Piers had hoped would be the foundation for a reformed communal life.

But Piers's rejection of the managerial ethos of the manorial economy did not mean that Langland's half acre no longer excited hopes for an ordered world. The world-making project that estate management texts offer their readers is as much a fantasy of holistic ecological and economic balance on the manor as a practical managerial guide. Langland's extension of that fantasy to society as a whole in its overlapping material and spiritual functions in the first part of the plowing of the half acre is convincing enough for many of his early readers to have outweighed its subsequent breakdown. Poets soon began to instrumentalize the insights about land, labor, and power within the manorial hierarchy in their visions of total social reform. In Langland's vision of reeves supervising workers, judging idlers, and allying themselves with figures like the knight who punish such parasites, writers like the anonymous poets of *Pierce the Ploughman's Crede* and *Mum and the Sothsegger* saw a model for how a disordered society could be transformed—and for poetry's role in that process. Poetry could be a documentary guide that decodes corrupted forms of wealth in terms of agrarian land and labor and that directs the sovereign enforcement of work. While the famous *apologia pro vita sua* in the C-text of *Piers Plowman* acknowledges and responds to the charge that writing might not be legitimate work at all by offering qualified affirmations of clerkly existence, poets in the *Piers Plowman* tradition, from the *Crede*-poet to Edmund Spenser, imagine in different ways poetry's ability to complement the managerial documentation of social and ecological disruption. In poems where wandering narrators trace the networks of agrarian political ecology, writing in the *Piers Plowman* tradition makes the relations and processes of a complex whole thinkable and amenable to top-down change. For the subsequent *Piers Plowman* tradition, this function of writing made it an ambivalent but indispensable component of the political ecology of reform.

Chapter 2

Ecologies of Antifraternalism in *Pierce the Ploughman's Crede*

Shortly after *Piers Plowman* began circulating in the late fourteenth century, a corpus of alliterative poems that bear a clear stylistic and thematic relationship to William Langland's poem appears, which critics have dubbed a distinct "*Piers Plowman* tradition."[1] These poems adapt *Piers Plowman*'s alliterative form and use it to explore contemporary political and religious controversies. While poems in the *Piers Plowman* tradition are shorter and less theologically complex than their exemplar, works like *Pierce the Ploughman's Crede* and *Mum and the Sothsegger* respond to another aspect of their poetic model than its nuanced theology or its self-questioning instability—namely, its insistent return to agrarian work to imagine ecclesiastical and political reform. *Pierce the Ploughman's Crede* in particular exemplifies how *Piers Plowman*'s agrarian allegory drives reformist poets to move familiar polemical tropes from the archetypal to the quotidian in its attack on the fraternal orders.

The stereotypical characterization of friars upon which *Pierce the Ploughman's Crede* so frequently relies has led critics to view the poem as if it were merely transmitting a set of received images and epithets for fraternal corruption.[2] In this, it would be representative of a general tendency in antifraternal discourse to reinforce, in Penn Szittya's words, a "medieval perception of the friars . . . more symbolic than realistic, more theological than political or economic, concerned more with what the friars were *sub specie aeternitatis* than with what they actually did in the world."³ But if we see *Piers Plowman*'s allegorical engagement with agrarian political ecology as the primary inspiration for the *Crede*-poet's antifraternal analysis, *Pierce the Ploughman's Crede* demonstrates the inseparability of eschatological exegesis and worldly critique. For example, the poem taps into a long-standing association, made much of in Wycliffite writing, between Cain and the friars. Caim, an alternative Middle English spelling of Cain, was used as an acrostic in Wycliffite polemic to associate the four fraternal orders with the original fratricide: Carmelites, Augustinians, Jacobins (Dominicans), and Minors (Franciscans).⁴ As Margaret Aston notes, "Genesis used a phrase to describe cursed Cain that seemed perfectly fitted to the wandering mendicant. The condemned brother, 'a fugitive and a vagabond in the earth,' was identifiable as the vagrant friar." In addition to Cain's association with heretics as the first farmer who gave "wheat mixed with tares," he also "stood for . . . false possession—and indeed his name is associated with the Hebrew word meaning to acquire or get."⁵ *Pierce the Ploughman's Crede* exploits this cluster of images around the friars to set up an opposition between two fundamental relationships to the agrarian environment: acquisitive movement through it, or stable labor upon it. The prosopopoeic tactic of giving the overdetermined meanings of agrarian labor individualized human forms in *Pierce the Ploughman's Crede*'s portraits of friars and an idealized plowman allows the poem to knit abstract moral desiderata to concrete relations of production and consumption.

Antifraternalism as a discourse frequently rehearses tropes that emerged in the controversies over the existence and function of the mendicant orders shortly after their foundation in the early thirteenth century. Because this discourse was formed among learned disputants in the theology faculty of Paris, an exegetical bent marks even the vernacular adaptation of antifraternal satire, such that it, "like other traditional and topical aspects of medieval satire, . . . more often deals in well-established fictional stereotypes than in observed social reality."⁶ *Pierce the Ploughman's Crede*, in this reading, presents the friars as timeless enemies of the church. There is no need to worry, as Langland's dreamer might, about how best to relate to actual friars. This approach to the *Crede* captures much of what sets the poem apart from its longer, less strident model. But the necessary task of differentiating *Piers Plowman* from its polemical appropriations overlooks what the poems share, despite their apparently vast differences in length and complexity: the ambition to make visible the interactions of institutional power with the daily processes of making a living in an agrarian society. This response to Langland would persevere through the sixteenth century, and the *Crede* establishes a recurring tendency to convert Langland's exploration of the troubling interdependence of agricultural processes into a stable base for political hierarchy. Building on the conflicts of passus 6 of *Piers Plowman*, *Pierce the Ploughman's Crede* joins the antifraternal critiques of an ecclesiastical dissenter to the perspective of a manorial overseer as the poem translates manifestations of mendicant luxury into their ultimate source in the fields of Pierce the Ploughman.

The episode in *Piers Plowman* that instigates the *Crede*-poet's antifraternal satire is probably the opening of passus 8 (B.8.1–61), as Christina von Nolcken demonstrates, where the dreamer questions two friars about how to find Do-Well; but this only supplies the dialogic structure that the *Crede*-poet borrows and expands into the framework of his whole poem.[7] It is passus 6 that most appeals to the *Crede*-poet's desire to translate traditional stereotypes of antifraternal satire into specific conflicts over the population's relationship to the land in postplague England. *Pierce the Ploughman's Crede* traces the relationship of agrarian land and labor to a monetary economy that seems to enable only the squandering of the life-giving energies of the plowed field. The *Crede*-poet's engagement with *Piers Plowman*'s agrarian allegory shifts the exegetical commonplaces of antifraternal discourse into an immanent confrontation with the political ecological contradictions of ecclesiastical wealth.

"Money-Worth" versus Land and Labor: The Political Ecology of Antifraternalism

Pierce the Ploughman's Crede (ca. 1393–1401) survives in three manuscripts: one fragment from about 1460 to 1470, and the complete poem in two sixteenth-century manuscripts. *Pierce the Ploughman's Crede* was also printed by Reyner Wolfe in 1553, and Owen Rogers copied Wolfe's text in his 1561 printing of the *Crede* as an addendum to *Piers Plowman*.[8] The poem is a strident satire of the fraternal orders with roots in both contemporary Wycliffite critiques and older polemical attacks on the fraternal orders.[9] It depicts an unlearned narrator who seeks someone who can teach him the Apostles' Creed. Our narrator visits representatives of the four mendicant orders, only to find that a plowman named Pierce is the one who can teach him the basics of the Christian faith. In the narrator's quest, he visits representatives of the Franciscans, Dominicans, Augustinians, and Carmelites. During each exchange, the friars attack each other rather than offer any substantive instruction. Each episode follows the same structure: the narrator asks a friar about learning the creed, and then he names a rival order, which prompts the friar to launch an attack on that rival. The Franciscan (lines 32–134) denigrates the Carmelites, the Dominican (154–267) attacks the Augustinians, the Augustinian (268–334) insults the Franciscans, and two Carmelites (339–419) demean the Dominicans. When the narrator finally meets Pierce, he endures the plowman's lengthy condemnation of all kinds of friars before he finally learns the creed.

The interplay of institutional religion and agrarian economy that defines *Pierce the Ploughman's Crede*'s approach to antifraternalism appears most clearly in the section featuring the Dominican. The staggering wealth on display in the lavish Dominican convent—"all strong ston wall sterne upon heithe [ground]"—activates the poem's tendency toward accounting.[10] Like a surveyor who can eyeball some product of human labor and quickly rough out ways of measuring it in terms of work time, monetary value, or raw material, the narrator takes in the whole complex ("y hadde all y-toted" [219]) and calculates how much waste is on display: "The pris of a plough-lond of penyes so rounde / To aparaile that pyler were pure lytel" (169–70); a little further, "Though the tax of ten yer were trewly y-gadered, / Nolde it nought maken that hous half, as y trowe" (189–90); and again, "I trowe the gaynage of the ground in a gret schire / Nolde aparaile that place oo point til other ende" (197–98). The narrator notes the convent buildings and the accoutrements with which they are "appareled" before equating these visible performances of institutional staying power to the monetary measures of agrarian land and labor: pennies equivalent to the price of a plowland, the revenues of ten years of collected tax, and the total income from the agrarian produce ("gaynage of the ground") of a great shire. As Kate Crassons observes, "the plow-land . . . has value not only for its price . . . but as a fertile and renewable source of food for the community."[11] *Pierce the Ploughman's Crede* not only criticizes the waste of this resource. It also implies a legitimate, alternative order that can rightfully collect rents and taxes, unlike the illegitimate parasitism of the friars. The political hierarchy that manages the transformation of fertile lands into monetary value and benefits from it in the form of taxation and rents, the *Crede*-poet suggests throughout, is the legitimate beneficiary of agrarian wealth, not any fraternal order.

This goes beyond archetypal antifraternal polemic because it engages with the specific political economy of the Dominican convent in London. This passage apparently describes the actual convent of the London Blackfriars.[12] The London Dominicans did not receive income from any rents from agricultural lands because they did not own any property beyond their precinct in London (from which they did collect rents on dwellings they leased out).[13] Nevertheless, their income from the king was substantial, being only one of five mendicant houses who received annual contributions, a promised twenty pounds per year from 1345.[14] This closeness to royal power is what one of the *Crede*'s Carmelites seems to allude to when he complains, "They ben counseilors of kings Crist wot the sothe, / Whou they curry kings and her back claweth" (364–65). Their dependence, as with all the fraternal orders, on bequests and donations, especially those from royal and aristocratic supporters, also means that the narrator's keen attention to measurements of value based on manorial economic standards is entirely appropriate for bringing out the political implications of Dominican wealth. The mention of taxes specifically, as Helen Barr observes, alludes to the mendicants' exemption from taxation, which further underscores the friars' political liminality because they at once benefit from the value extracted from agrarian land and labor thanks to aristocratic largesse while also existing outside a political order that is in part constituted in, and realized by, the collection of taxes.[15] As Crassons notes, "the friars get the best of both worlds as they pursue and enjoy the privileges of lay power while disavowing their financial obligations to civil authority and the community at large."[16]

The *Crede*-poet is not worried about the wastefulness of fraternal convents as such, but only insofar as this wastefulness threatens the political hierarchies that govern the manorial economy as a whole. A building like the Dominican convent not only consumes resources that otherwise would support the king and commons, it also enables the Dominicans to become disturbingly king-like: the hall is suited for holding the household of "an heygh kinge" (204), and the kitchen, likewise, would better "an hyghe kinge in castells to holden" (210), while other buildings on the grounds are sufficient "to herberwe the queene"

(215). This survey of the convent concludes with a complaint about the common worker's plight:

> And yet thise bilderes wilne beggen a bagg-full of wheate
> Of a pure pore man that maie onethe paie
> Half his rente in a yer and half ben behynde.
>
> (216–18)

In *Pierce the Ploughman's Crede*'s political ecological imaginary, the king and the commons are united in their shared victimhood by a group of wasters who interpose themselves between the legitimate, productive toil of the agrarian worker and the legitimate consumption of the sovereign. The juxtaposition of the kingliness of the Dominican convent with the poverty of the tenant prompts a description of the Dominican's grotesque corpulence:

> A greet cherl and a grym, growen as a tonne,
> With a face as fat as a full bledder
> Blowen bretfull of breth and as a bagge hongede
> On bothen his chekes, and his chyn with a chol lollede,
> As greet as a gos eye growen all of grece;
> That all wagged his fleche as a quyk myre.
>
> (221–26)

The overfull flesh of this figure underscores the point that the "bagg-full of wheate" these quasi-sovereigns beg from the people disappears from its proper metabolic circulation, interrupting the link between the workers' fields and their subsistence, just as the Dominicans come between the commons and the king. The depiction of the Dominican as a kind of grotesque preemptively justifies the harsh disciplinary deprivation that Pierce eventually advocates to restore a stable hierarchy to the manorial political economy.

The wealth of the Dominicans, tallied up in terms of grain and revenues from agrarian land, also informs the Augustinian's attack on the Franciscans: "Sothly, somme of tho gomes hath more good himselue / Than ten knyghtes that y knowe of catell in cofers" (282–83). A singular Franciscan, these Carmelites allege, hoards more wealth than ten knights. *Pierce the Ploughman's Crede* does not object to the unequal distribution of wealth, but it detests the way that mendicants can amass such wealth without owning any of the ground from which it springs. All the fraternal orders, like this imagined Franciscan, capture monetary surplus not through the extractive mechanisms of the manorial hierarchy but through "iapes" (47), which the Francsican claims are the foundation of the Carmelite order. For the *Crede*-poet, tricks, plays, and deceptive performances allow each order to siphon off the surplus that should go to the land's owners and protectors.

The destabilizing interchangeability of monetary exchange defines nearly all the fraternal speakers in the poem when they repeat a near-identical formulation to ask the narrator for a donation. Each time, money is suggested alongside its equivalent values in grain, bread, bedclothes, jewelry, or other useful goods. The Franciscan asks for:

> Other bell other booke or breed to our fode,
> Other catell other cloth to coveren with our bones,
> Money or money-worthe[.]
>
> (115–17)

The Augustinian seeks:

> All that amendeth oure hous in money other elles,
> With corne other catell or clothes of beddes,
> Other bedys or broche or breed for our fode.
>
> (321–23)

The Carmelites insist "that thou amenden our hous with money other elles / With som katell other corne or cuppes of siluer" (396–97). The Dominican does not make such a request because, as we have seen, the description of his convent provides the *Crede*-poet with occasion to decode fraternal wealth as the monetary form of agrarian goods. The other friars' requests capture a dynamic attested to in the wills of fraternal supporters, which would often include bequests of beds and bedclothes, silver utensils, cloth, textiles, and firewood.[17] To see this practice as the provision of items that were useful to the daily maintenance of a fraternal priory, however, does not accord with the *Crede*-poet's characterization of the friars as defined by fungibility. The clothes, beds, accoutrements, and food they repeatedly request of the narrator are not sought as use-values but are immediately converted into their "money-worth." In a prescient rehearsal of the confrontation between the use-value of a commodity and the monetary appearance of its exchange-value (Karl Marx's *Tauschwert*), the *Crede*'s friars delight in money's ability to "extinguish all distinctions."[18] When the Carmelites finish attacking the Dominicans, they promise the narrator "To taken all thy penance" (394), as long as he gives money or some equivalent.

What is striking here is not so much the familiar complaint about the selling of spiritual goods but the way this sale is situated within the broader circulation of useful goods in a monetary economy, or what Marx calls "social metabolism" (*Stoffwechsel*), a term he first introduces in his discussion of monetary circulation.[19] In the basic form of this social metabolism, "the product of one kind of labour replaces that of another," but in the exchange process, "commodities as use-values confront money as exchange-value."[20] Commodities and money thus relate to each other as a "unity of differences," which enables a series of metamorphic substitutions like those between "money-worthe" and bread.[21] The *Crede*-poet emphasizes how the fraternal orders' facility in the realm of monetary exchange separates them from the scene of agrarian production, where the growing of food takes place and whose use-value is ultimately the means of the population's survival. Money mediates the friars' participation in the social metabolism in a way that the *Crede*-poet contrasts with the narrator's penniless condition, which he describes in response to the Carmelite's request for donations: "I haue no good ne no gold but go thus abouten, / And travaile full trewlye to wynnen withe my fode" (400–401). The Carmelites scorn the narrator's desire, in their view, to get something for nothing. But the narrator articulates his penniless condition in a way that highlights money's role not just as an object of fraternal cupidity but as a medium through which anything, especially the life-sustaining conjunction of agrarian land and labor, can become fungible and movable. The narrator is a landless laborer who wanders and works to eat, while the friars wander in pursuit of the ultimate medium of deceptive substitution.

The permanent structures to which the friars retreat symbolize the effacement of agrarian labor that defines their grasping for donations. While the fraternal speakers present their buildings as the legitimate manifestation of their orders' prestige, the *Crede*-poet locates their true meaning elsewhere, playing on a contradiction that was inherent in both the historical and architectural foundations of the mendicant orders. As Anne Müller puts it, "As 'wandering monks' the whole wide world, *totus orbis*, was the room for their work. . . . However, in order to embody their claims of lasting presence in the medieval cities and to guarantee the performance-based establishment of their identity, the mendicants needed, of course, their own fixed *loci*."[22] The orders used buildings to stage their own histories. According to Müller, "the communities' claims of validity drawn from their own institutional history could be visualized . . . in architecture, décor, accoutrements, or even rites."[23] *Pierce the Ploughman's Crede* relishes the hypocrisy of a mendicant order spending freely on impressive buildings in order to celebrate founders committed to poverty. But more than just exposing this contradiction, the *Crede* presents it as a symptom of the fungibility of the marketplace in which the use-value of agrarian commodities can be subordinated to the tokens of an inscrutable exchange-value. Not only does the monetary form of this value obfuscate its agrarian origins, but the friars also obtain it by offering something seemingly even more abstract and fungible, namely, the beautiful but empty words that elicit the people's generosity. For the *Crede*-poet, the exchange of words and money that fraternal mendicancy necessitates expresses the fundamentally illegitimate substitution that justifies the existence of the mendicant orders: that preaching can replace manual toil as a beneficial contribution to the Christian community.

Pierce the Ploughman's Crede's Franciscan embodies this critique in an appeal to the narrator for a donation, in which he moves seamlessly from the order's founding ideals of poverty to glorious architectural display. He explains how his brethren have taken up the task of preaching in poverty so that their example might help the souls of the populace:

> We hauen forsaken the worlde and in wo lyveth,
> In penaunce and pouerte and precheth the puple
> By ensample of oure life soules to helpen;
> And in pouertie praien for all oure parteners
> That gyueth vs any good god to honouren:
> Other bell other booke or breed to our fode,
> Other catell other cloth to coveren with our bones,
> Money or money-worthe, here mede is in heven.
> For we buldeth a burwgh—a brod and a large—
> A chirche and a chapaile with chambers a-lofte,
> With wide windows y-wrought and walles well heye,
> That mote bene portreid and paynt and pulched ful clene,
> With gaie glittering glas flowing as the sonne.
>
> (110–22)

This self-flattering account of the Franciscan mission almost succeeds in eliding the financial partnership that lies at the heart of its ascetic enterprise. The prayers for their "parteners / That gyueth vs any good god to honouren" introduce the spiritual coin of intercessory prayer into circulation with other, indifferently substitutable media of exchange. The Langlandian echo of "mede," recalling *Piers Plowman*'s personification of the circulation of gifts, wages, and bribes, here captures the socially and spiritually corrosive effects of monetary exchange. As the friar goes on, the *Crede*-poet mimics the easy substitution of use-value for exchange-value in the fluent speech of the practiced preacher whose rhetoric dazzles as much as the building he describes.[24]

The friar's speech rushes from exemplary penance and poverty to a glorious, light-filled convent, culminating in the alliterative exuberance of "gaie glittering glas flowing as the sonne." He demonstrates the very capacity for seductive performance that accomplishes the destabilizing transformations of which the *Crede*-poet accuses him: "any good," whether it be books, bread, clothes, money, or its equivalent in value, will become heavenly reward because it will be used to build a worldly structure that will honor God. The social surplus of "any good" becomes the foundation of a soteriological and material economy in which the dazzling glass window "flowing as the sonne" visibly manifests the "partnership" of donors and the friars who pray for them. But *Pierce the Ploughman's Crede* despises the wealth exchanged in this financial partnership because it elides its making. When the scene of the poem shifts from the fraternal convents to Pierce's muddy field, the *Crede*-poet supplies the hitherto absent vision of the toil that makes this wealth.

Pierce as Counterimage and Figure of Discipline

When the poem shifts from its series of speeches by mendicant brethren to the narrator's encounter with Pierce in a plowed field, Pierce extends the critique of fraternal convents to a critique of their social mobility. Against the dubious combination of lavish buildings and vagrant preaching, Pierce represents both spatial and social fixity in the plowed fields. This is why Pierce objects to the friars' elevation of commoners to quasi-sovereign status rather than to the existence of the elite stratum itself. Instead of the "laweles" (609) elevation of commoners that the fraternal orders enable, Pierce wants the privileges of ecclesiastical lordship to remain in circles of aristocratic kinship:

> They schulden maken bichopes her owen brethren childre,
> Other of some gentil blod and so it best semed,
> And foster none faytoures ne swiche false freres
> To maken fatt and full and her fleche combren.

(756–59)

The friars embody a disruption of stable and essentialized class distinctions. They eat without working and grow fat on the misplaced wealth that ultimately springs from the land and labor of Pierce and his fellow agrarian toilers. Pierce constructs these figures as threats to England's political ecology by situating their excessive consumption in relation to the misused social and natural resources of "erthe" and "trauail":

> Bote loke whou this lorels labouren the erthe,
> But freten the frute that the folk full lellich biswynketh.
> With trauail of trewe men thei tymbren her houses[.]
>
> (721–23)

The energy expended by agrarian laborers ("trewe men") in order to grow the "frute" of the fields does not return to those workers to help sustain their life but instead is transmuted into the lavish buildings the poem had earlier described and accounted for in terms of the monetary equivalents of agrarian land and labor. In a kind of late medieval "metabolic rift," to borrow John Bellamy Foster's phrase for Marx's account of how capital interrupts the metabolism between humans and nature, the cycle of working, eating, and fertilizing the land with excrement is interrupted by friars whose consumption does not issue in fertile dung but in the wastefulness of fraternal luxury.[25] When the poem describes Pierce "in the fen almost to the ancle" (430), it offers an image of cyclical metabolic relations ("fen" means both mud and excrement) that opposes the image of the Dominican friar and the quaking "quyk mire" (quagmire, 226) of his ample flesh.[26] As Helen Barr remarks, "As a keeper of animals and fertilizer of fields, the peasant was ripe for comparison to manure and other forms of animal waste.... Alongside the insistently bodily portrayal of the peasant class—a group, which, if their detractors were to be credited, had no control over their sphincter muscles—was their representation as dirt, or pollution."[27] *Pierce the Ploughman's Crede*'s critique of mendicant wealth turns this association with excrement into one of Pierce's positive attributes. It evokes the quotidian ecological process of fertilization to allegorize the total social circulatory system that the friars disrupt. By robbing both workers and soil of life-sustaining nutrients, instead becoming "fatt and full" quagmires themselves, the friars embody their inability to offer spiritual sustenance to the narrator.

After the narrator leaves the friars in disgust, he sees Pierce at work in a muddy field with his wife while their young children look on.

Pierce's manual toil with his wife reminds us that while the friars are unmarried and lustful, Pierce is part of an idealized, fundamental (re)productive unit:[28]

> And at the londes ende laye a litell crom-bolle,
> And thereon lay a litell childe lapped in cloutes,
> And tweyne of tweie yeres olde opon a-nother syde,
> And alle they songen o songe that sorwe was to heren;
> They crieden alle o cry a carefull note.
>
> (437–41)

Even though his children, wrapped in "cloutes" like their bedraggled father, cry for hunger, Pierce still offers to help the narrator with an offer of food in the Langlandian idiom of "lijflode," echoing Holy Church's description in *Piers Plowman* of the earth's provision "of liflode at nede," including "mete at meel" (B.1.18, 24). Pierce offers help in a manner that suggests he is an agent of the God-given potential of the earth to meet human need:

> Sely man, why syghest thou so harde?
> Yif the lake lijflode lene the ich will
> Swich good as God hath sent.
>
> (444–46)

Pierce is the antifriar: where friars are idle, lecherous consumers, Pierce generates both food and future workers in the form of his children. With this image of the plowman working alongside his family, the *Crede*-poet offers an emblem of the naturalized conjunction of land and labor in the figure of Pierce: place-bound, sharing the fruits of the soil, and joining a work ethic to properly regulated sexuality in the procreative family unit.

Pierce's emblematic status as a counterimage to fraternal luxury is explicitly tied to the soil in the description of his and his wife's muddy, ragged clothes. In this detailed image that rivals the descriptive richness of the fraternal convents, Pierce's family's immersion in the earth recalls the unnatural, rootless wandering of the friars and their luxurious buildings that obfuscate the agrarian origins of the wealth they squander:

> His cote was of a cloute that cary was y-called,
> His hod was full of holes and his heer oute,
> With his knopped schon clouted full thykke;

> His ton toteden out as he the londe treddede,
> His hosen ouerhongen his hokschynes on eueriche a side,
> Al beslombred in fen as he the plow folwede;
> Twey myteynes, as mete, maad all of cloutes;
> The fyngers weren for-werd and ful of fen honged.
> This whit waselede in the fen almost to the ancle,
> Foure rotheren hym by-forn that feble were worthen;
> Men myghte reken ich a ryb so reufull they weren.
> His wijf walked him with a longe gode,
> In a cutted cote cutted full heyghe,
> Wrappen in a wynwe schete to weren hire fro weders,
> Barefote on the bare ijs that the blod folwede.
>
> (422–36)

The *Crede*-poet drapes Pierce in clothes that conspicuously bear marks of hard use: his hair, fingers, and toes poke out of their ragged holes. Each "cloute" functions as a protective covering that offers only openings, reversing the dynamic that defines the friars' permeable enclosures; where the latter allow the friars to consume and retreat, Pierce's clothes emblematize his productive union with the land. The wife who accompanies Pierce in the field figures the mutual interaction of the working body and earth as she tracks blood on the frozen, unplowed mud. The inseparability of Pierce and his family from the agrarian ecosystem is further registered in Pierce's stockings, "Al beslombred in fen"; in his mud-soaked mittens; and in the muck he wades through "almost to the ancle." "Fen," as we have seen, means both mud and dung, and the mention of his four heifers in the line following the description of his mucky immersion further connects Pierce to the process of fertilization. Fertilizer represents productive waste, the metabolic relation between bodies and the land that sustains them. This description of Pierce's and his wife's mud-soaked, laboring bodies personifies the ecological relations of the agrarian economy. Body and earth merge to support the commonwealth, and this image of an agrarian landscape, so shaped by toil, indicts those religious figures who would squander this union of living blood and fertile earth for dead stone and glass. But this construction of the antifriar through a celebration of the generative capacities of blood and soil signals the extent to which this naturalization of peasant labor legitimates violence against those who could be construed as threatening the social order.

The counterimage of Pierce in the plowed field prepares the way for the explicit modes of coercion that this ideal figure advocates when he launches his extended attack on the fraternal orders. In *Pierce the Ploughman's Crede*, Pierce assumes an authoritative stance not unlike that of Piers the Plowman in passus 6. Although Pierce is not as clearly in an authoritative role over a group of other workers, Pierce's speech characterizes him as an overseer of worker indiscipline. For Pierce, any friar is the equivalent to Langland's Wastour in passus 6. What makes it so galling that a friar might be, in Pierce's words, "serued as a souereine and as a lorde sitten" (584) is not just the hypocritical contradiction of the rules of an order founded on poverty but that these upstarts are, by nature ("kynde"), meant for manual toil: "For her kynde were more to y-clense diches / Than ben to sopers y-set first and serued with siluer" (760-61). Pierce, then, is more like Piers than at first seems in his condemnation of the friars as wasters because he is setting himself up as an arbiter of class status and an enforcer of labor discipline: he recognizes who should be working and thinks hunger is the best way to make them do so.

The Pierce of the *Crede* wants to compel the labor of these pleasure-seeking idlers: "Y might tymen tho troiflardes to toilen with the erthe, / Tylyen and trewliche liven and her flech tempren" (741-42). He hopes to do so through depriving them of rich foods and replacing them with the scraps of bare subsistence:

> A great bolle-full of benen were betere in his wombe,
> And with the bandes of bakun his baly for to fillen,
> Than pertriches or plouers or pekokes y-rosted
> And comeren her stomakes with curious drynkes,
> That maketh swiche harlottes hordome vsen,
> And with her wicked worde wymmen bitraieth.
>
> (762-67)

As Pierce winds up to the climax of his tirade, he brings together the initial themes of sexuality that had defined the Franciscan's first attack on the Carmelites while tying them to the charges of gluttony and sociospatial disorder: "God wold her wonynge were in wildernesse, / And fals freres forboden the fayre ladis chaumbres" (768-69). Here, the *Crede*-poet brings together the architectural, social, sexual, and dietary themes of the preceding attacks on fraternal corruption. The friars avoid their natural status as workers, just as they defy ascetic ideals by living in lavish urban foundations, so they should be compelled to work by being deprived of all but the barest subsistence, like beans and bacon rinds. This would, in turn, solve the problem of their consumption of rich foods and "curious drynkes" that inflame their lust, and removes the physical incitement to their verbal trickery that betrays credulous women. In his indictment of fraternal luxury and his vision of their disciplining, Pierce combines the techniques of manorial surveillance with the biopolitical management of both diet and sexuality.

Pierce's adoption of this disciplinary perspective extends to his treatment of the friars' social and spatial mobility, where they appear as both prowling outsiders and as lordly consumers. They at once singly menace the productive countryside and collectively consume its produce like a parasitic swarm. These "wer-wolues" (459), "when bernes ben full," stalk about like threatening raiders: "Thanne comen cursed freres and croucheth full lowe; / A losel, a lymitour ouer all the lond lepeth" (595–97). The figure of mere idler turns into the threatening raider who lurks on the margins of a properly ordered society and feasts on the food that is its product and foundation. Pierce relies on a longer tradition of antifraternalism rooted in the polemics of the Parisian schools as he links such threatening mobility with "the kynrede of Caym" (486):

> With-outen any trauaile vntrewliche lybbeth.
> Hy beth nought maimed men ne no mete lakketh,
> Y-clothed in curious cloth and clenliche arrayed.
> It is a laweles lijf as lordynges vsen,
> Neyther ordeyned in order but onlie libbeth.
>
> (606–10)

The friars are disordered in both their physical embodiment and their paradoxical social formation as a threatening collective and as singular agents that "onlie libbeth" (live alone, singly), beyond any order and "with-outen any trauaile." The friars' bodily habitus is surveyed for signs of disability or desperate starvation (they are "nought maimed men ne no mete lakketh") that would justify their begging. Pierce sees clean, luxurious clothes, indicating a "laweles lijf as lordynges vsen," once again aligning fraternal disorder with the friars' illegitimate ascension to the level of wasteful consumption that is justifiable only when it is practiced by the lordly class. Pierce protects the interests of that class as assiduously as a dutiful reeve in his defense of a natural hierarchy that confers upon the nobility alone the privilege to hoard and consume agrarian surplus.

The paradox of individuality and collectivity that defines Pierce's account of the fraternal threat also divides any convent against itself: "Though for fayling of good his fellawe shulde sterue, / He wolde nought lenen him a peny his lijf for to holden" (740–41). The *Crede*-poet reflects the reality of social inequality in the orders, where brothers from wealthy families and those who succeed in attracting wealthy supporters would enjoy more income and gifts than brethren from poorer families. Yet bequests by London citizens were made that specifically targeted *fratri indigenti* in both acknowledgment of and attempt to remedy that inequality.[29] *Pierce the Ploughman's Crede*'s contradictory imagery of single marauders and parasitic swarms bespeaks the social contradiction of a communal form of life that partially rebukes but also fully participates in a stratified political economy. Pierce swings between the figure of the unregulated individual to that of the undifferentiated mass in his construction of the fraternal threat to the realm's political ecology:

> And right as dranes doth nought but drynketh vp the huny,
> Whan been withe her bysynesse han brought it to hepe,
> Right so, fareth freres with folke opon erthe;
> They freten vp the furste-froyt and falsliche lybbeth.
>
> (726–29)

The *Crede*-poet invokes the same cluster of images around friars and drones that informs Chaucer's antifraternal simile in "The Summoner's Prologue":

> Right so as bees out swarmen from an hyve,
> Out of the develes ers ther gonne dryve
> Twenty thousand freres on a route
> And thurghout helle swarmed al aboute[.][30]

But where the Summoner plays on the trope of the disordered innumerability of the friars, the *Crede*-poet makes the swarming friars into parasitic drones to emphasize their unearned gluttony. As we will see in *Mum and the Sothsegger*, the construction of the figure of the idle waster gains much from the image of the inhuman mass of deceptive, invasive drones. The structural similarity of the fraternal "dranes" to the sovereign consumption of knights and kings is not a problem for Pierce (nor will it be for the *Mum*-poet) because this is the naturalized order of things that they construct from the existing class hierarchy. The *Crede*-poet's objection to fraternal wealth is founded on the conviction that, while lordly domination enables social reproduction by enforcing labor on the manorial estate, fraternal domination weakens social reproduction by parasitically interrupting the relationship that should exist between work and "lijflode."

The image of the drone justifies the disciplinary threat of hunger that Pierce repeats at the conclusion of his speech. Pierce elaborates on how he might fulfill his desire to force the friars to work and tame their flesh (742–43). Pierce wants to return the friars to their proper place of toil on the land by reducing their diets to bare subsistence levels:

> Thei schulden deluen and diggen and dongen the erthe,
> And mene-mong corn bred to her mete fongen,
> And wortes flechles wrought and water to drinken,
> And werchen and wolward gon as we wrecches vsen[.]
>
> (785–88)

Pierce holds up his own labor of digging and dunging the earth and his own rough garments ("wolward gon") as the norm to which all friars must conform. In contrast to their errant, gluttonous existence, Pierce prescribes hard labor and a meager diet in a way that echoes the diligent labor that the starving populace takes up in exchange for peas, beans, and loaves of rough bread in *Piers Plowman* at B.6.183–98. But in a departure from Langland that would continue to define the *Piers Plowman* tradition, Pierce does not share Piers's ambivalence about Hunger's effects on wasters. Instead, Pierce embraces rather than questions a managerial ethic in which workers kept lean will toil rather than aspire to ease. Pierce's reckoning of fraternal malfeasance turns the watchful eye of the overseer on the mendicant orders rather than the manorial field, but Pierce still finds there the waste and unlicensed mobility that threaten the ideal manorial demesne.

Literate Self-Contradiction

Once Pierce concludes his rant against the friars, he finally teaches the narrator the creed. This act of instruction sits uneasily with Pierce's condemnation of fraternal literacy and education. Much like Langland must address the impression that he might be a mere wandering poet and not a true worker in the famous apologia of the C-version of *Piers Plowman*, Pierce attacks literate upstarts in a way that belies anxieties about a deeper resemblance between reformist poets and the targets of their verse:

> Now mot ich soutere [shoemaker] his sone setten to schole,
> And ich a beggers brol [brat] on the booke lerne,
> And worth to a writere and with a lorde dwell,
> Other falsely to a frere the fend for to seruen.
>
> (744–47)

If any poor commoner can aspire to read and write, Pierce implies, then it will not be long before lords are tainted by their service or the fraternal orders are filled with new recruits for their fiendish activities. Pierce wants to redraw the social boundaries that the threatening mobility of the friars has erased, restoring these parasites to their rightful place within the social body by "taming" them with a harsh diet: "Y might tymen tho troiflardes to toilen with the erthe" (742). For Pierce, fraternal education undermines the social order he believes his labor upholds. As John Scattergood points out, however, Pierce attacks the means through which the reformist desiderata of Bible study and vernacular instruction can be achieved.[31] Pierce concludes his presentation of the creed with the assurance that "all that euer I haue written is soth, as I trowe" (837). In this, the *Crede*-poet is like the Chaucer who imitates the rhetorical mastery of the friars as he attacks them in "The Summoner's Tale."[32] The *Crede*-poet is likewise aware of the literary prowess of the mendicant orders but is suspicious of its learned and otiose origins. But, as Bruce Holsinger points out in his description of the poem's "situated aesthetics," *Pierce the Ploughman's Crede* is highly artful in a way that suggests ample time to read, analyze, and imitate its masterful exemplar.[33] As we will see, the contradiction of a style that sometimes purports to reject the material conditions for having a style—that is, leisure and learning—is one that bedevils poets who wish to make agrarian labor the foundation of a renewed social order.

This moment of literate self-contradiction coincides with an ambiguity about who is the speaker because the following line reads: "And for amending of thise men is most that I write" (838). As Barr describes this moment, "the voices of author, narrator, and Pierce all merge."[34] This ambiguous moment, in which the speech of Pierce and its written form overlap each other in a surfeit of potential speakers, marks *Pierce the Ploughman's Crede*'s self-defeating attempt to assert the foundational role of productive manual labor over and against the textual work of those who have succumbed to the temptation to "on the booke lerne, / And worth to a writere" (745–46). This moment exhibits the poem's attempt to make sense of the fraught relationship between manual labor and intellectual labor, capturing its own reformist art within a satirical trap laid for religious brethren. This is an enduring hallmark of Langland's influence on the literary self-consciousness of the *Piers Plowman* tradition. While a reader of Langland like the *Crede*-poet retains a positive valuation of the coercive powers of hunger that Langland rejects, one of the uncertainties of *Piers Plowman* that its otherwise strident imitators seem unable to shake off is the place of the poet in an efficient, orderly political ecology. The *Crede*-poet seeks to disavow the resemblance between his work and that of mere performers and luxurious scribblers by engaging in truer performances. In chapter 3, we will see how the *Mum*-poet develops a solution to this problem by imagining the reformist poet as an adviser to sovereign power, carving out a provisional niche for the writer within the realm's idealized political ecology. But for the *Crede*-poet, allegories of agrarian ecology cannot easily maintain the distinctions between winning and wasting, generation and decay, that the poem tries to map onto the social division between laborers and friars.

Nevertheless, it is precisely that distinction that structures *Pierce the Ploughman's Crede*'s vision of fraternal reform through hunger and toil. The indelible image of Pierce and his family's immersion in the agrarian environment suggests the implicit task this poem imagines for an unspecified agent of sovereign authority: making sure no one in the non-noble population can escape this toilsome entanglement with the earth. Where the *Crede* only states its desire for enforced labor and identifies the indirect means by which it can be coerced through hunger, it will be up to *Mum and the Sothsegger* to specify the nature of royal authority as a force that can regulate the realm's agrarian political ecology. Both *Pierce the Ploughman's Crede* and *Mum and the Sothsegger*, as we will see in chapter 3, consider how a community can be constituted and transformed not just in terms of political institutions and ecclesiastical forms but in the daily labors of making a living and reproducing life. These texts tie the moral and political abstractions of antifraternalism (or advice to princes, in the case of *Mum*) to the landscapes and labor practices that allow the growth of food and the sustenance of the population. In so doing, they think through the insoluble problem of the relationship of writing to reform, whether ecclesiastical or political, which brings these poems hard up against the contradictions of seeking to construct a vision of a socioecological totality and at the same time trying to stand outside it in order to direct its proper repair.

Chapter 3

The Drone and the Sovereign
Labor and Consumption in Mum and the Sothsegger

In chapter 2, we saw how *Pierce the Ploughman's Crede* uses its Langlandian source to ground antifraternal biblical exegesis in the everyday conflicts of England's late medieval agrarian political ecology. In another part of the *Piers Plowman* tradition, a small cluster of poems written in similar alliterative form eschews narrowly ecclesiological polemic and embraces the aspects of *Piers Plowman* that glance at royal and parliamentary controversy.[1] *Richard the Redeless*, *Mum and the Sothsegger*, and *The Crowned King*, all written early in the fifteenth century, consider the broken relationships among the king, his close circle, his subjects, and the legal and parliamentary institutions that ought to guide those relationships during the vexed reigns of Richard II and the Lancastrians. But their shared Langlandian model leads these poems to treat these high political controversies in ways that analyze the nature of sovereignty in relation to the manorial political ecology that is the source and subject of these troubled mechanisms of governance. The high political poems of the *Piers Plowman* tradition find in William Langland's totalizing social and religious allegory a means to join the theory and practice of monarchy to the manorial ecosystem. This analytical construction of the social whole includes not only the legal and political facets of landed wealth (i.e., the documents and parliamentary representatives with which these poems deal) but also the conflicts over land and labor that supposedly produce national wealth. From this perspective emerges a precarious vision of sovereignty in which the king must have vigilant advisers who know how to direct the sovereign to protect the productive union of land and labor from which the king may extract his "certayne substance."[2] If corrupt advisers and feckless magnates interpose themselves between the sovereign and the working commons, then the sovereign's power will be diminished—unless he finds truth-telling counselors. In *Mum and the Sothsegger* especially, the mutual dependence of king and agrarian worker belies a dynamic of conflictual interaction that defines manorial political ecology. But unlike Langland's recognition that ecological interdependence complicates disciplinary violence as a solution to conflicts over labor, these poems explore sovereign violence as a means to separate workers from idlers permanently. In this way, they extend the surveillance and coercion of manorial political ecology to a national context, at the top of which sits a vulnerable, dependent sovereign.

Mum and the Sothsegger seeks a form for imagining a public, reformist voice that contributes to a longer literary history of the formation of what Arthur Ferguson once called the "articulate citizen" of late medieval and early modern England.[3] More recent scholars have specified the institutional discourses and documentary forms that *Mum and the Sothsegger* deploys in its investigation of the state of the realm around the time of Richard II's deposition. Whether taking up the mode of fraternal correction, parliamentary petition, or the forms of legal documentary culture, the alliterative *Piers Plowman* tradition has fruitfully been read as an attempt to make poetry from the textual resources of a broadly defined, emergent public sphere.[4] This chapter argues, however, that the importance of *Piers Plowman* as a model for a poem about political advice is that it keeps in view the political ecological task of sovereign rule to maintain the land and labor upon which it depends. As such, this chapter extends the intervention of scholars who have called attention to the entanglement of legal, parliamentary, and clerical documentary cultures with the management of a variety of ecosystems.[5] The pervasive concern with public documentary culture and the crisis of royal counsel might seem to pull the politically focused *Piers Plowman* tradition away from the messy details of agrarian work that *Piers Plowman* and *Pierce the Ploughman's Crede* emphasize. None of these poems show a plowman mired in his fields or stage a dispute among laborers. Instead, a poem like *Mum and the Sothsegger* seems primarily to worry over the work of governance as it is carried out in and through legal and political institutions and practices. Nevertheless, the Langlandian model that inspires these poems ensures that their investigation of the nature of sovereignty never strays from the agrarian ecologies that sustain the commons, the king, and the intermediaries that come between them.

The King, Advice, and Agrarian Work

The problem that besets England in *Mum and the Sothsegger* inheres in the precarious political ecology of sovereignty itself. One of the key affordances of the Langlandian idiom to the political poems in the *Piers Plowman* tradition is that it brings the conflictual dynamics of manorial political ecology closer to the problem of kings, counselors, and advice. Like the ideal bailiff of the manorial demesne, the true adviser's role is to transmit knowledge about the realm to the king so he can better protect the source of his wealth and power.[6] *Mum and the Sothsegger*'s vision of kingship and the role of sovereign violence in maintaining England's political ecology finds theoretical echoes in the shorter poems of the *Piers Plowman* tradition. *The Crowned King*, for example, asserts succinctly the sovereign's dependence on agrarian land and labor for the very accoutrements and buildings that perform and realize his sovereignty:

> The playnt of the pouere peple put thou not behynde,
> For they swope and swete and swynke for thy fode;
> Moche worship they wynne in this worlde riche,
> Of thy gliteryng gold and of thy gay wedes,
> Thy proude pelure, and palle with precious stones,
> Grete castels and stronge, and styff walled townes.
> And yit the most preciouse plente that apparaill passeth,
> Thi pouere peple with here ploughe pike oute of the erthe,
> And they yeve her goodes to gouerne hem euen.
> And yit the peple ben well apaid to plese the allone.[7]

The king's glittering costume, his castles, and his fortified towns are essential manifestations of kingship, but even they are not "the most preciouse plente." That rare abundance is what the people "with here ploughe pike out of the erthe." While the luxuries and buildings that derive from the wealth produced by laboring commoners are important, the food that they "pike" from the earth sustains it all. The people's willingness to please the sovereign by rendering this surplus to him is, the narrator informs the king, a gift from God (76) that can only be threatened by heeding "glosyng of gylers mowthes" (glossing of beguiler's mouths, 86). This "glosyng" is what prevents the king from hearing "the playnt of the pouere peple." As the brief poem goes on to counsel, the king requires "a faithfull philosofre that flater woll never" (110). Despite affirming the sovereign's essential authority, the poem also cannot conceive of sovereignty without reference to the obligations of rule, especially the duty of protecting the sustenance of the common laborer. This job requires the king to learn about the material conditions and complaints of his subjects. But the king's mediated knowledge of his realm means that it is impossible for a sovereign to experience directly the problems of the people, the land, and the labor that create the wealth upon which he depends.

The literature of counsel is replete with the contradictions of sovereignty and advice because royal advising exposes, in Judith Ferster's words, "the king's paradoxical dependence on those he rules."[8] For Georges Bataille, the contradiction Ferster identifies in the advice-to-princes genre is inherent in the concept of sovereignty itself as an economic, and not just political, force in the world. Sovereignty, in Bataille's view, refers entirely to the practice of consumption, while any consideration of production—including any practical, future-oriented, useful knowledge—is fundamentally servile.[9] From this perspective, any advice a counselor might seek to impart to his king about the daily productive capacities of the realm simply seeks to make sovereignty go against its essence. The *Mum*-poet, as we will see, captures something of this dynamic in its dual figuration of vulnerable sovereigns, one human and one apian, who sit atop their respective hierarchies, consume what their subjects produce, and remain insulated from any direct knowledge of their realm, let alone any direct contact with the processes of production that support them. Sovereignty's weakness in *Mum and the Sothsegger* is its inability to gain true knowledge about human and natural resources. In this, *Mum and the Sothsegger* confirms what medievalists and early modernists alike observe about the interdependence, or even co-emergence, of sovereignty and biopolitics—rather than the two representing successive historical moments that correspond to the medieval and the modern.[10] As *Mum and the Sothsegger* discloses, medieval observers feared that the sovereign, dependent as he was on questionable advice, could not sustain England's political ecology.

Mum and the Sothsegger: The Waking World

Mum and the Sothsegger uses the Langlandian framework of the allegorical dream vision to coordinate its analyses of the interdependent discursive and material foundations of royal power. The poem presents a world run entirely by followers of Mum, the personification of wary silence. The narrator seeks a defender of Sothsegger, the personification of fearless truth telling. His search ends in frustration, and he falls asleep and dreams a vision of impossible agrarian plenty. As he wanders in his dream, he comes upon a garden in which a franklin tends his beehive. This figure takes up the cause of the Sothsegger and encourages the narrator to write what he has learned when he wakes from his dream.

Throughout the first waking part of the poem, the king is at once idealized and utterly dependent on intermediaries to know anything about the daily lives and material conditions of his subjects. Because the Sothsegger is, according to the narrator, "seruiselees," or unemployed, the king cannot benefit from his blunt truthfulness. Instead, the Sothsegger is scorned because

> He can not speke in termes ne in tyme nother
> But bablith fourth bustuely [boisterously] as barn vn-y-lerid [unlearned person];
> But euer he hitteth on the heed of the nayle-is ende,
> That the pure poynt pricketh on the sothe
> Til the foule flessh vomy for attre [vomit forth poison].
>
> (49–53)

A particular style of speech flows from this figure, boisterous and unlearned, a commoner's voice that lances the boils of an infected social body. And the pierced "foule flessh" that vomits poison anticipates *Mum and the Sothsegger*'s ultimate image of truth telling: the narrator, having woken from his dream, "vnknytte[s] . . . a bagge / Where many a pryue poyse [secret poetry] is preyntid withynne" (1343–44). The Sothsegger's role combines that of the surgeon with those of the petitioner and the reeve: he ought to extend to the king the kind of detailed account that a manorial lord might demand from his reeve or offer a true grievance as a parliamentary petitioner might, just as a doctor ought to inspect an infected sore thoroughly to treat it. Such a truth teller would allow the king to know, for example, "Hough grotz [coins] been y-gadrid and no grief amendid" (134). In learning about the discrepancy between the gathering of taxes and the material improvement of his subjects' lives, the king could, the poem optimistically imagines, "amende that were amysse into more ease" (138).

What follows, however, is the narrator's frustrating discovery that no existing institution can tell the king what he needs to know. The seven liberal arts at the universities offer no help (323-91). The four fraternal orders are likewise engaged in a familiar pursuit of profit and illegitimate power: they "gouuernen the grete and guilen the poure" (465). The friars, as expected, upend hierarchies and religious rules as they wander seeking gain, but the enclosed religious also fail to open their doors to the poor narrator (550-52). Left to wander, the narrator seeks help in cathedrals, only to find his insistent questioning about Mum ignored by priests who would rather gorge themselves like livestock in a barn:

> Thay wolde not intremitte of ner nother side,
> But euer kepte thaym close to cracche and to mangier,
> And fedde so the foule flesh that the velle ne might
> Vnethe kepe the caroigne but yf hit cleue shuld[.]
>
> (559-62)

The language of "foule flesh" swollen near to bursting again recalls the image of an infected body politic that a Sothsegger would cure by lancing the boils that grow when the king is unaware.

These cathedral priests are not just figures of infection but also of illegitimate consumption. The turn here to the clergy's appetites shows just what is gained by the *Mum*-poet's adaptation of *Piers Plowman* to the *speculum principium* genre in its opening up of conventional sources of political dysfunction to an expansive vision of agrarian waste. The poem strengthens the link between corrupt silence and parasitic consumption when the narrator visits his final failed representative of institutional knowledge: the parish priest. As the narrator attends mass, the priest's call for offerings displays a verbal excess that suggests the waste of agrarian plenty that the king and his agents should protect against:

> He taughte thaym by tyme thaire tithing to brigne
> Of al manier grene that groweth vppon erthe
> Of fructe and of floze in felde and in homes,
> Of polaille and of peris, of apples and of plummes,
> Of grapes and of garlic, of gees and of pigges,
> Of chibolz and of chiries and of thaire chese eeke,
> Herbaige and oygnons and alle suche thinges
> That grown in thaire gardynes, lete God his parte haue,

> Of hony in your hyves and of your hony-combes,
> Of malte and of monaye and of all that multiplieth,
> Of wolle and of wexe and what-so yow increceth
> Or newith yow, the ix partie nymeth to your self,
> And trewly the tithing taketh hooly churche.
>
> (600–612)

A corrector to the manuscript, perhaps caught up in this vision of excess, adds three lines:

> of lyke and lynne seede of lambes and egges
> of coltes and of calues that the cow lycketh
> of benes and of boutre that bele doo make[.][11]

In a list of foods that echoes the catalogue of goods brought to Hunger in *Piers Plowman*, the parish priest abuses his authoritative position: instead of truthfully guiding his parish, he seeks to consume its sustenance.[12] The list of foods bespeaks an impulse to account for the productive potential of the parish's land and labor, even if this is ultimately an account of misused plenty by yet another follower of Mum. This enumerative approach to the *Mum*-poet's satire of the parish priest exemplifies how the influence of *Piers Plowman* invites the poem to situate useless, uninformative speech in relation to useless consumption. The priest's words are not just spiritually empty, but they catalogue the potential loss of foods that would otherwise fill the empty bellies of his parishioners. As a kind of poetic accountant of this imaginary consumption, the *Mum*-poet, as in the *Crede*-poet's calculations of fraternal waste, acts here as an estate manager who sits between the physical labor and ecosystemic processes of the manor, on the one hand, and their textual mediation for the sovereign lord, on the other. This lord, so the poet hopes, can set things right once he knows what is being wasted on his demesne and by whom. He just needs to find a truth teller first.

Mum and the Sothsegger: The Dream World

The narrator, now frustrated and exhausted after the failure of the parish priest, "lay dovne on a lynche to lithe my boones, . . . And ere I were ware, a wynke me assailled" (857, 869). A "lynche" is a ridge, "especially one used as a boundary marker," which marks the narrator's passage into his dream of a perfect natural landscape.[13] The narrator falls asleep on marginal, unproductive agrarian land as a vagrant might. "Lynch" is a term that could denote a boundary marker between plowlands in a legal document, but here it serves as a boundary between the waking and somnolent worlds of the poem. This detail indicates the poem's attunement to the imbrication of legal documentary culture with experience of the agrarian environment.[14] In this liminal position, the narrator dreams of an ideal landscape that, like the one Piers describes to the would-be pilgrims of passus 5, is marked by natural features that are nevertheless products of human labor:

> I lifte vp my eye-ledes and lokid ferther
> And sawe many swete sightz, so me God helpe,
> The wodes and the waters and the welle-springes
> And trees y-traylid fro toppe to th'erthe,
> Coriously y-courid with curtelle of grene,
> The flours on feeldes flavryng swete,
> The corne on the croftes y-croppid ful faire,
> The rennyng riuyere russhing faste,
> Ful of fyssh and of frie of felefold kind,
> The breris with thaire beries bent ouer the wayes
> As honysoucles hongyng vppon eche half,
> Chesteynes and chiries that children desiren
> Were loigged vndre leues ful lusty to seen.
> The havthorne so holsum I beheulde eeke,
> And hough the benes blowid and the brome-floures;
> Peris and plummes and pesecoddes grene,
> That ladies lusty loken muche after,
> Were gadrid for gomes ere they gunne ripe;
> The grapes grovid a-grete in gardyns aboute,
> And other fruytz felefold in feldes and closes;
> To nempne alle the names hit nedith not here.
>
> (889–909)

The narrator opens his eyes to a dream world and finds himself enjoying the sovereign pleasures of drinking in "many swete sightz" in a well-managed landscape that he has done no work to create. The copiousness of this passage echoes the priest's list of foods he will accept as payment, although here the emphasis is on aesthetic delight rather than gourmandizing. Nevertheless, most of the nouns in this descriptive survey refer to edible goods that require labor to grow or gather: grain in arable fields; fish in rivers; berries, chestnuts, cherries, beans, pears, plums, peas, grapes, and an ineffable number of fruits grown in fields, crofts, and gardens—in spaces created by human labor.

The description's shift to animals in no way diminishes the sense that this dream landscape is made by human work, and it further underscores the narrator's temporary standpoint as a sovereign voyeur. Rabbits sneak from their warrens, hares bound from coverts and dodge hunting dogs, sheep lounge by hedgerows, cows and horses gambol about their pasture. While these animals are mostly livestock, useful for food, work, and wool, even the noble deer of various sorts live plentifully in a hunting park that is just as much a managed space as an enclosed pasture or a rabbit warren:

> Hertz and hyndes, a hunthrid to-gedre,
> With rayndeer and roobuc runne to the wodes,
> For the kenettz on the cleere were vn-y-coupled;
> And buckes ful burnysshid that baren good grece,
> Foure hunthrid on a herde y-heedid ful faire,
> Layen lowe in a launde a-long by the pale,
> A swete sight for souurayns, so me God helpe.
>
> (925-31)

This "swete sight for souurayns" is described in a way that emphasizes the dependence of sovereign pleasure upon the labor that makes the infrastructure in which natural delights flourish. The relationship between gardens and sovereign rule undergirds this dream vision of the *locus amoenus*, but the dream landscape of *Mum and the Sothsegger* is expansive, covering a wide range of environments made by a variety of human labors.[15] The visionary scene takes full advantage of an alliterative poetics of plentitude that at once suggests an inexhaustible source of sovereign enjoyment *and* the utilitarian accounting of laboriously managed landscapes that enable any act of sovereign consumption.

The poem does not remain with the sovereign's perspective of passive, purely visual enjoyment. Instead, the dreamer moves down from the hilltop toward a scene of work in a franklin's garden: "I moued dovne fro the mote to the midwardz / And so a-dovne to the dale" (932-33). This downward movement signals the poem's concern with making visible the links between sovereign consumption and agrarian production. At the bottom of the dale, the narrator finds "a faire hovs with halles and chambres, / A frankeleyn-is fre-holde al fresshe newe" (945-46). This franklin is not a manorial servant or a wage laborer but a member of the non-noble gentry. And he is rich, too—a prosperous country gentleman with a large house, either recently built or renovated "al fresshe newe," and a garden.[16] He could be a member of Parliament, as Matthew Giancarlo argues, and the emphasis on his legal status and political function in the realm overlaps with his role as an agent within the political ecology of manorial husbandry.[17] As Stephen Yeager shows, the franklin "resembles the figure of the *procurator*" from the parable of the laborers in the vineyard, which was commonly translated into English as "reeve."[18] In this view, the franklin embodies the position of the reeve of high medieval husbandry manuals, at once directly involved in the maintenance of England's agrarian infrastructure, accounting for its system of rents and labor services, and in the coercive maintenance of that infrastructure in the service of a higher lord. The poem leads us to this social position as the narrator moves to a site that replaces the passive gaze of a king with the direct knowledge and labor of an ideal agrarian manager and freeholder.

The franklin and his garden allow the poet to replicate the sovereign's hierarchical authority but at a lower social level where direct work on the land is still possible, much closer to the social level of the ideal audience of estate management literature—educated and able to manage the operations of an estate but not performing the toil of the landless laborer or tenant. The independent franklin can be the ultimate authority within his minimal territory, but—unlike a king or member of the higher nobility—he is still directly involved in the maintenance of his household, and he is not dependent on the mediation of servants and their written "gloses" on the state of things. The garden is also a reduced and enclosed space, small enough to be maintained by the efforts of its owner. It allows the poet to skip the complexities of labor management and present a simplified picture of sovereign rule as the direct application of care and/or violence.

A key aspect of sovereignty's limitations in *Mum and the Sothsegger* is the dependence of sovereign enjoyment on the labors of commoners, but the poem evades the detailed ethical consideration of labor management and discipline that defines Langland's approach to the manorial economy. The *Mum*-poet offers a simpler vision in which wasters do not need to be accommodated to a Christian community but simply destroyed. In this way, the *Mum*-poet's treatment of the franklin's garden simplifies and occludes the relations of force and necessity that guide actual manorial production. It shares this quality with another major work of fifteenth-century agrarian poetry, albeit one that exists at an even further remove from Langland's aesthetic and religious orientation: the Middle English poetic version of Palladius's *De re rustica*, commissioned by Humfrey, Duke of Gloucester, and written from 1439 to 1443. Palladius's silence in *De re rustica* on matters of the labor force, its discipline, and its organization makes its practical advice on establishing an agrarian estate more portable, in a sense. None of its advice is specific to a particular political economic order, even as its choice of crops, like olives and vines, favor the specific ecological conditions of the Italian peninsula.[19] But this silence also allows Humfrey's *On Husbondrie* to enact an ideal, fantastical form of useful knowledge for sovereign control over the land. Shorn of the complexities and conflicts of labor management that define the detailed treatises on the hierarchy and responsibilities of different kinds of laborers on manorial estates, *On Husbondrie* presents knowledge of and control over the lord's productive landscapes as an aesthetic project, as a literary achievement in which the aristocratic patron's sponsorship enables his direct knowledge of the cultivation that makes his rule possible. Only the translator-poet mediates, but this is done in collaboration with an expert patron and not the ranks of potentially unruly servants that populate the manorial estate in earlier examples of husbandry manuals.[20] In the same way, the dream garden of *Mum and the Sothsegger* and its franklin keeper allegorize the kind of unmediated knowledge of and direct action on the realm's political ecology that is impossible for the king in the poem's waking world. The Middle English *On Husbondrie* emphasizes how, through seeing and knowing the air, water, land, and bodies of the people that live in these elements, proper political ecological governance can be achieved. The proem to Humfrey's commissioned translation, as Lynn Staley observes of Charles V of France's earlier "georgic" translation program, establishes a tightly interlocking set of associations between knowledge, writing, and agrarian husbandry as foundations for royal power.[21] As such, it is analogous to *Mum and the Sothsegger*'s brief, somnolent vision of a fecund and aesthetically refined agrarian landscape from which the realities of class conflict, surveillance, and labor coercion have been banished and the contradiction between sovereign authority and its need for advice has been temporarily suspended.

But the turn to *Mum and the Sothsegger*'s exemplary beehive restores to view the coercion that was occluded in the narrator's vision of the franklin's freehold as the poem confronts the violence necessary to maintain its vision of sovereign consumption and servile production, purged of all parasitic intermediaries. The franklin, "an olde auncyen man of a hunthrid wintre" (956), not only works the garden in the freehold but also destroys the parasites that threaten its flourishing:

> He houed ouer a hyue, the hony forto kepe
> Fro dranes that destrued hit and dide not elles;
> He thraste thaym with his thumbe as thicke as that come,
> He lafte noon a-live for thaire lither taicches.
>
> (966–69)

This image of a man, old but "right stronge," poised to bring swift destruction on idle parasites, suggests that any program of ameliorative political speech that the narrator sought in the waking world will need to be joined with force. Here, the *Mum*-poet marks an incipient recognition that the most effective kind of reformist poetry will be able to provoke and guide the violent enforcement of those reforms.[22] It is curious that the figures that occupy actual royal office (bee or human) do not have the capacity for such effective violence but only the franklin does. His relationship to the garden is direct, his regulation of his beehive immediate. In this way, he could be thought of as a figure for a God who protects by punishing.[23] He recognizes the drones that waste his honey and acts decisively to destroy them, unlike the dependent and misinformed king of the first part of the poem or the feeble bee king of the dream.

The franklin claims ownership of the garden in terms of the work he does to keep it flourishing:

> "I am gardyner of this gate," cothe he, "the grovnde is myn owen,
> Forto digge and to delue and to do suche deedes
> As longeth to this leyghttone the lawe wol I doo,
> And wrote vp the wedes that wyrwen my plantes;
> And wormes that worchen not but wasten my herbes,
> I daisshe thaym to deeth and delue oute thaire dennes.
> But the dranes doon worste, deye mote thay alle;
> They haunten the hyue for hony that is ynne,
> And lurken and licken the liquor that is swete,
> And trauelyn no twynte but taken of the beste
> Qui non laborat non manducet. Bernardus.
> Of that the bees bryngen fro blossomes and floures."
>
> (976–86)

He pulls weeds; crushes worms and digs out their dens; and, most of all, exterminates drones because they "doon worste." Like the deceptively mobile friars of *Pierce the Ploughman's Crede* that "lurken in her selles" (60), these drones "haunten the hyue" to luxuriate in the sweet honey that they do no work to earn. This prompts the *Mum*-poet to insert at line 985 a quotation of 2 Thessalonians 3:10, "Qui non laborat non manducet," wrongfully attributed to Saint Bernard.[24] This quotation is one of several scriptural loci that undergird antifraternal exegesis from the thirteenth century on, but here it extends beyond ecclesiological critique to encompass any number of alleged idlers who share qualities with the parasitic drone.[25] The quotation is an odd fit here, unless, as Helen Barr suggests, we understand it as a lightly obscured critique of the fraternal orders, which otherwise have no allegorical counterpart within *Mum and the Sothsegger*'s bee society.[26] Given the venerable history of the verse from 2 Thessalonians in antifraternal polemic, such resonances are inescapable here, but it does not help solve the problem of understanding what kind of sovereign agency the franklin might represent at this moment. The tag from 2 Thessalonians implies the kind of indirect punishment and coercion that Piers the Plowman invokes in passus 6 when he asks Hunger to attack the idle wasters. But the franklin does not merely let the drones starve; he actively destroys them with his own hands. In this way, part of *Mum and the Sothsegger*'s innovation within the *Piers Plowman* tradition becomes clearer: it puts forward an agent of political coercion that uses violence to maintain the productive assemblage of land and labor. Where Langland and the *Crede*-poet invoke the managerial tactics of the manorial economy to address ecclesiastical conflict, the *Mum*-poet crafts the franklin's garden to envision sovereign violence as the ultimate savior of England's political ecology.

The Beehive within the Franklin's Dream Garden

The above reading of the franklin leaves open the question of the significance of the beehive that he protects. *Mum and the Sothsegger* channels a long tradition of representing the society of bees as an example for human political organization and economic activity, taking as its most immediate source Bartholomaeus Anglicus's *De proprietatibus rerum*. The beehive is a rigidly hierarchical space; in *Mum and the Sothsegger*, the king bee literally sits atop the hive and also commands full obedience from the swarm:

> Thay haue a king by kinde that the coroune bereth,
> Whom that doo sue and serue as souurayn to thaym alle,
> And obeyen to his biddynge, or ells the boke lieth.
>
> (999–1001)

Within the rest of the hive:

> eche a place hath a principal that peesith al his quarter,
> That reuleth thaym to reste and rise whenne hit nedith,
> And alle the principallz to the prince ful prest thay been at nede,
> To rere thaire retenue to righte alle the fautes;
> For thay knowen as kindely as clerc doeth his bokes
> Wastours that wyrchen not but wombes forto fille.
>
> (1012–17)

From the king's unquestioned place at the top of the hive, authority descends to "principallz" that rule over their own sections of the hive, each ready to muster their retinues whenever "fautes" must be amended. These faults, we learn, are idleness and waste, which these principals know "as kindely as clerc doeth his bokes." This is the second time the *Mum*-poet quotes this line from *Piers Plowman* (B.5.538) in which Piers asserts his natural knowledge of Truth as his manorial servant. Here, as if compressing the entire episode of Piers's failed attempt to organize the plowing of his half acre before journeying to Truth, the principal bees do not have natural knowledge of anything so transcendent as Truth but rather of the sort of Wastours that prevented Piers and his followers from seeking Truth. At first, this change might seem like it wrecks the simile between Piers's "kindely" knowledge of Truth and clerical knowledge of books by eliminating the element of abstract knowledge that is the basis of the comparison: a cleric can potentially come to know Truth through books, as Piers knows Truth "kindely." The bees, by contrast, know "Wastours," which is a different kind of knowledge than the clerical study suggested in the original Langlandian simile. However, if we think of the clerkly books in this passage from *Mum and the Sothsegger* not as scripture or theological texts but as the documentary records of the manorial bailiff or reeve, who would have had training in the clerkly arts of law and household management, then this seemingly awkward quotation of *Piers Plowman* becomes more apt. The bee leaders' kindly knowledge of wasters is thereby associated with the literate practices of record keeping on the manorial demesne as each term of the simile is then associated with the surveillance and disciplining of labor. This kind of useful knowledge about waste and disorder, which the principal bees know by nature and clerks know by the surveys and extents in their "bokes," is the necessary precondition for coercive or punitive violence against any waster.

The relationship between the political order of the beehive and the ordering of labor becomes clear in the next lines, further solidifying the link between useful knowledge of husbandry and the nature of sovereignty in *Mum and the Sothsegger*'s political imagination:

> Thaire works been right wondreful wite thou for sothe,
> For sum, as thou sees thay shape thaym to the feldes
> To sovke oute the swettenes of the somer floures,
> And sum abiden at home to bigge vp the loigges,
> And helpen to make honey of that thay home bringen,
> And doon other deedes thorough dome that is among thaym;
> And sum waiten the wedre, the wynde and the skyes,
> Yf hit be temperate tyme to trauaylle or to leue.
> Thay eten alle at oones and neuer oon by hymsilf,
> Thorough warnyng of thaire warthour leste waste were among thaym.
>
> (1018–27)

There is an echo here, with its catalogue of interdependent laborers, of the ideal manorial workforce as described in husbandry manuals, in which some work to gather the fruits of the fields, others work on the infrastructure of the estate, others work to process the produce, others observe local conditions to determine when it is best to labor, and all are watched over to ensure that waste does not get a foothold within this productive assemblage. Hierarchy, labor management, and surveillance turn out to be the shared features of the manorial demesne, the dream beehive, and the realm as a whole in *Mum and the Sothsegger*'s bureaucratic vision of political ecology.

This is why the *Mum*-poet pauses to linger over the bees' shared language that even "the leste of thaym" (1030) understands. For such an interdependent, hierarchical system to function, the kind of transparent communication that is absent in the poem's waking world must be present here in the dream's beehive:

> The bomelyng of the bees, as Bartholomew vs telleth,
> Thair noyse and thaire notz at eue and eeke at morowe,
> Lyve hit wel, thair lydene the leste of thaym hit knoweth.
>
> (1028–30)

In the beehive, a universally understood vernacular contributes to a totalizing political allegory in which daily struggles over work and waste are intimately connected to the status and survival of the king.

The bee king's status and his survival are curiously precarious, however. The king bee is not dominant or forceful. The king bee is "The most merciful among thaym and meekest of his deedes" (1031). In fact, the king apparently even lacks the capacity for violence: he is "spereless, ... Or yf he haue oon, he harmeth ne hurteth noon in sothe" (1033-34). This king does not need the threat of a stinger because he relies on reason and consent to rule, not "venym": "To reule thaym by reason and by right-ful domes, / Thorough contente of the cumpaignie that closeth alle in oone" (1036-37). Between force and consent, the king bee needs only the consent of his subjects because his reason, transmitted through the bees' vernacular, is enough to win their support, even if the king is so physically weak that he cannot visit colorful flowers without a supportive retinue in case he falters: "And yf he fleuble or feynte or funder dovneward, / The bees wollen bere hym til he be better amended" (1042-43). This king bee is in no way a figure of imposing rule. He resembles the drones more than he does the franklin. Even if the king bee speaks to and learns from his agents so that his rule becomes more effective, it is not so effective that his hive is ever safe from parasitic infestation by drones, whom we meet after this description of the king's faint powers, and of whom, we are told, "is al the doute" (1044) in the otherwise perfect functioning of the hive.

Drones are idle, deceptive, and gluttonous. They cannot be guided by the king bee's reasoned command because they are already external to the totally efficient, interlocking system of labor and communication that the true hive represents. In a hive where each bee is defined by its place in the hierarchy and the tasks it pursues, the drones are mere stomachs:

> But of the drane is al the doute, the deueil hym quelle,
> For in thaire wide wombes thay wol hide more
> Thenne twenty bees and trauaillen not no tyme of the day,
> But gaderyn al to the gutte and growen grete and fatte
> And fillen thaire bagges brede-ful of that the bees wyrchen.
>
> (1044-48)

The focus on the drones' "wide wombes" makes them consumers without a purpose, filling their guts as if they were the bloated cathedral clerics of the poem's waking episodes or the festering sores on the body politic that Mum creates. This emphasis on the corrupting uselessness of the drones' consumption is one of the poet's departures from Bartholomaeus, who affirms that consuming surplus honey *prevents* the poisoning of the hive. In John Trevisa's translation, "Also been sittiþ vppon þe hyues and soukeþ þe superfluyte þat is in honycombes, and hit is isayde þat ȝif þay deden nouȝt soo, þereof schulden attercoppes [spiders] ben igendred of þat superfluyte and been schulden deye" ("Also, bees sit upon the hives and suck the superfluity that is in honeycombs, and it is said that if they did not do this, then spiders would be engendered of that superfluity and bees would die").[27] According to this account, consuming the "superfluyte" is necessary in order to prevent the spontaneous generation of spiders from the stagnation of excess honey. Wastefulness here serves a purpose; at a certain point, excess must be expended in a fit of consumption. In the realm of *Mum and the Sothsegger*'s beehive, however, an ecological vision in which a Bataillean squandering of excess is necessary, and thus not wasteful in the most pejorative senses that the *Piers Plowman* tradition assumes, cannot fit with the poem's political ecological approach to sovereignty and counsel. The state cannot be exemplified by a self-regulating, peaceful, homeostatic system according to *Mum and the Sothsegger* because the maintenance of polities requires surveillance, discipline, and violence. The franklin mimics this function of the state because *Mum and the Sothsegger* is not concerned to recuperate so-called wasters within a Christian community but rather considers the elimination of idle parasites as part of the basic task of keeping the realm productive and secure.

The beehive is not a naturally functioning exemplum in *Mum and the Sothsegger* because it requires external human assistance to function. As the franklin explains, there would be little honey:

> But yf [unless] the gardyner haue grace and gouuerne hym the bettre
> And wisely a-waite whenne dranes furste entren,
> And nape thaym on the nolle ere that thaire neste caicche;
> For been thay oones ynned his eyen shal be dasid
> Fro al kinde knowlache, so couert thaym helpeth.
>
> (1059–63)

The franklin must take on this role of surveillance and extermination because the king bee is stingless and the other worker bees are too busy to notice the infiltration of their hive by drones. So a gardener has to destroy them before they are "ynned," otherwise they will be able to disguise themselves among the bees. As he goes on to explain, however, eventually the bees "see thaire swynke is y-stole," and upon realizing they've been robbed, the bees "quellen the dranes quicly and quiten alle thaire wrongz" (1084–86). The king bee cannot kill the drones, even if he could identify them; the gardener can and does identify and kill the drones before they establish themselves in the hive; and the worker bees, only after the fruits of their labor are stolen, identify and kill the drones. The franklin's attack on the drones renders the king bee superfluous, like the drones themselves who grow fat on others' labor (1072), even as the franklin himself is, as Giancarlo observes, "the ultimate parasite on the hive as a whole, implicitly extracting from it a heavy tax of honeyed wealth." However, as Giancarlo continues, "He stands as a singular figure and speaker, but a speaker *for* this community of the hive of which he is, and is not, an integral part," making him fundamentally a personification of "licit parliamentary power" insofar as he "stands both with, and across from, the sovereign social structure he is charged to speak for and protect."[28] This reading of the franklin not only explains his puzzlingly redundant status as a kind of supplemental sovereign to the king bee but also suggests a further, more speculative and abstract possibility for the franklin's significance. In this sense, I regard *Mum and the Sothsegger*'s franklin as an exemplary instance of Katharine Breen's "moderately realist personification" that is on its way to becoming a speculative "nominalist personification" with its riddle-like opacity.[29] The king bee and the franklin do not embody abstract, Platonic ideas of kingship but rather are composed of a number of identifiable qualities that the reader must coordinate and cognize in order to arrive at a novel concept—such as the ideal of parliamentary authority. But there are other elements of the franklin's relationship to his garden and hive that exceed his equation with Parliament and that invite further speculation. In this way, the sense that the franklin and his hive do not entirely fit together allegorically prompts readers to imagine a challenging political-economic intersection that lacked a clear conceptual terminology: the site where kingship and counsel, text and knowledge, land and labor converge. There is something enigmatic about this relationship between franklin and bees. The franklin inhabits a productive agrarian landscape, within which he maintains a garden and beehive through close surveillance, destroying any idle parasites. His actions suggest that the *Mum*-poet is seeking a figure not just for the proper government structure that could supplement royal power. He also seeks to figure the mechanism that would connect changes in governance to the daily material interactions on the land of the manorial estate. Such a figure would be a kind of ideal combination of sovereign violence and biopolitical "power-knowledge," the two constituting each other in relation to the ecological and economic pressures of the manor.[30] The regulating power of the state thus combines the administrative-epistemological acumen of the "sothsegger" with the necessary force to protect the realm's material conditions from any idlers, parasites, or wasters that the truth-telling adviser identifies. In this way, the franklin embodies a kind of economic and extraeconomic coercion that complements the transmission of accurate knowledge about the realm because the *Mum*-poet seeks a figure for the violent maintenance of the manorial hierarchy that ultimately supports the dependent and isolated king.

Return to the Waking World and the Bag of Books

As the poem draws toward its end, the *Mum*-poet imagines effective political counsel in variously material terms—as documents, of course, but also as a kind of medical device that enables the healthy venting of discontent rather than the harmful circulation of angry, libelous speech.[31] When the narrator wakes up, he sets out to follow the advice of the franklin, which allows the *Mum*-poet to fantasize about the most effective reception that writing can have when it reaches the highest authorities of the realm. As the franklin puts it shortly before the dream's end:

> Sith thou felys the fressh lete no feynt herte
> Abate thy blessid bisynes of thy boke-making
> . . .
> And lete the sentence be sothe, and sue to th'ende;
> And furst feoffe thou therewith the freyst of the royaulme,
> For yf thy lord liege allone hit begynne,
> Care thou not though knyghtz copie hit echone,
> And do write eche word and wirche there-after.
>
> (1280–87)

Being given to the sovereign, this book takes the place of the human adviser and begins a top-down reformation of the corrupt political system that motivates the poem's composition. The "blessed bisynes" of bookmaking provides a means to deliver frank truths to the king. When the narrator wakes up, he imagines himself as a doctor who softens "the soores to serche thaym withynne" (1338). When he opens his bag of books, it contains a slew of records of clerical corruption, the documentary "attre" that poisons the realm. As it turns out, it is not (only) poetry "in balade-wise made" (1345) that the narrator delivers to the king but a collection of records of legal and political misdeeds, the discursive evidence of an ailing kingdom. *Mum and the Sothsegger* imagines a process of reform in which books reach directly to the sovereign and guide his decisions.

Without the circulation of such written forms of counsel and complaint, "the fals felon fester with-ynne," the franklin warns—far better "Whenne the anger and the attre is al oute y-renne" (1124–26). Unless "shire-men" speak of the "fautes and founde thaym to amende" (1131–33), then Mum will cause them all to carry "a bagge ful of boicches vn-y-curid" (1139) back to England's agrarian hinterlands, spreading an infection that mars the body politic. The counterimage to this festering sack of stifled resentment appears after the dreamer wakes up and begins the process of amending his realm by sharing a vast written record of its many problems:

> Now forto conseille the king vnknytte I a bagge
> Where many a pryue poyse is preyntid withynne
> Yn bokes vnbredid in balade-wise made,
> Of vice and of virtue fulle to the margyn,
> That was not y-openyd this other half wintre.
>
> (1343–47)

This image of a bag full of texts has received a deserved amount of attention as central to the poem's argument about the legal and governmental procedures and documents that might enable the reform of a dysfunctional political system. But it also suggests how the idiom of agrarian allegory rooted in *Piers Plowman* activates the *Mum*-poet's bureaucratic critique. The spaces of the freehold, the garden, and the beehive evoke manorial territory and its hierarchical relations, which in turn depend on documentary accounting. This links writing and agrarian labor in ways that go beyond the traditional analogy between penning lines and plowing furrows.[32] In *Mum and the Sothsegger*'s vision of sovereignty, the king ensures the productivity of common labor and agrarian land, which then means he ought to receive "a certayne substance . . . / To susteyne this souurayn that shuld vs gouerne" (1637–38).

The king's ability to access that substance depends, however, on its effective calculation and collection, a complicated and conflictual operation to which many of the documents in the narrator's bag of books are addressed, such as the "papir of penys" or legally binding IOUs for sums that bishops will misuse (1350), or the "rolle of religion" that tells how monastic incomes have been (mis)used "sith the pestilence tyme" (1364–69), or the "scrowe" that tells of squires who ignore the injustice of nobles "that piled han poure men of penys and of goodes" (1489–91), or, finally, the "copie of couetise" that recounts how conscience is corrupted when it gets rich "thorough ryfling of the people" (1683, 1686). These documents, though aimed at familiar satirical targets, nevertheless drive the point home that documentary records can either enable or impede the healthy circulation of agrarian wealth to all members of the body politic, even if for now such documents only seem to register "an unholy alliance between unprincipled authority and literate technology," as Richard Firth Green puts it.[33] The material consequence of such an unholy alliance is that both the commons and the king are in danger of being deprived of their sustenance by the drone-like corruption attested to in these documents.

The exemplum of Ghengis Khan that interrupts the catalogue of documents serves to assert the priority of loyalty to a strong king as the cure for such corruption, but it recenters the *Mum*-poet's focus on sovereign violence as a response to the failure of counsel to maintain the productivity of agrarian land and labor. Ghengis Khan's test of loyalty first requires the spectacular violence of making his subordinate lords murder their sons and then requires they "sese" or legally yield (enfeoff) their lands to him (1435–39). The exemplum asserts that violence is necessary to the king's ability to maintain the law and control the land on which the entire substance of the realm depends. In this sense, Ghengis Kahn is not so much an absolutist counterfigure to the franklin's parliamentarianism, as Giancarlo argues, but another manifestation of the poem's analysis of the imbrication of sovereignty, violence, and land in a kind of protocolonial political ecology.[34] After all, Ghengis Kahn's effective violence and control of his lords' lands enabled the Mongols' widespread territorial conquests, having both regained

> The lande and the lordship that thay loste had,
> And conquered cuntrees, as Cathay-is lande,
> That is the richeste royaulme that reyne ouer houeth.
>
> (1454–56)

Key to this poetic fantasy of a violently maintained order of productive work and transparent documentation that also enables the further expansion of national control over rich agrarian territory is the hope that vernacular poetry itself will not be a superfluous distraction from the vital labors of the commonwealth but an agent of collective amendment.

Conclusion: Centralization and Colonization in the *Piers Plowman* Tradition

Mum and the Sothsegger has been read as a harbinger of Tudor public complaint in which the critique of England's political, economic, and religious structures find form in humanist tracts, satirical pamphlets, and poetry of the early to mid-sixteenth century. For Arthur Ferguson and Andrew Wawn, *Mum and the Sothsegger* represents the incipient growth of this literature of "articulate citizenship" that would become more widespread in the sixteenth century, while Giancarlo complicates this reading of the poem by teasing out the contradictions between its advocacy of public complaint and "the fantasy of strong-willed, univocal centralized authority that comes across, perhaps startlingly, as a proleptic portrait of Tudor-era absolute monarchy."[35] One reason that *Mum and the Sothsegger* seems proleptic of the Tudor period is its vision of royal authority that insists on the violently enforced, top-down unification of land and labor into a productive assemblage, a dynamic that continues into the era of the dissolution of the monasteries and the expansion of English colonial projects in Ireland and the New World. The *Mum*-poet adapts *Piers Plowman*'s vision of an ideal social whole based on toil to articulate the relationship between sovereign power and the workers and advisers that make it function. For much of the poem, sovereign power is at once dependent on and responsible for the fundamental, biopolitical operation of controlling the population by controlling the workforce's relationship to the earth. Absolute royal power hardly seems a possibility until the exemplum of Ghengis Kahn. For this to be the fantasy that the *Mum*-poet invokes in contrast to the apparent weakness of the English king presages the response of many readers of *Piers Plowman* who incorporate its vision of agrarian toil into an appeal to an expansive view of sovereign power. The uncanny echo between Ghengis Kahn's actions and the policy of "surrender and regrant" in Tudor Ireland bespeaks the compatibility of the Langlandian idiom with a colonial vision of reform, as we will see in chapter 5.[36]

But this approach to the violent enforcement of the manorial hierarchy also drives early Reformation responses to the agrarian crises of the sixteenth century.

Chapter 4 turns to the era of so-called primitive accumulation to show the centrality of a medieval poetics of agrarian labor to English Reformation literature, which sought to represent the interactions of ecclesiastical wealth and agrarian land and labor as threats to the political ecology of the realm. Sovereign power becomes an agent of environmental transformation in this tradition insofar as it takes up the role of answering these threats through both economic and extra-economic means.

CHAPTER 4

The Political Ecology of Primitive Accumulation in English Reformation Literature

The first half of the sixteenth century has long been understood as an era of crisis. Enclosure, inflation, rural depopulation, vagabondage, and the varied upheavals related to the dissolution of the monasteries seemed to dissolve stable structures of social reproduction in the blink of an eye. Poets from John Skelton to Robert Crowley, alongside prose polemicists like Simon Fish, worked these developments into their texts as they sought to understand how the sustaining relations of the agrarian ecosystem were abstracted into monetary wealth and consumed by illegitimate princes of the church. Early Tudor poets and polemicists extended Langlandian approaches to manorial political ecology to a new context, registering both the continuities of its exploitative structures and seemingly novel crises in an era of increased transfer of arable land to pasture. I approach these large-scale economic and ecological developments via the resolutely practical and detail-oriented works of John Fitzherbert, whose *Boke of Husbandry* and *Surveying*, both printed first in 1523, were the successors to *Walter of Henley* as the most widely read works on estate management in the sixteenth century. In his irenic vision of well-informed freeholders and landlords coordinating their disparate goals of diversified farms on the one hand and monetary accumulation on the other, Fitzherbert registers perennial contradictions between the localized ecologies of the manor farm and the lordly imperative to accumulate profit.

After a reading of Fitzherbert's books as witnesses to the political ecological contradictions of the early sixteenth century, I turn to three works from the 1520s: John Skelton's *Collyn Clout* (1522), Jerome Barlowe and William Roye's *Rede Me and Be Nott Wroth* (1528), and Simon Fish's *A Supplicacyon for the Beggars* (1528). I then take up *Philargyrie of Greate Britayne* (1551) by *Piers Plowman*'s sixteenth-century editor, Robert Crowley, which brings together the prophetic strains of the *Piers Plowman* tradition with a historical and structural analysis of wealth creation both before and after the Reformation.

The fact that Crowley, the latest writer in this chapter, is the strongest link back to *Piers Plowman*, while Skelton, the earliest writer, forms the strongest link ahead to Edmund Spenser, reflects the elusive literary genealogy of the *Piers Plowman* tradition in the first half of the sixteenth century. Crowley's edition of *Piers Plowman* is obviously the best evidence there could be of his close knowledge of the poem. But Skelton's familiarity with *Piers Plowman* must be deduced through the less certain means of verbal echoes, shared thematic concerns, and a common affinity for prophecy and personification.[1] Barlowe and Roye exhibit even less evidence of engagement with *Piers Plowman*, although their familiarity with Skelton's work is assured.[2] Fish might have known Skelton's work, given that he moved in the same circles of early Protestant exiles as Barlowe and Roye, who definitely read Skelton.[3] But as a prose writer, Fish fits uneasily within a *Piers Plowman* tradition defined by prophetic, prosopopoeic agrarian poetry, and there is little specifically Langlandian about his *A Supplicacyon for the Beggars*. Nevertheless, his attack on purgatory and church wealth, printed in Antwerp and smuggled to England in 1529, was widely influential, provoked a response from Thomas More, and would soon be celebrated for supposedly catching the attention of Henry VIII in John Foxe's *Acts and Monuments* (1563), which also reproduced the text (it had been printed in England for the first time in 1546).[4] Fish's analysis of the political ecological unity of agrarian crisis and ecclesiastical landownership has much in common with Barlowe and Roye's. In their compression of a broad crisis into an attack on singular pillars of the institutional church, Fish's *A Supplicacyon for the Beggars* and Barlowe and Roye's *Rede Me and Be Nott Wroth* both amplify Skelton's foundational indictment of Cardinal Wolsey in *Collyn Clout*. Crowley's editorial work on *Piers Plowman* emerges from a constellation of mid-Tudor literary efforts to join prophetic, personifying poetry to a critical analysis of manorial political ecology under the pressures of monastic dissolution and agrarian capitalism, and Skelton's *Collyn Clout* was an early and influential exemplar of this kind of writing.[5] The results of Crowley's immersion in *Piers Plowman* combined with his sympathy for the critical agrarianism of Skelton, Barlowe and Roye, and Fish are fully manifest in *Philargyrie of Greate Britayne*'s account of the dissolution of the monasteries and the nature of monetary accumulation. Skelton and Crowley bookend a cultural moment in which Langlandian poetry addressed crises of land, labor, sovereignty, and economic power in ways that would be taken up by one of the most consequential readers of Skelton and Crowley, Edmund Spenser—as we will see in chapters 5 and 6.[6]

Enclosure, Primitive Accumulation, and the Metabolic Rift: The Changing Political Ecological Situation in the Work of John Fitzherbert

Both John Fitzherbert's *Boke of Husbandry*, appearing in twenty editions between 1523 and 1598, and his *Surveying*, appearing in eleven editions between 1523 and 1567, offer practical advice and a general moral outlook that promises readers a chance to thrive in challenging times.[7] Despite Fitzherbert's best efforts to focus on the useful knowledge of the yeoman farmer and estate surveyor rather than any hint of social crisis, he cannot, like his predecessor in *Walter of Henley*, avoid the conflicts that rive the agrarian estate. Fitzherbert expands and elaborates on the kinds of traditional ecological knowledge that informed the great estate management treatises of the high Middle Ages. Given that the means of production—plows, human and animal labor power, soil, rain, and sun—had not much changed from the fourteenth to the early sixteenth centuries, the novelty of Fitzherbert's writing often emerges from shifts in relations of production. Such shifts were felt to be catastrophic—an agrarian crisis defined by a rising population at a time when more land was used as pasture and when rising prices outstripped any gains in wages from the beginning to the middle of the sixteenth century.[8] Landowners large and small, as well as more prosperous tenant farmers, were seeking new ways to profit from the wool trade and to gain monetarily by "improving" their lands via engrossing and enclosure—the merging of several smaller holdings into large estates, and the depopulation and fencing of arable lands and commons to create pasturelands. These processes allowed landowners to produce more profitable commodities like wool, but they led to widespread reports of an increase in idleness, vagabondage, social dislocation, and moral decline. For example, the 1489 "Acte Agaynst the Pullynge Doun of Tounes" describes the consequences of enclosure as causing both economic and spiritual decay because evicted agrarian workers lost both their livelihoods and their ties to the local parish: "for where in somme Townes two hundred persones were occupied and lived by their laufull labours, nowe ben there occupied two or three herdemen and the residue fall in ydelnes, the husbondrie whiche is one of the greatest commodities of this realme is gretly decaied, churches destroied, the service of God withdrawen."[9] This late fifteenth-century legislation registers the implication of agrarian political ecology in ecclesiastical dysfunction in a way that presages the sectarian verve of Reformation-era poetry on agricultural crisis.

Fitzherbert studiously avoids direct comment on ecclesiastical politics, but he cannot escape the tensions between the market orientation of the revenue-hungry landlord and the needs of poorer agrarian households. This contradiction explicitly shapes the complementary framing he gives to *Boke of Husbandry* and *Surveying*. Fitzherbert sees his two books as addressing two halves of a social whole because they mirror what he hopes to show is the inherent compatibility of the laboring and noble estates. This can be seen in the way he introduces *Husbandry* and *Surveying* in their respective preambles. In *Husbandry*, Fitzherbert begins with the fundamental question of human purpose:

> This is the questyon. Whervnto is euery man ordeyned. And as Job saythe, Homo nascitur ad laborem, sicut auis ad volandum. That is to saye, a man is ordeined and borne to labor, as a byrde is ordeyned to flye. And the apostle sayth, Qui non laborat: non manducet: debet enim in obsequio dei laborare, qui de bonis eius vult manducare. That is to saye. He that laboureth nat, sholde nat eat, & he ought to labour & do goddes warke that wyll ete of his goodes or gyftes, the whiche is an harde text after the lyterall sence. For by the lettre the kynge, the quene, nor al other lordes spirituall & temporall sholde not eat, without they sholde labour the whiche were vncomely, & nat conuenyent for such estates to labour.[10]

The answer, attested by Job and Paul in 2 Thessalonians, is that everyone must labor; if they do not, they should not eat. Fitzherbert quickly acknowledges, however, that this universal law must be amended to accommodate sovereigns and "all other lordes spirituall and temporall."

How should we understand the survival of this group that does not labor and yet eats plenty? In *Boke of Husbandry*, Fitzherbert avoids the question with a quick reference to the "Boke of the Moralities of Chess," which he cites to support his naturalization of the social hierarchy by analogy to the board game. In the preface to *Surveying*, however, he takes up the question directly: "Howe & by what maner, do all these great estates and noblemen and women lyue and maynteyne their honour and degre? and in myne opinyon, their honour and degre is vpholden and maynteyned, by reason of their rentes, issues, reuenewes, and profytes that come of their maners, lordshippes, landes & tenementes to them belongyng."[11] Fitzherbert answers his own question: the nobility both survives physically and maintains "honour and degre" thanks to the revenues they gather from their lands.

As Fitzherbert goes on to explain in the preface to *Surveying*, noble dependence on the productivity of their lands joins his two books in one purpose: he wrote *Boke of Husbandry* for farmers and tenants "that they may more surely, easely and profitably encrease and sustayne their pore housholde, wyues, and chyldren: and also truely to paye their rentes customes, and seruyces vnto their lords and the honoures of their fermes and tenauntryce."[12] *Husbandry* helps the small-scale producer help the large estate owner by showing the former how to pay the latter "truely." *Surveying* promises to teach landlords how to know if they are being paid "truely" by accurately measuring and valuing the extent of their holdings.

In this move toward social harmonization, however, Fitzherbert already traces the fault lines between the need of tenants to "sustayne their pore housholde" and the need for lords to get revenue via "their rentes." The origins of this conflict, Fitzherbert later explains, have deep historical roots: the lords who followed William the Conqueror first divided their lands among their bonded laborers; later lords, realizing the injustice of holding people in bondage, converted their status to that of free tenants, who continue to sustain themselves and pay rent to the noble estate.[13] Fitzherbert turns to a semilegendary history of the Norman yoke and its gradual, voluntary amelioration to construct an ideal political ecology in which the lords' virtuous division of the land in the past, after an initial violent seizure, prompts the virtuous labor of the free tenant.

This is characteristic of Fitzherbert's desire to harmonize the division between tenant and lord, between ecology and economy. Regardless of whether he convincingly achieves that goal, he establishes the contours of political ecological conflict within the manorial system. *Surveying*, as

Andrew McRae argues, reflects the uneasy coexistence of the personal bond between lord and tenant (defined by "customes, and seruyces") and the already prevalent tendency to monetize that relationship in the form of rents.[14] While Fitzherbert glides over this tension, the fact that *Surveying* begins with a translation of and commentary on the text of the *Extenta Manerii*, or the form for surveying an estate's holdings codified after the Statute of Westminster II to allow lords to prove accusations of fraud against manorial officers, reveals the role of legal coercion underlying the extraction of rents. The goal of achieving greater control over land as property depended on the increased standardization of quantitative measurements, mapping techniques, and legal standards.[15] This increasing standardization had its roots in the coercive instruments of manorial administration because the *Extenta Manerii* allowed landlords to survey the total value of their estates in order to prove (and punish) any instances of fraud or theft on the part of their reeves or bailiffs. The relationship between *Boke of Husbandry* and *Surveying*, then, mirrors the conflicted relationship between the ecological conditions of daily labors on the farm and their economic and legal abstraction.

Fitzherbert takes pains to present this process as if it composed a seamless social, ecological, and economic whole. But the seams show even in the opening premise of *Husbandry*'s advice on farming, founded on the ecological principle of the complementarity of animal and arable husbandry: "An husbande can not well thryue by his corne without he haue other cattell, nor by his catel without corne. . . . And bycause that shepe in myne opinyon is the moost profytablest cattell that any man can haue, therfore I purpose to speke first of shepe."[16] In the first sentence, corn and cattle mutually enable the farmer's prosperity because corn and stubble will feed cattle, whose manure will improve future yields of corn in a virtuous ecological cycle. The second sentence shifts abruptly and without comment, however, from ecological to mercantile logic, asserting the profitability of sheep rearing as guiding the order of instruction in the book. Yet mercantile calculation threatens the homeostatic, ecological balance of the farm and, by extension, the reciprocity of the laboring and lordly estates.

Fitzherbert avoids direct comment on this potential contradiction between grain and wool production, but as *Boke of Husbandry* continues, his vision of an ideal smallholding is shown to be one of diversified, interacting parts, which require detailed scrutiny by the farmer—an arrangement that increasingly proved to be at odds with the drive toward sheep rearing. Fitzherbert describes the varied micro environments and animals that the farmer must attend to, writing in his "paire of tables" anything amiss with the "closes, pastures, feldes, ... hedges, ... horses, mares, beestes, shepe, swyne, or geese" he might encounter, such as "a gap, or a sherde in his hedge, or any water standyng in his pastures vpon his grasse." Problems arise, but they remain amenable to managerial supervision: "For a man alwaye wandrynge or goynge about somwhat fyndeth or seeth that is amysse and wold be amended. And as soone as he seeth any suche defautes, than let him take out his tables and wryte the defautes. And whan he cometh home to diner, souper, or at nyght, than let hym call his bayly or his heed seruaunt, and to shewe hym the defautes, that they may be shortly amended."[17] Fitzherbert's *Husbandry* constructs a political ecology of the small manorial farm in which landscapes, animals, infrastructure, servants, and writing are united through the supervision of the diligent freeholder.

This devotion to the details of the agrarian ecosystem enables their eventual abstraction into the alienable medium of marketable commodities. *Surveying* explains how an expert in measuring and calculating extents and revenues can ensure that the full amount of value is captured from a manor's lands. In this text, Fitzherbert worries about what losses will occur if any aspect of a lord's knowledge of his lands proves incomplete. "Wherefore it is necessary," he asserts, "that euery great estate ... shulde haue a Surueyour." If every kind of land held by a lord is "extended, surueyed, butted, bounded, and valued in euery parte," then "the said estates shulde nat be disceyued, defrauded, nor disheryted of their possessyons, rentes, customes, and seruyces."[18]

For Fitzherbert, this complete and careful record ensures peace: "it wolde be as a perpetuall and sure euydence for euer, to put away all strife and varyaunce."[19] But he is trying to ameliorate conflicts that were rooted in processes already well underway, as is clear in his moralizing charge to his imagined lordly readers: "I aduertyse and exorte on goddes behalfe, all maner of persons as well lordes as other. That whan the lords or freholders, knowe where their landes lye and what euery pasture or percell is worthe by the yere. That the lordes nor the owners therof do nat heyghten their rentes of their tenauntes, or to cause them to pay more rent or a gretter fyne, than they haue ben acustomed to do in tyme past."[20] Once Fitzherbert has described the power that the surveyor's document holds to settle all disputes, he acknowledges that the lord could abuse that power.[21]

As Fitzherbert knew, maximizing revenue did not necessarily depend on having lots of tenants growing grain on ecologically diverse small farms when pasturing sheep provided more income. He seeks to assuage his concern that this project would have negative consequences for the rural commoner by begging landlords to eschew rapid rent hikes, like the ideal lords of the distant past who voluntarily ended bondage on their estates. But this emphasis on individual moral agency belies the implicit acknowledgment of the ecological and economic forces that shape any farmer's or landlord's actions in *Boke of Husbandry* and *Surveying*. Fitzherbert was describing different aspects of a process of value creation in which investment in agrarian improvement both transformed the ecological relations of the manor farm and enabled the increased accumulation of monetary wealth. He was, in other words, thinking through the nature of what later theorists would call "primitive accumulation."

The Metabolic Rift of Primitive Accumulation

The procedures that enable ecological knowledge to be quantified and abstracted in the form of husbandry manuals, the survey of extents, and the collection of revenue are fundamental to the political ecology of capitalism's historical emergence. As Jason Moore theorizes the late medieval roots of capitalism's "world-ecology," he modifies both Karl Marx's account of so-called primitive accumulation and Immanual Wallerstein's world systems theory to emphasize capitalism's reliance on both human and nonhuman work. Moore's analysis of the enlistment of natural forces in the accumulation of value allows us to see how agrarian writing and surveying are part of the process whereby "capital, science, and state transform work/energy into value."[22] It is possible to see, mutatis mutandis, the marketing of wool, husbandry manuals, and the *Extenta Manerii* as cognate, respectively, to Moore's trifecta of "capital, science, and state." The investments of landowners, the ecological knowledge of the estate manager, and the juridico-political power of the manor courts each represent different aspects of the social relations that enable the monetization of agrarian ecosystems. The role of surveying in debates about colonization in early modern England likewise demonstrates how technologies of measurement effected ecological transformations beyond England's shores.[23]

With Fitzherbert, we can see how the process of so-called primitive accumulation, as Marx narrates it, relates to another central concept that appears elsewhere in *Capital*: the "metabolism" between humans and nature and its disruption under conditions of capitalist agriculture and urban industrialization. John Bellamy Foster has illuminated this concept in his account of the "metabolic rift" in Marx's thought, which is rooted in Marx's recognition that capital increases productive capacities only "by simultaneously undermining the original sources of all wealth—the soil and the worker."[24] In volume 3 of *Capital*, Marx expands on this dynamic:

> Large landed property reduces the agricultural population to an ever decreasing minimum and confronts it with an ever growing industrial population crammed together in large towns; in this way it produces conditions that provoke an irreparable rift in the interdependent process of social metabolism, a metabolism prescribed by the natural laws of life itself. The result of this is a squandering of the vitality of the soil, which is carried by trade far beyond the bounds of a single country.[25]

Marx's idea of the "metabolism" (*Stoffwechsel*) between humans and nature emerged in part from his study of soil science, which offered a way to think through capital's effects on the sustaining conjunction of land and labor.[26] In short, the rift inaugurated by the rise of capitalist agriculture and large-scale urban industry was the rift between eating and excreting. As human and animal waste no longer restored the soil's fertility, monetary accumulation proceeded at the expense of the total metabolic interaction of human nourishment and the nourishment of the soil.

Marx is referring to a later era of large-scale urban industry and industrial agriculture in the passage from volume 3, but in identifying the ecological consequences of the expansion of monetized exchange as the primary motivator for agrarian production, Marx had already located the germ of the metabolic rift in his account of so-called primitive accumulation at the end of volume 1. From the fourteenth to the sixteenth centuries, the creation of a landless workforce went hand in hand with enclosure and rural depopulation as landlords bowed to "the power of powers": money.[27] This new power breaks the virtuous cycles of metabolic interaction among labor, manure, and arable land that Fitzherbert had wishfully described in *Boke of Husbandry*. The concept of the metabolic rift allows us to see enclosure or monastic disendowment as not only economic upheavals but as ecological events.

Poets and polemicists from Skelton to Fish approached the rift between socioecological reproduction and monetary wealth via the contradiction of the church's pastoral function and its status as England's largest landlord. The church's massive involvement in the process of agrarian production gave rise to the hope that the disendowment of the church might lead to the total transformation of the realm. This hope underwrites the mingling of humble agrarian labor and grand prophetic visions of renewal undertaken under the aegis of an apocalyptic sovereign in the sixteenth-century *Piers Plowman* tradition. These texts, as we will see, encourage the "centripetal" violence of the sovereign against the "centrifugal" violence of the clerics as the former recolonizes England's pastures with agrarian laborers enlisted from the ranks of the latter.[28] Despite the starkly opposed tone of scabrous writers like Skelton or Barlowe and Roye to that of the irenic Fitzherbert, they all relied on a similar analytical perspective on agrarian political ecology that allowed them to hold in view the conflicted interactions of land and labor as these were transformed into monetary wealth.

Collyn Clout, Enclosure, and the Wandering Prophet-Poet

The relationship between early sixteenth-century agrarian poetry and *Piers Plowman* registers both a continuous interest in the conflicts of manorial political ecology and gaps in direct literary influence. The works of Fitzherbert allow us to see continuity and change in manorial political ecology from the time of *Walter of Henley* to the early sixteenth century, just as Crowley's *Philargyrie of Greate Britayne* shows how William Langland's poem could shape literary responses to Reformation-era conflicts. John Skelton, by contrast, presents a more challenging mixture of continuity and change. As Eric Weiskott observes, Skelton shares Langland's bilingual poetics of Latin and English, but formally Skelton remains "an enigma" whose Skeltonic meter evinces no obvious affinities with his predecessors.[29] Skelton's formal eccentricity makes it hard to fit him into the history of early modern engagement with *Piers Plowman* epitomized by Crowley's attempt to understand and imitate Langland's alliterative verse.[30] As noted above, however, many critics have found commonalities substantial enough to justify the view that Skelton knew *Piers Plowman*, even if his engagement with the poem is less overt than his explicit invocations of Chaucer or John Gower.[31] *Collyn Clout* especially seems to channel a Langlandian approach to ecclesiastical and economic crises. In the opposed figures of Collyn Clout—the wandering "ragged farmer"—and the unnamed Cardinal Wolsey, Skelton avails himself of personification and prophecy in ways that make his knowledge of Langland difficult to discount.[32] This sets *Collyn Clout* apart from the other fifteenth- and sixteenth-century texts that feature plowmen but otherwise exhibit no obvious familiarity with *Piers Plowman*.[33] In *Collyn Clout*, there is no plowman. But neither is there one in Crowley's *Philargyrie of Greate Britayne*, and each poem exhibits a Langlandian ambition to address religiopolitical crisis through a totalizing critique of the contradictions of manorial political ecology.

Skelton's satires of Cardinal Wolsey—*Speke Parott*, *Collyn Clout*, and *Why Come Ye Nat to Courte?* (ca. 1521-1523)—launched durable attacks on worldly clerics that would appeal to many readers who did not retain Skelton's loyalty to the established church.[34] *Collyn Clout* is perhaps the most influential of those satires, which everywhere alludes to Wolsey's notorious reputation as a domineering, grasping prince of the church.[35] In part, this lasting influence has to do with the way Skelton insinuates Collyn within the early Tudor agrarian crisis insofar as everything he says, and the style in which he says it, emerges from his apparent vagrancy as he wanders, listens, and reports on the ecclesiastical culprits of England's overall decay. From this humble position he crafts a version of the worldly *vates*, the prophetic seer who is also imbued with the furor poeticus that allows him to transmute his totalizing critique of the English church into a vision of total reform.[36] Or rather, it would had he not discovered that his vision requires a closer contact with the executive violence of the sovereign than he really enjoys, resulting in his intimidated silence at the poem's close.

At the poem's start, Collyn embodies the contradictions that we saw in Fitzherbert's texts between the authoritative management of the manorial ecosystem and the social dislocation it causes. The figure of Collyn combines characteristics of the vagrant displaced by enclosure and the freeholder who wanders about noting faults and recording them in writing. This contradictory figure mirrors the poem's dual claims to offer both the rough voice of the commons and Skelton's voice of inspired poetic authority. *Collyn Clout* inhabits the immanent tensions of the agrarian crisis and looks to transcendence via the prophetic poet. This dynamic of the inspired outsider is one that many critics have noted as a singular achievement of Skelton's poetic reflections on his ambivalent relationship to political power.[37] But this ambivalence inheres not just in Skelton's precarious relationship to courtly and religious authority but also in the economic and ecological rifts that Collyn everywhere records in his reports on the gluttonous consumption of the church. *Collyn Clout*'s enactment of the contradictions between textually mediated authority and the impoverished wanderers it creates is mirrored in the amended 1598 edition of Fitzherbert's *Boke of Husbandry*, in which the reviser, James Roberts, enjoins: "Sith then thou art in such large chaines bound unto the Earths bridall, close not the closets of thyne eyes with sloth, keepe measure, not extending to ryot, and thy riches will increase, as numbers flow in the fire-inflamed braine of the diuinest Poet."[38] Here, Fitzherbert's careful measurement of the earth becomes the measured numbers of the "fire-inflamed braine of the diuinest Poet," evoking Skeltonic (and Spenserian) versions of the poet as *vates*. Roberts uncannily echoes Skelton's dialectic of earthy observation and poetic inspiration in *Collyn Clout* because the cataloguing of ecclesiastical waste of agrarian commodities forms the substance of Skelton's inflammatory poetic measures. Collyn embodies this contradiction between the quotidian struggles of England's political ecology under Wolsey and the frustrated vision of ecclesiastical reform guided by the prophetic authority of the poet.

The first forty-six lines of the poem expound upon the futility of speaking out to an indifferent public, but this does not stop Collyn Clout from announcing himself as a documentarian truth teller:

> And yf ye stande in doute
> Who brought this ryme aboute,
> My name is Collyn Cloute.
> I purpose to shake oute
> All my connynge bagge,
> Lyke a clerkely hagge.
> For though my ryme be ragged,
> Tattered and jagged,
> Rudely rayne-beaten,
> Rusty and mothe-eaten,
> Yf ye take well therwith
> It hath in it some pyth.[39]

As John Scattergood notes, the image of Collyn emptying his "connynge bagge / Lyke a clerkely hagge" echoes *Mum and the Sothsegger*, which concludes when the dreamer "vnknytte ... a bagge / Where many a pryue poyse is preyntid withynne" (1343–44). While there is little reason to think that Skelton knew a poem that only survives in one damaged manuscript, it nevertheless puts Collyn in the position of the compiler of textual evidence who, like a manorial bailiff or surveyor, uses verbal and documentary scraps to understand the agrarian infrastructure through which he moves and to guide its rectification.[40]

Outdoor mobility defines Collyn's description of his poetic style, rain-beaten and ragged like the cloak of either a vagrant or an out-riding manorial servant. While this raggedness recalls the threadbare poverty of Pierce of *Pierce the Ploughman's Crede*, for example, Collyn is not fixed in the muck of his plowland like the ideal worker but instead moves across such spaces in an ambivalent combination of the landless laborer, the reeve, and the roving dreamers and social critics who typify *Piers Plowman*, *Pierce the Ploughman's Crede*, and *Mum and the Sothsegger*. Collyn's authority stems from his wandering in the world, transforming his social marginalization into a source of vital information about the realm:

> Thus I, Collyn Cloute,
> As I go aboute,
> And wandrynge as I walke,
> I here the people talke.

(285-88)

As Collyn wanders, he gathers evidence against the princes of England's church like a manorial auditor. Going about both defines the poem's self-consciously "tattered" style and manifests the consequences of the political ecological crises that the poem attributes to clerical greed, idleness, and social mobility. Collyn embodies the contradictions of the agrarian crisis by figurally combining the opposed social positions of the manorial overseer and the landless worker. But this seeming contradiction belies a deeper unity in their opposition to the common enemy: Wolsey and his prelates.

Collyn's first report attacks bishops who seek only

> to crepe
> Within the noble walles
> Of the kynges halles,
> To fatte theyr bodyes full[.]

(125-28)

These lines efficiently combine the dual ruptures that Skelton's clerics perpetuate in the agrarian ecosystem that harm reeve and laborer alike: their class mobility and their grotesque consumption. They escape from spaces of productive toil to occupy the sovereign space of noble consumption illegitimately. Once there, they squander the food they eat, wasting the energies of the realm's political ecological system without helping to sustain it. Collyn calculates the ecclesiastical role in the agrarian crisis by cataloguing their excessive consumption and their disruption of the supposedly innate relationship between commonborn workers and the land.

Skelton's satirical energy in *Collyn Clout* often derives from the use of linguistic plenitude to evoke a sense of material waste.[41] The alliterative momentum that lends itself to the listing of foods in a poem like *Mum and the Sothsegger*, for example, also animates Skelton's rhymes, giving them a sense of potential limitlessness that mirrors the insatiable appetites of the religious estate. The friars seek fees with their preaching, but rather than stopping at the monetary abstraction of a simple payment, Collyn lists the contents of a larder to emphasize the interruption of life-sustaining energies that the friars embody:

> As many a frere, God wote,
> Preches for his grote,
> Flatterynge for a newe cote
> And for to have his fees,
> Some to gather chese
> Lothe they are to lese
> Eyther corne or malte,
> Somtyme meale and salte,
> Somtyme a bacon flycke
> That is thre fyngers thyche
> Of larde and of grece,
> Theyr covent to encrease.
>
> (836–47)

A friar will not just seek monetary payment but cheese, corn, malt, salt, bacon, or lard to "encrease" the convent, an accusation that turns the fraternal convent into an extension of the corpulent clerical bodies that define *Collyn Clout*'s unsubtle references to Wolsey's notorious fleshiness. Both convents and cardinals eat up the commons' dietary staples and grow to grotesque proportions while others starve.

The clerics of *Collyn Clout* require such a great quantity and variety of stuff—food, buildings, clothes, lands, and animals—that they allow Skelton to speak of and for a social whole by writing catalogues of commodities that metonymically evoke agricultural productivity. The expansive pull of Skeltonics suggests the vast efforts of the population as Collyn tallies instances of the clergy's unregulated consumption. In a pointed allusion to Wolsey's special permission to eat meat during Lent due to a stomach ailment, Collyn reports the cries of the people against the abuse of spiritual authority to gain profane delights:

> They crye and they yell
> ...
> Howe some of you dothe eate
> In lenton season flesshe meate,
> Feasauntes, partryche and cranes;
> Men call you therfore prophanes.
> Ye pyke no shrympes nor pranes,
> Saltfysshe, stockfyssh nor herynge,
> It is nat for your werynge,
> Nor in holy lenton season
> Ye wyll neyther beanes ne peason.
> But ye loke to be let lose
> To a pygge or to a goose,
> Your gorge nat endued
> Without a capon stued,
> Or a stewed cocke
> Under her surfled smocke
> And her wanton wodicocke.
>
> (199–219)

Foods both licit and illicit during the season of Lent fill out this complaint, with reference to the diet of fish and vegetables that Wolsey avoids contributing to the picture of a country whose abundant food supplies are squandered and misused. Lent, which ought to be a season of self-denial, becomes instead an occasion to observe how unbounded appetites among the religious elite end up affecting every aspect of England's political ecology.

The accounts of wasteful consumption are only half of the poem's analysis of the religious estate's negative effects. The avoidance of labor defines Skelton's prelates as much as their appetites. "Bysshoppes dysdayne," he reports, "Sermons for to make, / Or suche laboure to take" (133–35). This dereliction complements the poem's dismay at the clergy's unnatural rise from their supposedly innate status as agrarian workers. The problem is not the plight of the poor but the topsy-turvy change to the relations of agrarian production. As Collyn laments, "Ye growe nowe out of kynde" (661). The church leadership breaks the order of nature ("kynde") by rising above their station. Wolsey's (in)famous rise from butcher's son to cardinal is the local reference, but this biographical detail stands for a critique of the church hierarchy, which enables a new distribution of the population in servile and sovereign roles:

> For you love to go trym,
> Brought up of poore estate,
> With pryde inordynate,
> Sodaynly upstarte
> From the donge carte,
> The mattocke and the shovll
> To reygne and to rule;
> And have no grace to thynke
> Howe ye were wonte to drynke
> Of a lether bottell
> With a knavysshe stoppell,
> Whan mammockes was your meate,
> With moulde brede to eate—
> Ye coude none other gette
> To chewe and to gnawe
> To fyll therwith your mawe—
> Lodged in the strawe,
> Couchynge your drousy heddes
> Somtyme in lousy beddes.
>
> (641–59)

Here, the accumulative tendencies of Skeltonics enable an account of agrarian toil that is both contemptuous and attentive in tone. Skelton lingers over the details of what the clergy leave behind when they take orders. Having embraced "dyssymulynge and glosynge" (356) in order to fatten themselves at the king's board, these church leaders have abandoned the tools and spaces of agrarian toil. They have forgotten the deprivation that they ought to continue to experience as a kind of agrarian proletariat who have only their labor to sell in exchange for "mammockes" (scraps) and moldy bread. Skelton is not condemning the fact that such deprivation exists, nor even the gap between such poverty and the plenty enjoyed by the ruling class; rather, he is condemning the movement from one status to the other, which the corrupt church hierarchy facilitates.

This is not just a matter of social dislocation, as Skelton's agrarian spokesman attests, but an instance of a metabolic rift between agrarian land and agrarian workers. As rich prelates "growe... out of kynde," they break a kindly distribution of workers on the landscape. The church diverts laborers from the dung cart and shovel and toward sites of sovereign consumption. Collyn blames the clerics themselves for seeking an ecclesiastical route away from poverty and toil, but it is the church that creates a path from "lousy beddes" to luxurious comfort. Clerical class mobility appears as a political ecological catastrophe because it severs the natural link between land and labor. The poem unsurprisingly entertains the fantasy of reversing their ascent to leisured status:

> A preest without a letter,
> Without his vertue be greatter,
> Doutlesse were moche better
> Uppon hym for to take
> A mattocke or a rake.
>
> (270–74)

This familiar dream of reinforcing class divisions sutures a moralizing analysis of the church's social function to its effects on broader economic and ecological processes.[42] When a laborer leaves behind the dung cart and the mattock, their luxurious consumption does not just damage their own souls. *Collyn Clout* frames the church as an environmental force because of how it separates a certain segment of the population from agrarian toil and simultaneously enables them to consume more than their fair share.

Skelton's analysis of the metabolic rift perpetuated by the spiritual lords of the realm grows from his expansive accounting of their idleness and waste, but the implied suggestion of a solution in the form of coerced labor is comparatively brief. As the poem concludes, we see why. Collyn has embodied the contradictory position of the wandering vagrant who also surveys the realm and calls out illegitimate idlers as if he were a manorial bailiff. At the poem's end, this ambivalent role turns out to be quite precarious. His railings catch the attention of an offended cleric who asks the "wardeyn of the Flete" (1165) to send him to prison. The sovereign violence Collyn might have wanted to direct against the religious estate is now turned against him. Collyn falls into frightened silence. Characteristically for Skelton, as Jane Griffiths has shown, fears about "the liberty to speak" obtrude on the most grandiose possibilities for poetic authority as the poem ends with ominous threats to imprison and punish this fearless truth teller.[43] This makes it all the more striking that Skelton ends the poem with a Latin epilogue that asserts Collyn's exclusive poetic authority as a divinely inspired *vates*:[44]

> *Colinus Cloutus, "Quanquam mea carmina multis*
> *Sordescunt stulte, sed pneumata sunt rara cultis,*
> *Pneumatis altisoni divino flamine flatis.*
> *Unde mea refert tanto minus, invida quamvis*
> *Lingua nocere parat, quia, quanquam rustica canto,*
> *Undique cantabor tamen et celebrabor ubique,*
> *Inclita dum maneat gens Anglica."* (1–8)

> Although to the multitude my songs are foolishly contemptible, yet they are rare inspirations to the cultivated who are inspired by the divine breath of the sublime spirit. Whence, it concerns me much less, although the envious tongue is prepared to injure me, because, although I sing rustic songs, nevertheless, I shall be sung and celebrated everywhere while the famous English race still remains.[45]

The contrast between the popular voices that Collyn compiles and the contempt here for "the multitude" (*multis*) that cannot join the ranks of "the cultivated" (*cultis*) echoes Collyn's disdain for the abject poverty of the rural workers for whom he claims to speak. This tension is manifest in the very choice of the exclusionary medium of Latin for this self-conscious defense of *"Colinus Cloutus"* as, in Robert S. Kinsman's words, the "prophet-hero" of the poem.[46] Collyn's description of his poetry as rustic suggests the agrarian dimension of the preceding critique, but if the hope was that vernacular poetry about the agrarian crisis could guide sovereign correction, the poem's conclusion shows the precarity of this hope and the need to resort to the literary refuge of Latinate self-aggrandizement. If the poetic *vates* is going to repair the rift between the people and their sustenance, then he will need more secure access to sovereign power than Collyn enjoys. Skelton's more radical readers in the later 1520s, however, were far enough from centers of political power to imagine in their own works a less complicated relationship between the role of the reformist writer and the execution of sovereign violence.

Barlowe and Roye: Skelton's Reformed Imitators

Compared to Skelton, Jerome Barlowe and William Roye were true religious and political outsiders, former Franciscans exiled to the continent where they worked with William Tyndale, Simon Fish, and other radical reformers.[47] Perhaps because of this liminality, their wide-ranging critique in *Rede Me and Be Nott Wroth* makes no claims for elevated poetic authority along Skeltonic lines but instead embraces and elaborates upon *Collyn Clout*'s incipient systemic analysis. Notwithstanding Skelton's hostility toward reformed religion, his satires of Wolsey "are categorically clear and irrefutable sources" for Barlowe and Roye's poem.[48] *Rede Me and Be Nott Wroth*, printed in Strasbourg in 1528 by John Schott and soon after smuggled into England, adopts Collyn's infrastructural critique of clerical waste in a way that seems at first like it will reprise Skelton's individualized focus on Wolsey's failings.[49] They do not observe Skelton's caution about naming the prelate, opening their book with a parody of Wolsey's coat of arms beneath the text "I will ascende makynge my state so hye, / That my pompous honoure shall never dye."[50] However, *Rede Me and Be Nott Wroth* goes further than focusing on Wolsey as an individual and instead situates ecclesiastical corruption within larger processes of wealth accumulation and their historical roots during the course of its lengthy dialogue between Watkyn and Ieffraye.

The most far-reaching moment of this structural analysis appears when Ieffraye seeks to justify his accusation that great abbeys and religious houses have caused the agrarian crisis. As Ieffraye asserts, "All husbande men they have vndone / Destroyinge the londe miserably" (2753–54), a charge he proves with a lengthy causal narrative of how abbots have destroyed the realm's agrarian base:

> Ief.   Take hede howe farmers go backwarde,
> And thou shalt se it with thyne ey.
> For the londes welth pryncipally,
> Stondeth in exercyse of husbandry,
> By encreace of catell and tillynge.
> Which as longe as it doth prosper,
> The realme goeth backwarde never,
> In stabill felicite perseverynge.
> The abbeys then full of covetyse,
> Whom possessions coulde not suffyse,
> Ever more and more encroachinge.
> After they had spoyled gentill men,
> They vndermyned husbande men,
> In this manner theym robbynge.

>   Wheare a farme for xx.lj. was sett,
>   Vnder. xxx. they wolde not it lett,
>   Raysynge it vp on so hye a some.
>   That many a good husholder,
>   Constrayned to geve his farme over,
>   To extreme beggary did come.
> Wat.   I have hearde saye of myne elders,
>   That in Englonde many fermers,
>   Kept gaye housholdes in tymes passed.
> Ief.   Yet that they did with liberalite,
>   Sheawynge to povre people charite,
>   But nowe all together is dasshed.
>   Of ryche farme places and halles,
>   Thou seist nothynge but bare walles,
>   The rofes follen to the grownde.
>   To tourne fayre houses into pasture,
>   They do their diligent cure,
>   The common well to confownde.
> Wat.   Howe have the abbeys their payment?
> Ief.   A newe waye they do invent,
>   Lettynge a dosen farmes vnder one.
>   Which one or two ryche francklynges,
>   Occupyinge a dosen mens lyvynges,
>   Take all in their owne hondes a lone.
>
>   (2756–93)

Watkyn and Ieffraye attempt a comprehensive social analysis of how religious institutions can be responsible for "destroyinge the londe miserably." As long as husbandry prospers, Ieffraye avers, "The realme goeth backwarde never," but ever since "abbeys then full of covetyse" began "encroachinge" on the estates of great lords and squeezing their tenants, they also began engrossing smaller landholdings, so that a multitude of smallholders is replaced by "one or two ryche francklynges." Like the ruined monasteries of *Collyn Clout* that now house fowl and livestock, the "ryche farme places" have become "bare walles" and "pasture" because the former tillers of the arable soil are no longer attached to the land. They have been dispersed by engrossing franklins who seek cash returns by pasturing sheep.

But rather than laying the blame solely on the moral shortcomings of these rich franklins, as Fitzherbert might do, Barlowe and Roye consider structural motivations. This leads them to the real culprit—the great, landowning abbeys. They find that these few rich franklins empty households and villages because they need to recover the losses they incurred quickly "to get the abbottes consent" (2806) to lease the engrossed estate. Driven by this economic imperative, franklins resort to the production of wool, which might provide a good cash return but which also has socioecological consequences:

> Pover cilly shepperdes they get
> Whome into their farmes they sett,
> Lyvynge on mylke, whyg, and whey.
>
> (2812–14)

The shepherds here not only personify the consumption of inordinate resources by a few people to the detriment of the common laborer, but also the consumption of resources for the purposes of gaining profit, rather than sustaining a rural community. Such a vision of overconsumption provokes a reactive fantasy of recolonization in response to rural depopulation. In the sheep/shepherd pairing that replaces the agrarian community, the diet of the shepherds symbolizes their separation from agrarian labor and the locatable, accountable communities it sustained. During the idealized past the poem constructs, prosperous farmers supported whole households, villagers, and beggars with the food they grew. These smallholders were settled in place, growing food from the ground they and their workers tilled. In contrast, the shepherds eat in mobile isolation with their flocks, sustaining themselves only with milk, cheese, and whey. They are like nomads on the newly deserted English countryside in an uncanny prolepsis of Spenser's construction of Irish cattle-herding practices in *A View of the Present State of Ireland*. If the realm "goeth backward never" when husbandry prospers, as Barlowe and Roye suggest, then husbandry's impairment will drive the realm back to some primal, deserted state. They do not locate such a powerful regressive force in the individual moral failings of a Wolsey or a greedy franklin but in the church's determining role in the realm's political ecology as it pursues monetary accumulation instead of the care of souls. Once this developmental track has been taken, *Rede Me and Be Nott Wroth* argues, then it does not matter how sternly a Fitzherbert might warn his landowning readers not to rack-rent or evict tenants; they will have no choice but to pursue money above any other good, opening a metabolic rift in the past unity of the ideal landed estates they imagine.

Barlowe and Roye's vision of ecological destruction motivates their preferred solution: restoring an older vision of agrarian ecological balance through enforced labor. While the scattershot approach to the invective in *Rede Me and Be Nott Wroth* means that Ieffraye does not follow up with a remedy for this crisis, the poem's introductory "lamentacion" (110), which precedes the dialogue, shows how the elimination of the Catholic mass would force the religious estate to become laborers again. When they can no longer dispense the saving mass, the priesthood will no longer be able to "spretually sow [and] temporally mowe" (2830–31). Instead, the lamentation's priestly speaker fears,

> Oure effeminate flesshe and tender bones
> Shalbe constrayned to faule vnto laboure
> For why decayed is all oure honoure[.]
>
> (176–78)

The clergy's ventriloquized "lamentacion" imagines the priestly body as a source of the realm's decadence, and as such its disciplining by labor will enable the realm's renewal. England will be recolonized by the religious idlers who had caused its desertion. While Fitzherbert avoids acknowledging the contradiction between the smallholder's diversified farm and the need to maximize profit by raising sheep, Barlowe and Roye make it central to their critique of the church. They pry apart these conflicting ecological and class imperatives, showing how ecclesiastical landlords explode the compact that once held landowners, tenants, and laborers to grain-producing ecosystems.

A Supplicacyon for the Beggars

A Supplicacyon for the Beggars (ca. 1528) was published around the same time as *Rede Me and Be Nott Wroth* and emerges from the same milieu of exiles to the European continent that produced Barlowe and Roye's poem. Fish's *A Supplicacyon for the Beggars* likewise seeks to repair the agrarian crisis by removing a central institution of the church, in this case, the doctrine of purgatory. In both *Rede Me and Be Nott Wroth* and *A Supplicacyon for the Beggars*, theological proof matters less than the causes and effects of the church's parasitic role within England's political ecology. But where Barlowe and Roye emphasize the threat to laborers and small landowners, Fish addresses the ambitions of his king.

The whole tract is presented as an appeal to Henry VIII written in the voice of England's beggars, but this fiction of direct address does not exhaust the authorial poses Fish adopts. *A Supplicacyon for the Beggars* echoes earlier poetic traditions of social critique in its reliance on the distinction between true and false beggars that animates Langlandian anticlericalism.[51] Rainer Pineas, meanwhile, notes how Fish's use of hearsay is similar to "the reportorial technique with which Skelton had protected himself in his anti-Wolsey poems."[52] At times, Fish writes as if he were a surveyor, reporting extensive calculations of acreage, households, incomes, and commodities. At other times, he narrates the conditions of England's spiritual and material downfall as if he were a historian of ancient Britain. For Fish, reform of the church requires both the measurement of land and labor and the construction of the history of their interaction. Fish deploys these varied rhetorical stances to craft a vision of English history as a political ecological contest between sovereign and church over the territorial resources that sustain an industrious population.

A Supplicacyon for the Beggars argues that the doctrine of purgatory has enabled the church to interrupt an ideal metabolic interaction that existed in England's mythic past, in which the land, the people, and the king's military strength mutually supported each other. But before he immerses his readers in an ideal past of ecological balance and unimpeded political sovereignty, Fish takes on the role of the surveyor. Fish presses Henry VIII as if he were a diligent steward urging the lord of his estate to approve a firm hand against idlers who are fleecing him of his profits. According to Fish, England's beggars "for verey constraint . . . die for hunger," while bishops, abbots, priors, and an innumerable "idell, rauinous sort" set "all laboure a side" but get "[t]he goodliest lordshippes, maners, londes, and territories."[53] Fish translates the general political categories for units of landed property—lordships, manors, lands, and territories—into a list of the material commodities they produce: "corne, medowe, pasture, grasse, wolle, coltes, calues, lambes, pigges, gese, and chikens. Ouer and bisides, the tenth part of euery seruauntes wages, the tenth part of the wolle, milke, hony, waxe, chese, and butter."[54] This litany of agricultural produce and infrastructure encompasses everything from different uses of land (pasture and meadow) to the wages of the landless laborers who work in such spaces and the commodities they make. The list conjures rural plenty in order to illustrate the enormity of its waste.

To reinforce his account of England's contemporary decay, Fish constructs a historical comparison to show how bad things have become. The idealized past of *A Supplicacyon for the Beggars* presents a sovereign unimpeded by the expropriations of the religious estate: "Oh greuous and peynfull exactions thus yerely to be paied! from the whiche the people of your nobill predecessours, the kinges of the auncient Britons, euer stode fre.... The danes, nether the saxons, yn the time of the auncient Britons, shulde neuer haue ben abill to haue brought theire armies from so farre hither ynto your lond, to haue conquered it, if they had had at that time suche a sort of idell glotons to finde at home."[55] Fish uses the story of Britain's early medieval colonization to envision a relationship between sovereign power and the land it controls that had not yet been interrupted by religious institutions. Fish invokes Henry VIII's legendary ancestor to further drive this point home: "The nobill king Arthur had neuer ben abill to haue caried his armie to the fote of the mountaines, to resist the coming downe of lucius the Emperoure, if suche yerely exactions had ben taken of his people."[56] This not only touches on a sense of Tudor "family pride" but also plays on feelings of geopolitical insecurity rooted in the loss of agrarian productivity at home.[57] The myths of ancient Britain, with its waves of invasion and occupation, allow Fish to construct the interdependence of agrarian ecology and sovereign power. Colonization and expansion depend on being unencumbered by the church, Fish argues, perhaps in a canny appeal to an incipient interest in New World colonization. As we will see in chapter 5, one of Fish's contemporaries and a member of Thomas More's circle who joined in the controversy sparked by Fish's pamphlet, John Rastell, had put together a failed colonial venture to the northeast coast of America about a decade before *A Supplicacyon for the Beggars* was printed.

According to Fish, the most consequential invasion that led to the downfall of ancient Britain's prosperity was that of the Roman church. Of this event, he laments, "Oh the greuous shipwrak of the comon welth, whiche yn auncient time, bifore the coming yn of these rauinous wolues, was so prosperous, that then there were but fewe theues!"[58] Fish interprets the historical decline from ancient Britain to the present as a story of an invasive species destroying a homeostatic political ecology. These "rauinous wolues" will have no place in Fish's reformed society, which will no longer create niches for the flourishing of "theues" that now wander England. These stories of the realm's ancient conquests before the establishment of the Roman church usefully blur the boundaries between religious change and the political ecology of colonization.⁵⁹ In Fish's view, Henry VIII must recolonize his territory by forcing the "idell glottons" of the church to work.

For the king to protect his realm from ravenous clerical appetites, *A Supplicacyon for the Beggars* proposes violent coercion to work and marry:

> Set these sturdy lobies a brode in the world, to get theim wiues of theire owne, to get theire liuing with their laboure in the swete of theire faces, according to the commaundement of god, Gene. iij. to gyue other idell people, by theire example, occasion to go to laboure. Tie these holy idell theves to the carts, to be whipped naked about euery market town til they will fall to labor, that they, by theyre importunate begging, take not awry the almesse that the good christen people wolde giue vnto vs sore, impotent, miserable people, your bedemen.⁶⁰

Relying on an understanding of the injunction to labor in Genesis 3 as requiring manual toil, Fish dismisses the legitimacy of the spiritual labor of the clergy and fraternal orders. The religious must be coerced into physical labor through the direct violence of the king. The gendered counterpart to the curse of toil in Genesis 3—pain in childbirth—also informs Fish's fantasy of coercing the clergy to marry. Requiring the religious to work and marry enables a new form of control over the realm's population:

> Then shall, aswell the nombre of oure forsaid monstruous sort, as of the baudes, hores, theues, and idell people, decreace. . . . Then shall you haue full obedience of your people. Then shall the idell people be set to worke. Then shall matrimony be moche better kept. Then shal the generation of your people be encreased. Then shall your comons encrease in richesse. Then shall the gospell be preached. Then shall none begge oure almesse from vs. Then shal we haue ynough, and more then shall suffice vs; whiche shall be the best hospitall that euer was founded for vs. Then shall we daily pray to god for your most noble estate long to endure.⁶¹

The anaphoric repetition of the word "then" at the beginning of each sentence underscores the causal thinking that links the ecology of agrarian land and labor to national "richesse," the preaching of the gospel, and the longevity of Henry VIII's "noble estate." The enforcement of labor ensures a generative agrarian landscape and provides a general "hospitall" for the needy of his realm who speak this supplication. But care for beggars is manifestly secondary to the main thrust of Fish's persuasive strategy, which is to excite Henry VIII's imagination about the squandered agrarian wealth of the nation and to suggest that a new regime of labor on arable land seized from the church would strengthen the king's economic and military position. Fish's emphasis on sovereign violence complements the analysis of economic compulsion in *Rede Me and Be Nott Wroth*. While Barlowe and Roye explain why processes like enclosure can be blamed on the church, Fish puts forward a stark vision of what can be done about it. Robert Crowley would combine the analytical and prescriptive aims of each of these texts in *Philargyrie of Greate Britayne*. Yet the changed ecclesiastical circumstances after England's break with Rome in 1534 necessarily affected Crowley's analysis of an agrarian crisis that, as it turned out, did not need a singular ecclesiastical culprit to wreak its havoc. What remains the same, however, is the role of sovereign violence as the final defense of the realm's political ecology.

Robert Crowley's Metabolic Rift: *Philargyrie of Greate Britayne*

Robert Crowley was a prolific writer, but arguably his most monumental achievement was his 1550 edition of *Piers Plowman*. While scholars had once seen this edition largely as a tendentious Protestant appropriation of Langland's poem, subsequent refinements to this view have led to a wider appreciation of Crowley's attempt to make sense of the poem's historical, linguistic, and formal alterity while also remaining attuned to its resonances in Crowley's present.[62] The effects on his own writing of editing and annotating Langland's poem can be seen in his allegorical indictment of the English Reformation published a year after the *Piers Plowman* edition, *Philargyrie of Greate Britaine* (1551). *Philargyrie of Greate Britayne* adapts Langland's agrarian allegory, especially the conflict between Hunger and Waster, to understand the aftermath of the dissolution of the monasteries as an ongoing political ecological crisis. Evidence for how he might deploy the insights he gained from a reading of the plowing of the half acre can be seen in his annotation of the passage describing Hunger's effects with the lines "Faitors worke for fear of honger" and "How begers mai be made to work."[63] Crowley emphasizes the causal relationship between hunger and work in ways that will inform his approach to the interplay of economic power and sovereign violence in *Philargyrie of Greate Britayne*. Previous critics are inclined to see mainly traditional economic moralism in Crowley's critique, but this discounts the degree to which Langlandian personification enabled Crowley to undertake a precocious structural analysis of the usefulness of scarcity and its selective amelioration.[64]

The dissolution of the monasteries in the 1530s and 1540s provided timely evidence for novel developments in England's political ecology, as did midcentury controversies over international trade. An act passed in 1555 of Mary I's reign asserts—in language that uncannily echoes the critique of the export trade in Crowley's *Philargyrie of Greate Britayne*—that despite previous legislation against it, the persistence of "unsatiable persons seking their onely lucers and gaynes, hathe and dayly doth carye and convey innumberable quantitie aswell of Corne Chese Butter and other Victuall, as of Wood, out of this Realme into the parties beyond the Seas," causing in turn "a wonderfull dearthe and extreame pryses."[65] Meanwhile, in the decade or so before the publication of *Philargyrie of Greate Britayne*, the fate of former monastic assets offered tangible manifestations of the process by which the lands and livings of smallholders could become "the golden showre of dissolued Abbey lands," as Richard Carew put it in his 1602 account of one such transfer.[66] The scramble for former monastic lands formed part of a generally more active land market throughout the middle of the sixteenth century. The greatest beneficiaries from the acquisition of these assets could expect either new sources of annual revenue, as did the great lords who received the most extensive holdings, or resaleable assets that could be sources of cash for those who acquired smaller, more piecemeal holdings.[67] At the same time, increasing numbers of people were moving to cities seeking waged work, prompting some observers to advocate for the restoration of arable farming as the primary use of English land and labor; such positions were in part an indictment of the failure of the dissolution to redress the plight of the poor, which, Larry Scanlon argues, also motivated Crowley's annotations to passūs 5 and 10 that predict or advocate "the suppression of the Abbayes" as a reminder to its Protestant readers of this failure.[68] As a writer steeped in the agrarian perspective of the *Piers Plowman* tradition, Crowley would have had ample occasion to see how the marketing of parcels of land after the dissolution could disrupt processes of social reproduction.

The dissolution augmented the revenues of some great lords, but it also provided opportunities to commoners like John Braddyll, who recalls in his will that, thanks to Henry VIII's dissolution, his "firste rising and gaine was gotten by byenge and sellinge of lande and other dive [*sic*, diverse] bargaines."[69] Similarly, operators like John Bellow and

John Broxholme amassed a number of small properties to be sold for cash.[70] There was also a more literal and direct transformation of religious infrastructure to fixed capital to be observed in the movement of industries like ceramics and glassmaking into the stone buildings of former priories alongside the use of such large buildings in places like Canterbury for cloth manufacture.[71] The point here is not so much that Crowley's poem is an accurate record of an empirically verifiable transition to capitalism after the dissolution but rather that Crowley was surrounded by opportunities to observe the quantitative abstraction and alienation of living land, labor, and infrastructure into money that could be used to make more money. For Crowley, Langlandian allegory allowed him to make this process legible because its mode of personification likewise foregrounds the constant interplay of materiality and abstraction that is at the heart of wealth accumulation.

Philargyrie of Greate Britayne tells the story of four personifications. Philargyrie is a rapacious giant who invades Britain in a vaguely distant "long tyme before" and convinces "a legion" to follow him, giving them a free hand to steal whatever they want as long as they bring him gold, the only substance he can digest.[72] After a while, Hypocrisy suggests that Philargyrie can get gold more easily by eschewing forceful plunder and convincing the population to buy their salvation from purgatory instead. This arrangement fails because Hypocrisy, repulsed by Philargyrie's insatiable consumption, attempts to win the people to his side and to follow him exclusively, and Philaute rises to take his place. Philaute informs Philargyrie of Hypocrisy's betrayal and hatches a plan to undercut the usurper by preaching reformed theology. He succeeds in supplanting Hypocrisy but fails to find enough gold to satisfy the giant by selling Hypocrisy's assets, causing Philargyrie to beat the population with the "rode / Of hunger" (1326-27). This leads to such an outcry that finally Truth tells of the people's suffering to the King, who takes up the sword and drives out Philargyrie.

Crowley recognized from his immersion in the *Piers Plowman* tradition that luxurious consumption depended on the transformation of land, labor, and food into the inert abstractions of moneyed wealth, and so both the phenomenon and his analysis of it are not new. But in the wake of the dissolution of the monasteries, there is something newly unsettling about this process to Crowley: no longer is there a singular, identifiable culprit in the form of the church or the fraternal orders as there was for the *Crede*-poet, Barlowe and Roye, or Fish. Instead, Crowley recognizes in the process of the creation of wealth a permanent state of political ecological crisis. He invents Philargyrie to be the visible, singular culprit for a structure of exploitation that depends on a fundamental metabolic rift that the church alone did not create and that cannot be resolved by the church's reform alone. Crowley seeks to describe a general process whereby the creation of wealth depends on the creation of conditions that separate people from the land, which will allow Philargyrie to wield his ultimate weapon, "the rod / Of honger" (246–47).

Philargyrie's arrival "long tyme before" echoes Fish's vision of a legendary age of territorial sovereignty and agrarian plenty ruined by an occupying force of wolfish clergy. In the opening narrative section of Crowley's poem, however, Philargyrie's religious valence is not as a representative of a foreign church but as a self-styled deity in his own right. He is, in one sense, just greed, plain and simple, but this transhistorical vice needs historically specific conditions upon which to work, and Crowley will supply these in further detail. At first, though, the narrative remains sparse. Philargyrie gathers "a legion" of followers, pledging that all who join him will "lyue in playe and sporte" (56–58), as long as they:

> honoure him as God
> Wyth Baggis of golde
> In many folde
> In number euen or odd[.]
>
> (61–64)

They are instructed to obtain this wealth, the narrator specifies, with "force and stronge hand" (71). When Philargyrie begins his oration in the next section, he tells his piratical band to:

> Catch what you can
> From euery man
> And hold it for your owne
> Reape, let me se
> And brynge to me
> That other men have sowne.
>
> (113–18)

The historical terms of the allegory remain vague early in the poem, which Christopher Warley notes as a lack in Crowley's economic analysis.[73] But the vagueness is important to Crowley's point: he simultaneously wants to describe a general process of wealth expropriation and to understand the historically specific features of what appears to be its recent intensification. He is seemingly muddling different historical moments because the interplay of economy, ecology, and coercive power are blended over time in an emergent process that can bring long-past moments of expropriation into the present. For all the writing, both in the early Tudor period and in subsequent centuries, about a sixteenth-century break between a stable, reciprocal manorial system and a new and exploitative market system, the tensions between these two coexisting possibilities were evident by the mid-fourteenth century, as Crowley would have learned from *Piers Plowman*'s trenchant economic critiques. Thus, Crowley does not seek a historical allegory with an easily locatable "before" and "after" but is, at this stage, crafting an analysis of the general process by which wealth is made through the interaction of land, labor, and violence.

Making wealth from this interaction involves abstract measurements of value that enable both simple expropriation by force and circulation by exchange. Philargyrie thus commands the use of force, hoarding, and exchange together:

> And where you spye
> Commoditie
> Ther plant your dwelling place
> And then employe
> Your whole study
> To get it up apase
> And by eche porte
> Where is resorte
> Se that ye do conueye
> All maner thynge
> Whereof myght sprynge
> Profyte to this contrey
> For so shall ye
> Enriched be
> And haue money in store
> For you shall sell
> > Thyngis twyse so wel
> > As men dyd heretofore.
>
> (137–54)

Instead of a precise historical allegory, Crowley opts for a narrative that progresses not according to chronological sequence but rather via the logic of expropriation, which at first involves only force but almost immediately includes mercantile exchange and economic coercion. Obtaining goods and marketing them involve occupying particular places and using specific infrastructures to create new political ecological conditions in which agrarian produce can be "conueye[d]" away and become "money in store."

As Philargyrye continues, he expands on the nature of wealth in a catalogue that suggests how its abstract, monetized form depends on an initial seizure of a dynamic agrarian ecosystem:

> The woule, the lead
> The corne for breadde
> The bere butter and cheese
> Wyll be well solde
> Wherefore be bolde
> By them you can nought leese.
>
> (155–60)

Beginning with a list of commodities, Crowley works back to the land, labor, and infrastructure that produces them:

> You muste therfore
> Haue euermore
> All those thyngis in your hande
> Wherin sprynge
> Of euery thynge
> And fyrst encrease doeth stande.
>   The pasture grownde
> That feadeth sound
> You must in no case lacke
> All maner mynes
> And myllis that gryndis
> Must helpe to fyll your sacke
>   Copsis of wodde
> Be verye good
> For you to have in hande
> You must nedes haue
> Greate fermes a thraue
> Wyth all good fruitfull lands.
>
> (173–90)

Philargyrie does not want only an inert storehouse of goods but a dynamic system that continuously generates more and more wealth. The verbal accumulation that cannot resist listing more and more sites for the production of value expresses Crowley's expansive vision of economic expropriation. Philargyrie assures his followers that pastures, mines, mills, woodlands, and farms are the most sustainable sources of monetary wealth because they are renewable—they are where "fyrst encrease doeth stande."

Philargyrie teaches his crew that it is essential to "have in hande" the combined land, labor, and infrastructure that produces the sustaining energies of life. Philargyrie surveys primal landscapes for the harvest of use-values that sustain the basic needs of the population, but this is only the first step in a process that will reduce this diversity into the homogenizing medium of gold. Philargyrie teaches his followers that the process of gathering these goods and selling them causes restrictions on supply, which activates a mercantile logic that cuts against the logic of sustainable use. Once his followers have obtained this infrastructure, they are to restrict the distribution of whatever goods they produce to boost exchange value:

> Short tale to make
> You muste all take
> And whorde up styll in store
> Tyll that be scant
> Whereof no want
> Was euer sene before.
>
> (191–96)

Simple expropriation by force quickly gives way to economic coercion once the process of exchange creates new kinds of scarcity. The regenerative capacities of arable and pasture have now been yoked to the process of creating monetary wealth rather than food.

This contradiction between the imperatives of sustenance and the accumulation of money is central to the significance of Philargyrie's need to eat gold. Gold is the only substance that he can digest, so the compelling force of the mortal body's need for food is intimately familiar to him. This allows him to understand that, in the last resort, he can rely on the populace's need to eat to drive them to work for his satisfaction. In this postdissolution revision of Langland's Hunger, Philargyrie cannot be appeased, even temporarily, by the simple arrival of harvest.[74]

He always seeks a further transformation of agrarian land and labor not just into food but into that mysteriously powerful medium of exchange: gold.

The process of getting gold for Philargyrie's consumption shows Crowley's prescient grasp of the need for endless growth that defines capitalist accumulation. Philargyrie needles his followers never to relent in their quest for gold (221-26). Like Langland's Hunger, Philargyrie will eat what is brought to him, but he will not go away. Philargyrie personifies the transformation of dynamic components of a living agrarian ecosystem into the unchanging medium of gold, and this process is unending. It fuels only Philargyrie's continued life, who figures in this aspect the accumulation of monetary wealth that never returns to the lands and bodies that first made it. Phylargyrie's strange metabolism personifies the interruption of the collective metabolism of humans and the earth.

Philargyrie's power stems not only from his initial promise to his followers of a life spent "in pleasure" (241) but also from the threat he utters if they do not work to keep him fed:

> I am your God
> And have the rod
> Of honger in my fyste
> Wherefore take hede
> Ye do me fede
> Wyth golde that is fynest[.]
>
> (245-50)

Here, a clear result of editing *Piers Plowman* is Crowley's absorption of Langland's portrayal of hunger as a manipulable weakness of the mortal body. Even if actual famines arise from myriad political, ecological, and economic interactions, Langland's personification consolidates those factors in a way that underscores hunger's role in maintaining structures of domination. Crowley, like the other writers in the *Piers Plowman* tradition, emphasizes the coercive manipulation of Hunger in Langland's allegory, ignoring Langland's exposure of its inability to function as a controllable tool of power that can be brought in and dismissed at will. But Crowley's approach to hunger serves a different purpose from other texts like *Pierce the Ploughman's Crede*. He is not suggesting that the strategic withholding of sustenance from a certain group—friars or idlers or clerics—will make them reliable workers. He is locating "the rod / Of honger" within a political ecological process that combines the threat of direct violence with the indirect violence of separating the population from the lands and infrastructure that sustain them.

To accelerate the process of economic coercion, Philargyrie advises mercantile export to further drain the realm of necessities like food and cloth. This turns out to have a double economic benefit for Philargyrie's crew: the implicit one of direct exchange for money on the foreign market and the explicit one that the resulting shortages will raise prices:

> Convey awaye
> These thyngis beyond ye fome
> Then shall the pryse
> Of that aryse
> That shal be lefte at home[.]
>
> (168–72)

In Crowley's version of international trade, commodities leave, realizing their exchange value in the form of the gold that Philargyrie eats, but nothing useful—nothing that feeds and houses the population—comes back. In this analysis, Crowley shares the assumptions of the act passed in 1555 of Mary I's reign quoted above. In Philargyrie's command to "convey awaye" such commodities, Crowley recognizes that it is not the mere reciprocity of trading goods for gold from foreign lands that will feed him but rather the price rise "at home" that will both increase the quantities of money his followers can demand for their hoarded commodities *and* enable Philargyrie to deploy the rod of hunger and thus compel their labor when they can no longer afford to buy those commodities.

Philargyrie's initial seizure of land, labor, and infrastructure inaugurates a political ecology geared toward the production of gold rather than useful goods. When the ecclesiastical figure of Hypocrisy suggests a new method for obtaining both gold and productive lands, Crowley asserts that clerical wealth is not just the abstraction of acres and rents described in a surveyor's register but the intervention in a dynamic system of labor and land. The church, as England's largest landlord, perpetuates this intervention, but it does not create it, Crowley argues, which is why the dissolution of the monasteries does not alter this fundamental arrangement. Philaute replaces Hypocrisy, but the structures of expropriation remain, just as Philargyrie's speech describing how to create those structures precedes the rise of religious fraud in the figure of Hypocrisy.

After Philargyrie's first speech, Hyprocrisy emerges from the crowd to propose an artful deception that will convince the population to give up their resources willingly. Hypocrisy predicts that if the people fear suffering in purgatory, they will pay to avoid it:

> So they wyll brynge
> To us althynge
> Whereof we shall stande nede
> Houses to buylde
> Boeth thackt and tylde
> And bye us fode and wede[.]
>
> (383–88)

Anticlerical satire often connects manipulative preaching and the seizure of wealth, but Crowley is more detailed in his depiction of the uses to which this wealth is put. The "houses" that Hypocrisy builds are not just purely wasteful, luxurious expenditures, like the glistering stained glass in the Franciscan convent of *Pierce the Ploughman's Crede* or the tapestry-lined walls of Wolsey's rooms in *Collyn Clout*. They are the means for Hypocrisy's church to further impinge on both the territorial sovereignty of the political hierarchy and the physical health of the population:

> Then in ech place
> That pleasante was
> He planted houses sure
> Of lyme and stone
> They were ech one
> Because they shoulde endure
>   Bulwarkis also
> A thousande moe
> Then any man can tell
> To beate them downe
> That ware the crowne
> If they dyd once rebell
>   So was that lande
> Whole in the hand

> Of Philargyries men ...
> 	But to couloure
> His endeuoure
> He dyd those places name
> Houses for clarkes
> And the bulwarckes
> Lodgyngis for blynde & lame[.]
>
> (527–50)

These buildings, disguised as housing for bishops and monks, limit royal sovereignty, but the military fortifications disguised as hospitals "for blynde & lame" also suggest the church's insidious control over bodies.[75] In this biopolitical supplement to economic power, Crowley envisions a more totalizing and subtle control over the physical existence of the population in its interactions with the environment. He recognizes that the political ecology of ecclesiastical domination depends not only on the seizure of natural resources but also the discipline of and care for individual bodies. At first, this domination only affects the ostensibly nonlaboring bodies of the disabled population. As Philargyrie's appetites persist, however, his bodily disciplining of the populace extends ever wider as he wields the rod of hunger at the poem's narrative climax. The prosopopoeic figuration of Philargyrie wielding hunger as a punitive weapon while also using hospitals as a cover for his domination exemplifies personification's capacity to compress processes of biopolitical and economic power through figures of sovereign violence.

The rod of hunger is used only after Philaute has taken power from Hypocrisy. Philaute seizes his chance to rule when Hypocrisy grows tired of working so hard to fill the giant's unfillable gut and attempts to usurp Philargyrie's dominant position. Philaute prevents Hypocrisy's scheme by alerting Philargyrie to his adviser's treachery and requests a new arrangement. He asks to "be sent / To preach in Lent" (1007–8) to draw people away from Hypocrisy's side. Philaute's strategy is to convince the people that they are wrong to seek salvation by paying Hypocrisy, "Sens all men muste / Be made iust bi Christis bloud" (1017–18). He invokes "Christis bloude" a second time (1022) as a power greater than Hypocrisy's masses and bells, and this repeated emphasis on "Christis bloud" leaves little doubt as to the ecclesiastical form Philaute personifies. Yet the truly justifying substance of Christ's blood appears here as just another means to manipulate the flow of worldly goods to

Philargyrie's gullet. Philaute's success cuts Hypocrisy out of the circuit of accumulation, and all the wealth he had amassed passes directly to Philargyrie and Philaute.

Philaute's plan has a major flaw, however: if he preaches that salvation cannot be bought, then he will not be able to squeeze gold from the credulous. This leaves only the sale of Hypocrisy's former assets as a source of gold. Once Philargyrie has eaten through that hoard, Philaute desperately feeds him "wyth leade / With stones, and wyth tymber" (1278–79). After selling off and dismantling the built infrastructure of Hypocrisy's reign, Philaute turns to the infamous practice Crowley and others perceived to be a worsening problem since the break with Rome: rack-renting. But even Philaute's raising of rents "from fyue grotes to a pounde" (1315) cannot satisfy the giant. Finally, Philargyrie uses the rod of hunger that always hovered as a threat behind the machinations of Hypocrisy and Philaute:

> Then gan this God
> To take the rode
> Of hunger in his fyst
> And sayde that he
> Woulde fylled be
> No man shoulde him resiste.
>   Then wyth strokes sore
> He smote the pore[.]
>
> (1325–32)

Crowley's analysis of the dissolution of the monasteries inverts Fitzherbert's strenuous attempts to ameliorate the conflict that inheres in the landowners' ability to survey and quantify potential revenues from their lands and to increase them, should they wish, by wielding the threat of eviction. Fitzherbert could only exhort them not to do so. Crowley, however, saw that no individual moral conscience had prevented the interruption of the rural population's embeddedness in an agrarian ecosystem that had long fallen out of sync with the need for monetary accumulation. Philargyrie personifies this impersonal force that wields hunger to drive people to work—not to obtain their food immediately but rather to accumulate surplus.

While this analysis departs from Fish's diagnosis of the Roman church as the cause of England's weakness, Crowley constructs a similar figure of correction to Fish's Henry VIII in his King. The King learns from Truth about Philargyrie's attack on the commons and announces to God:

> Thou hast chosen me
> Ouer thy flocke to raygne
> Make me of myght
> All wrongis to ryght
> And make all well agayne[.]
>
> (1404–8)

Although Philargyrie personifies the complexities of institutional religion's intersection with the manorial economy, his singular form as a character activates the concomitant fantasy that another, more powerful figure can solve the problems the giant represents by taking up the sword of state power. Crowley's King has apparently been ignorant of the plight of his people. He has not been involved in any of the preceding action in the poem, and he seems to stand above the system that exploits them. This very separation, however, allows him to intervene as a defensive figure—as long as he is informed by Truth first. In the poem's abrupt ending, the King

> chased oute
> This gygante stoute
> And then all thyngs were well[.]
>
> (1412–14)

These final lines register the possibility that sovereign violence can restore a fantastical equilibrium between the realm's agrarian land and its laboring population.

In this account of *Philargyrie of Greate Britaine*, Crowley uses what he learned from editing *Piers Plowman* to anatomize the political ecology of primitive accumulation, creating the figure of Philargyrie to personify the metabolic rift of agrarian capitalism. He, like Truth at the end of the poem, must persuade the sovereign to take violent action against the idlers and parasites that threaten the productive political ecology of the realm.[76] The role of Truth as adviser to a distant sovereign in *Philargyrie of Greate Britaine* seems less like a nod to Langland's transcendent Saint Truth and more like a possible figure for reformist poetry's ability to guide sovereign authority. The conclusion of *Philargyrie of Greate Britaine* suggests that poetry can participate in drastic material reforms as Crowley avoids Skeltonic anxiety about the poet's authority to speak.

Fitzherbert believed that writing could affect the political ecology of the realm in a different way—through practical texts on its daily management rather than polemical analyses of the expropriation of wealth in verse. Despite the differences between their respective literary projects, both Fitzherbert and the critical poets of the mid-Tudor years were attuned to the totalizing implications of writing about agrarian land and labor. Skelton, Barlowe and Roye, and Fish assert that the most far-reaching consequences of clerical corruption can be found in the church's effects on the agrarian economy, while Crowley uses the fact of wealth's origins in agrarian land and labor to attack the monetary accumulation of the churches of Rome and England. In each case, these poems eschew the mild tone of Fitzherbert's didacticism even as they explore the contradictions between the flourishing of rural workers and the imperatives of monetary accumulation that Fitzherbert tentatively outlines. In their critiques of the church's role in furthering the separation of workers from their toilsome relationship to the land, the poets and polemicists of the sixteenth-century *Piers Plowman* tradition seek, with varying degrees of confidence, to carve out a role for the prophetic writer to identify and correct all that is amiss in the ecology and economy of the realm. As we will see in chapters 5 and 6, Spenser seems to move between Crowleyan confidence and Skeltonic doubt in his renovation of the *Piers Plowman* tradition in Elizabethan Ireland. There, Spenser develops their insights about the fraught interactions of wealth accumulation, sovereign power, and the role of writing as a theorist and practitioner of colonial exploitation.

CHAPTER 5

Why Colin Clout Came to Ireland

The Piers Plowman *Tradition and Spenser's Late Pastorals*

John Rastell was a lawyer, writer, and printer who demonstrates the impact of the *Piers Plowman* tradition on the ideology of Atlantic colonialism. He was brother-in-law to Thomas More (and great-grandfather to John Donne). He was enmeshed in the literary scene that surrounded figures like Thomas More and John Skelton, and he was a would-be colonial adventurer. Rastell's career combined colonial thought and practice with literary engagement with the *Piers Plowman* tradition in a way that clarifies what Edmund Spenser might have found in this tradition when the latter put Colin Clout, his Skeltonically named pastoral persona, in Ireland in his late pastoral verse.

The colonial dimension of Rastell's engagement with English agrarian critique might seem surprising given that his contribution to the *Piers Plowman* tradition takes the form of a dramatic interlude he printed and perhaps collaborated in writing with John Heywood around 1525 called *Gentleness and Nobility*, which has been read as a radical critique of private property and class hierarchy.[1] Nevertheless, when set alongside Rastell's earlier interlude that advocates for the colonization of North America, *Four Elements* (1520), his celebration of agrarian labor takes on a different cast. There, the seemingly oppositional energies of the *Piers Plowman* tradition end up supporting a work ethic that appeals to the interests of a dominant class of landowners, notwithstanding the critique of class hierarchy that animates *Gentleness and Nobility*.

Gentleness and Nobility depicts a merchant, a knight, and a plowman who debate "who is a verey gentylman and who is a noble man and how men shuld come to auctoryte."[2] The dialogue is a compendium of economic and moral arguments in which each speaker affirms the virtue of each social estate. Despite the occasionally harsh tones of their debate, where the plowman acquits himself especially well, the play affirms that agrarian labor, craftwork, import and export of goods from other climates, and the improvement of property are the interlocking foundations of a just society. But consensus is elusive in the face of the uncompromising attacks of the plowman, who rejects class hierarchy and, in David Bevington's words, "represents a fusion of the exploited agrarian worker and the idealistic intellectual."[3] Bevington could just as well be describing Pierce from *Pierce the Ploughman's Crede* or Skelton's Collyn Clout. This is fitting because Rastell himself printed a selection of Skelton's works between 1525 and 1527.[4] Rastell also weighed in on the controversy between Simon Fish's and Thomas More's competing supplications with his own *A New Boke of Purgatory* (1530), in which he attempted to shore up More's orthodox position, even though he became a promoter of reformed religion later in life.[5]

In addition to his career as a writer and printer, Rastell pursued colonial designs on North America, organizing an ill-fated trading venture to the northern coast of the continent.[6] After having contributed funds for outfitting three vessels with trade goods and supplies, the ships' masters conspired to thwart the voyage, only making it as far as Cork Harbour in Ireland before Rastell had to resist the attempts of the crew to use the ships for piracy and was forced to allow the ships to sail to Bourdeaux for the sale of their cargo while he remained in Ireland.[7] Stuck there for two years (1517–1519), he wrote the didactic *Four Elements* (1520)—the first printed work in English to refer to the New World as "America."[8] This interlude exemplifies how the formation of colonial ideology could combine the construction of nature as a knowable object with a work ethic familiar from both estate management texts and the *Piers Plowman* tradition. The would-be colonial adventurer wrote a prosopopoeic drama in which Natura Naturata and Experiens school Humanity in elemental physics and cutting-edge geography on the spatial relationship between the Old and New Worlds by using a large globe likely based on maps of the world printed in the preceding few years.[9] This novel global perspective is matched, however, by familiar late medieval modes of imagining the role of labor within the social whole. To check the pride of the rich who "do no nother thyng / But bringe ryches to their own possessyon,"[10] the play asserts:

> [A]ll the ryches in the worlde that is
> Rysyth of the grounde by Goddys sendynge,
> And by the labour of pore mennys handys,
> And though thou, ryche man, have therof the kepynge,
> Yet is not this ryches of thy gettynge,
> Nor oughtyst not in reason to be preysed the more
> For by other mennys labour it is got before.
>
> (71–77)

Here, Rastell articulates an ideology of work, also prominent in *Gentleness and Nobility*, in which the source of England's wealth is really the soil and "the labour of pore mennys handys." While we have seen instances of this work ethic in the agrarian critique of church wealth in the *Piers Plowman* tradition, Rastell deploys it in a colonial context far different from the English countryside beset by enclosure.

Rastell takes a view that might seem to uplift the humble English worker and uses it to dramatize the benefits of colonial settlement and exploitation. After informing the audience about the discovery of a new continent (the Americas) "within this twenty yere" (736), Experiens tantalizingly speculates about "what commodytes be within" (747). No one knows the riches this continent holds, however, because of feckless idlers like Rastell's mutinous crew, who "wolde take no paine to saile farther / Than their owne lyst and pleasure" (758–59). Because of this idle greed, "Such kaytyffes have distroyed" (761) whatever chance the English had to be the first ones to occupy and exploit this rich land, to:

> take possessyon
> And ma[k]e furst buyldynge and habytacion,
> A memory perpetuall!
>
> (765–67)

These maritime English wasters are matched by the inhabitants of this new land: "Whiche as yet lyve all bestly" (780). They have no knowledge of God or iron tools: "Buyldynge nor house they have non at all, / But wodes, cotes, and cavys small" (787–88). Colonial adventurers have the chance to perform the "meritoryouse dede" of instructing these people who live only in woods and caves "to lyve more vertuously" (776).

But this is inseparable from the larger goal of expanding Henry VIII's territorial sovereignty and accessing a vast amount of material wealth. Experiens rhapsodizes about what

> an honorable thynge,
> Both to the realme and to the kynge,
> To have had his domynyon extendynge
> There into so farre a grounde[.]
>
> (768–71)

Experiens follows this wish with a catalogue of copper, timber, pitch, tar, and fish (793–810). Rastell surveys the potential wealth of the new continent and laments its waste caused by both the rapacious idleness of bad English sailors and the "bestly" life of the Indigenous inhabitants.

In Rastell's view, the only way to access the commodities of the New World is to enlist virtuous and hardworking Englishmen to sail and settle there, as he had just tried and failed to do himself before languishing in an Ireland that had not yet become the focus of the colonial ambitions that Spenser would articulate.[11] *Four Elements* reveals how the ideology of work associated with early Tudor reformism could be extended to the justification of colonial occupation in places where the land is fertile but allegedly remains unworked because of a lack of "pore mennys handys." The New World excited both Rastell's didactic literary ambitions and his desire for wealth to shore up Henry VIII's dominion. These found a familiar literary expression in the vernacular personifications and political ecological assumptions that mark both *Four Elements* and *Gentleness and Nobility*.

As for the Indigenous population of the New World in *Four Elements*, Experiens concludes:

> But howe the people furst began
> In that contrey or whens they cam,
> For clerkes it is a questyon.
>
> (817–19)

No more thought is given to these people or their land as Experiens moves onto another subject in his lesson. But at the end of the sixteenth century, Spenser would focus a great deal of attention on the origins and lifeways of the inhabitants of a much nearer colony: Ireland. Spenser sought to extend the dominion of another Tudor monarch to an Ireland that had become the subject of extensive colonial designs, especially in Munster, since the start of the second Desmond rebellion. He did so by both writing and settling on the Munster plantation, where he surveyed the potential wealth of Ireland and sought to describe how it could be accessed through a radical transformation of the island's political ecology. Like Rastell, Spenser found an earlier English literary tradition congenial to this aim, but he deployed it in a more ambivalent way to question both the limitations and possibilities of poetry's role in transforming Irish land and labor.

Why Colin Clout Came Back

In 1595, some sixteen years after the character's debut in *The Shepheardes Calender* (1579), Colin Clout reappears as an Irish shepherd in Spenser's epyllion, *Colin Clouts Come Home Againe*. One year later, in 1596, Colin Clout appears in *The Faerie Queene* as a shepherd in the recognizably Irish setting of the pastoral cantos of book 6. The return of Spenser's pastoral persona to his verse after such a long absence is one of the more puzzling aspects of Spenser's career, given that *The Shepheardes Calender* encourages its readers to see the work as a preparatory exercise for a development from pastoral to epic.[12] Why bring back a figure and a genre that suggested youth and pre-epic pastoral experimentation? For many critics, the late pastorals (and Colin Clout's reappearance) seem anomalous, disrupting the idea of Spenser's career as a linear, programmatic enterprise.[13] But the Skeltonic source of Colin Clout's name offers a clue to what pastoral meant to Spenser in Ireland, where he blended courtly bucolics with the prophetic and critical agrarian reformist verse of the earlier sixteenth century.[14] Spenser explicitly, if ambiguously, associates his pastoral beginnings with the Langlandian vein of English literary history after the final emblem of *The Shepheardes Calender*, which counsels his book not to presume to match the style of "the Pilgrim that the Ploughman played a whyle."[15] Here, Spenser associates his pastoral verse with the *Piers Plowman* tradition and folds it into a careerist self-presentation that also aligns his pastoral persona with the work of John Skelton. For Spenser, the return to pastoral in Ireland was also a return to the Langlandian and Skeltonic resonances of his earlier work.

Scholars have traced the importance of Skelton's *Collyn Clout* for *The Shepheardes Calender*.[16] Similarly, much of the work on Spenser's relationship to the *Piers Plowman* tradition focuses on *The Shepheardes Calender* and certain episodes of *The Faerie Queene*.[17] But the late Irish pastorals show Spenser responding to the massive upheavals in property regimes and agrarian practices in colonial Ireland that echoed the early Tudor crises that had provoked Skelton's Collyn's restless critique and Robert Crowley's editorial and poetic engagements with *Piers Plowman*. Spenser's reading of Skelton's *Collyn Clout* and of Crowley's edition of *Piers Plowman* furthered his ambition to make poetry out of the tension between transcendent visions and the immanent conditions in which reform must be enacted. In *Colin Clouts Come Home Againe* and book 6 of *The Faerie Queene*, Spenser returns to a pastoral indelibly linked to this poetic tradition of seeking poetry's place in relation to sovereign power by writing Colin Clout's song into the political ecology of Elizabethan Ireland.

Spenser and his fellow settlers sought to extend English modes of manorial political ecology to Ireland, especially in the Munster plantation. The "plantation" of Tudor Ireland describes the confiscation of Irish-owned land and its redistribution and settlement by the so-called New English, or recent settlers in Ireland as opposed to the "Old English" families who had been in Ireland since the twelfth-century conquest of Henry II (1171). Plantation was the rapacious dénouement to the violent suppression of Irish rebellion in Munster, which ended with the defeat and execution of the Earl of Desmond in 1583. As Andrew Hadfield summarizes the managerial mechanics of this expropriative endeavor in Munster, "It was vital to have as much information about the area as possible so that it could be controlled and governed by the undertakers on behalf of the crown. It was their duty to use the legal system and raise an army in order to transform the land from a rebellious backwater into a flourishing, anglicized outpost, an expansion of England."[18] However much some of Spenser's New English contemporaries might have seen themselves as independent developers of a new resource frontier, they—like the ideal freeholder of John Fitzherbert's husbandry manuals—depended on the English Crown and its attendant juridico-political hierarchies in order to wrest wealth from Irish soil, pastures, and woods.[19] In this way, the Munster plantation exemplifies the structural role of extra-economic violence in processes of primitive accumulation in sites of colonial expansion that occur long after the early-sixteenth-century moment narrated in Karl Marx's account of the "classic form" of primitive accumulation in England around the time of the dissolution.[20]

The project of extending a profit-minded manorial political ecology to the Munster plantation echoed the dissolution of the monasteries in the way state violence created the preconditions for the accumulation of wealth. English colonial settlement in Ireland in the 1570s and 1580s, according to William Smyth, was furthered by the "strategic absorption of the former Church lands" after dissolved monasteries were used "as key strong points in the reconquest."[21] Meanwhile, as Keith Pluymers observes, "The Munster Plantation was a project of unprecedented scale and bureaucratic complexity in Ireland, comparable to the seizure and redistribution of church lands in England by Henry VIII."[22] The similarity of political ecological reorganization between the dissolution of the monasteries and the establishment of the Munster plantation invites consideration of how the *Piers Plowman* tradition informed not only Spenser's overtly ecclesiastical satires in *The Shepherds Calender* but also his poetry that explicitly concerns Irish land and labor. Spenser himself leased former monastic lands from his earliest arrival in Ireland as the secretary to Arthur Grey, 14th Baron Grey de Wilton, lord deputy of Ireland, and the inseparability of ecclesiastical reform from the use of agrarian land would have been obvious to anyone involved in the attempt to take over dissolved monasteries in Ireland.[23] Spenser's poetry on Ireland situates poetry's place in the process of colonial primitive accumulation by weaving together themes of labor, leisure, and rapacious consumption that defined the literature of an earlier moment of primitive accumulation in England.

Book 6 of *The Faerie Queene* and Colonial Political Ecology

In *The Faerie Queene*, Edmund Spenser completed six books of a projected twelve on the "priuate morall virtues" of holiness, temperance, chastity, friendship, justice, and courtesy.[24] The first three virtues are treated in the three-book installment of 1590, while the latter three were added in a six-book version published in 1596. Book 6, the book of courtesy, follows the knight Calidore as he pursues the Blatant Beast, a figure for slander who is first introduced at the end of book 5, the book of justice. Book 5 deals most directly with Ireland's geopolitical situation and the harsh means that might be necessary to prevent its alignment with Spain or other enemies of England.[25] Book 6 continues book 5's engagement with Ireland but emphasizes the process of colonial reform as an intervention in the relations between people and place rather than between geopolitical blocs.

Spenser treats courtesy throughout book 6 as inextricably linked to the question of reform and its possibility for colonized populations and landscapes.[26] As Andrew Zurcher has shown, the virtue of courtesy speaks to the royal prerogative to correct criminal "border-crossers" of both physical and social boundaries by martial law.[27] Such a violent measure of eliminating a threat to the established order partakes of the abstractions of legal and political theory as justifications for sovereign intervention, but it also requires consideration of the daily labors that allow people to subsist either within or outside the "courtesy" of the realm. If any reform of colonial Ireland is to take hold, it must—as Irenius puts it in *A View of the Present State of Ireland* (1596)—ensure that all rebels be "brought to labour or civill Conuersacion."[28] Book 6 can be seen as an attempt to explore the violent nature of the conjunction that both separates and joins labor and "civill Conuersacion." The climax of this investigation is Calidore's encounter with Colin Clout as he leads the dance of the Graces in canto 10. But before turning to this scene's explication of courtesy's relationship to political order, we must consider the central cantos, from which Calidore is absent and which define the colonial implications of Spenser's approach to the work of reform.

In the central cantos of book 6, the narrative turns from its main knight and his quest for the Blatant Beast to the episode of Calepine, Serena, and the Salvage Man. In canto 4, the Salvage Man rescues Serena and Calepine from Turpine, a figure for the discourteous knight, and immediately turns his attention to caring for the wounded Calepine and the terrified Serena. He leads them to his wild forest home:

> Farre in the forrest by a hollow glade,
> Couered with mossie shrubs, which spredding brode
> Did vnderneath them make a gloomy shade;
> There foot of liuing creature neuer trode,
> Ne scarse wyld beasts durst come, there was this wights abode.[29]

There, in the otiose shade, the Salvage Man offers only "the frutes of the forrest," foraged for his guests because he does not grow any other food: "For their bad Stuard neither plough'd nor sowed" (6.4.14.6). Although the Salvage Man is a "bad Stuard" who eschews the plow, he has an innate sense of justice and hospitality. On the one hand, his neglect of the plow suggests the barbarous characteristics attributed to the Irish by English propagandists—as does his gloomy dwelling, which, though not subterranean, echoes other caves in *The Faerie Queene*, most notably those of the Brigants, which resemble Irish souterrains, or caves for storage and concealment.[30] On the other hand, his lack of labor suggests the exemption from manual toil that the ideology of heritable nobility allows, as does his instinctive recognition of right and the need to defend Serena violently. As Judith Anderson observes of the Salvage Man's nobility, "the issue of aristocracy is far from clear," just as "the issue of origins, of nature and nurture, seems equally open."[31] The Salvage Man's idleness and righteous violence are qualities that manifest "sparkes of gentle mynd" (6.5.1.8), promising his capacity to be reformed. Unlike the Salvage Nation that will attack Serena in canto 8, the Salvage Man is "of noble blood" (6.5.2.7). He represents the possibility that some people are capable of reform, while others are not.

As we will see in chapter 6, English colonial reform discourse about Ireland viewed the moral and spiritual conversion of colonized people as a desirable complement to their enlistment in structures of wealth extraction. For example, Irenius explains in the dialogue of Spenser's *A View of the Present State of Ireland* that once the Irish "applye themselues vnto honest trades of Civilitye" (178) and begin to live in or near towns "sowed and sprincked with englishe" (211), the next step should be to look to their education: "[E]uerye parishe shoulde be forced to kepe one pettie schollmaster adioyninge vnto the parishe Churche . . . whearby they [the children] will in shorte space growe vp to that Civill Conversacion" so that they "will loathe the former rudenes in which they weare bredd" (218). This argument allows us to see the Salvage Man episode as a development of the theme of courtesy as a movement away from "former rudenes" toward "Civill Conversacion" in places defined by settled agrarian labor. This is part of Spenser's poetic project of, in Richard McCabe's words, "facilitating the presentation of violent conquest as civil reclamation."[32] The Salvage Man remains poised between innate courtesy and an uncivil, which is to say, uncultivated, relationship to the environment. The Salvage Man's ambivalence as a nonlaborer capable of courteous acts mirrors the ambivalence of Tudor reformers of Ireland about the population they wished to colonize: Could an innate propensity for civility be restored there, or would an innate barbarism continue to block such efforts?

Spenser's wager, and that of the plantation enterprise in general, was that such reform was possible if the ecological and social relations of Ireland could be forcibly reordered. Not only would this involve surveying, calculating, and collecting revenues from Irish lands recently placed in the hands of English colonists like Spenser. It would also require new, justifying images for the hierarchical relation between sovereign and territory, as well as a work ethic to promote the kinds of labor that would enrich the new colonial landlords and their sovereign.

If the poet could be an agent of colonial reform, then it would be in the latter area. Book 6 tests the possibilities of this agency as it confronts vicious conflicts over Irish land and labor when the poem's focus returns to Calidore.

The resumption of Calidore's narrative in canto 9 begins with a summary of his quest for the Blatant Beast:

> Him first from court he to the citties coursed,
> And from the citties to the townes him prest,
> And from the townes into the countrie forsed,
> And from the country back to priuate farmes he scorsed.
>
> (6.9.3.6–9)

The knight has pursued slander from court to city, to towns, to the country, before returning to "priuate farmes." After this, Calidore arrives in a pastoral space that notably combines the herding of cattle ("neat") and sheep:

> From thence into the open fields he fled,
> Whereas the Heardes were keeping of their neat
> And shepheards singing to their flockes, that fed[.]
>
> (6.9.4.1–3)

This itinerary surveys the idealized political ecology of the colonizing reformer. The "priuate farmes" through which Calidore runs suggest the kind of smallholdings contributing to the revenues of a larger manorial hierarchy.[33] Meanwhile, his arrival in the pastoral space avoids the association made in *A View of the Present State of Ireland* between cattle herding and violent, raiding idlers. Instead, these herders are tending both "neat" and sheep, which, when placed next to "priuate farms," composes a picture of the peaceful coexistence of arable farming, sheep rearing, and cattle herding that is also the hoped-for result of the campaign of military violence that Spenser prescribes in *A View of the Present State of Ireland*. Spenser echoes the satirical itinerary of the wandering social critic in Calidore's journey, which surveys Ireland's ideal but unrealized order of combined arable and pastoral production.

The implicit order glimpsed in the summary of Calidore's arrival in the pastoral community does not last thanks to the raid of the Brigants. But before their attack, Calidore is granted a vision of the transcendent source of political order during his encounter with Colin Clout. One day, Calidore chances upon Mount Acidale, an exceedingly beautiful place where he witnesses Colin Clout leading the dance of the Graces (6.10.15). The description of Mount Acidale, like Calidore's itinerary, spatializes social distinctions in a way that emphasizes courtesy's relationship to the disposition of hierarchical social relations, including those that at once highlight the distinctions between high and low, ruler and worker, while also hinting at the material continuities between earthly toil and sovereign authority:

> It was an hille plaste in an open plaine,
> That round about was bordered with a wood
> Of matchless hight, that seem'd the earth to disdaine,
> ...
> And at the foote thereof, a gentle flud,
> His siluer waues did softly tumble downe,
> Vnmard with ragged mosse or filthy mud,
> Ne mote wylde beastes, ne mote the ruder clowne
> Thereto approch, ne filth mote therein drowne[.]
>
> (6.10.6.1–3, 7.1–5)

Mount Acidale stands apart from the world around it, rising above a flat plain with an encircling wood "Of matchless hight, that seem'd the earth to disdain." The moat-like river excludes "ragged moss," "wylde beastes," "the ruder clowne" and their "filthe," images that combine natural decadence and social lowliness. The "ragged moss" suggests shady stasis, while the wild beasts stand for animal vitality that has not been yoked to a productive order. The "ruder clowne" describes the innate, unreformed status of the lowborn rustic. Yet even lofty trees are rooted in the soil. Wild beasts may be tamed and uncultivated rustics enrolled in a political and economic order, as Spenser thought deeply about in *A View of the Present State of Ireland*. The emphasis on physical boundaries in the landscape also underlines Colin Clout's status as a mediating figure who sits between the Graces and the work of reform. Spenser makes him a figure for the mutual definition of colonial toil and poetic inspiration. But in book 6, this figure's role is limited. He lacks direct contact with the violence of colonial reform, which becomes Calidore's domain, and he also lacks the direct relationship to the land that defines the Colin of *Colin Clouts Come Home Againe*. As we will see, in *The Faerie Queene*, Colin explains the principles of hierarchical order that justify colonial domination as an extension of courtesy, but his art has little bearing on the violent conflicts that rage beneath Mount Acidale.

As Colin explains to Calidore, the three Graces:

> on men all gracious gifts bestow
> ... the complements of curtesie:
> They teach vs, how to each degree and kynde
> We should our selues demeane, to low, to hie;
> To friends, to foes, which skill men call Ciuility.
>
> (6.10.23.1-9)

Upon Mount Acidale, courtesy and its kindred "skill" of "Ciuility" flourish. For Spenser, "Ciuility" involves the political ordering of "degree" and "kynde," which explains why "Civill Conversacion" was such an important part of Spenser's vision of town life in *A View of the Present State of Ireland*. But this civility is also a work ethic because it depends on the practice of "honest trades of civility" that newly pacified Irish town dwellers would learn. The relationship between the scene atop Mount Acidale and Calidore's fight with the Brigants turns on the ability to defend the order of civility and the agrarian labor upon which it depends.

Colin Clout's appearance in *The Faerie Queene* ends with Calidore's departure from Mount Acidale and his confrontation with the Brigants. Even as the narrative returns to chivalric violence and leaves Colin behind, however, the Skeltonic resonance of his namesake continues. In the emphasis on the Brigants' isolated dwelling, their lack of agrarian labor, and their strikingly mercantile rapacity, the conclusion of book 6's pastoral reprises earlier Tudor visions of clerical corruption and the ravages of enclosure. In this way, Spenser seems to continue the Skeltonic dynamic seen in the Latin epilogue to *Collyn Clout* between addressing a crisis in rustic songs and withdrawing to the divine heights of poetic inspiration. While Colin withdraws, however, Calidore's violent response to the Brigants' rapacity suggests that, for Spenser in Ireland, the vatic power of the poet does not only ascend toward celestial power. It also descends toward considerations of how such power works, both within hierarchically ordered human communities and among those communities' varied relationships to the environment.

After the scene on Mount Acidale, the Brigants attack the shepherd community, stealing sheep and kidnapping shepherds to be sold into slavery, including Pastorella, the object of Calidore's affection. The stanza describing the Brigants' attack juxtaposes their violence with their avoidance of labor, reiterating a crux of colonial reformism that also marked the Salvage Man episode. While Calidore is away hunting one day:

> A lawlesse people, *Brigants* hight of yore,
> That neuer vsde to liue by plough nor spade,
> But fed on spoile and booty, which they made
> Vpon their neighbours, which did nigh them border,
> The dwelling of these shepheards did inuade,
> And spoyld their houses, and them selues did murder;
> And droue away their flocks, with other much disorder.
>
> (6.10.39.3–9)

Coming so soon after Calidore's conference with Colin on Mount Acidale, the description of the Brigants' otiose existence mirrors the leisured order of Colin's piping for the Graces. As Katherine Little points out, the Brigants invert Colin's upward-moving poetic inspiration and Calidore's legitimate chivalric violence.[34] The Brigants are figurally opposed to Colin and Calidore, but each grouping is defined in relation to the work of the plow—either by rising above the plane of agrarian production or, as we will see the Brigants doing, hiding beneath it. Such a symmetrical arrangement invites readers to think about how courtesy ought to mediate social relationships defined by labor.

The Brigant inversion of the scene on Mount Acidale continues in the description of their island home:

> Their dwelling in a little Island was,
> Couered with shrubby woods, in which no way
> Appeard for people in nor out to pas,
> Nor any footing fynde for ouergrowen gras.
>
> For vnderneath the ground their way was made,
> Through hollow caues, that no man mote discouer
> For the thicke shrubs, which did them alwaies shade
> From view of liuing wight, and couered ouer[.]
>
> (6.10.41.6–9, 42.1–4)

Their island, like Mount Acidale, is shielded from intruders by water and dense undergrowth. It is an exclusive, defensive space (not unlike the Salvage Man's forest home) beneath which the Brigants live in caves.

Unlike Colin who rises above the pastoral plain, the Brigants reach below ground, from whence they launch parasitic assaults on neighboring shepherds. As the Brigants break forth from their caves, they seek to gain not only from seizing sheep or food but also people. Returning with their captives, the Brigants intend:

> For slaues to sell them, for no small reward,
> To merchants, which them kept in bondage hard,
> Or sold againe.
>
> (6.10.43.4–6)

This grim practice not only makes the Brigants more dire adversaries but also introduces the process of exchange into Spenser's juxtaposition of transcendent order and immanent relations of land and labor. How should courtesy, as a political ideal of comportment within a hierarchy, deal with such a corrupt form of exchange? Spenser addresses this question by turning to earlier poetic accounts of the interplay of violence and exchange in the expropriation of rural workers.

The relationship between the Brigants' violent seizure of labor power and the necessity of exchange shapes Calidore's climactic rescue of Pastorella from the Brigants' cave. Her salvation follows a fight between the Brigants and the merchants who seek "by such trafficke after gaines to hunt" (6.11.9.2–4).[35] The brawl leads to the slaughter of all the captives except Pastorella, and so it is only she whom Calidore must rescue. Given the pivotal role of a dispute between two traders of enslaved people in its resolution, this episode bears out Maureen Quilligan's observation of the difference between slavery in classical epic and slavery in *The Faerie Queene* because in the early modern context of the latter, "slavery is *only* mercantile" rather than tied up with heroic conquests.[36] The Brigants' island condenses the vision of an Irish wasteland where violence, theft, and exploitative commerce in human labor prevent the establishment of an ideal political ecology of settled agrarian labor, commercial wool production, and literary achievement.

These are colonial manifestations of discursive formations with deeper roots in anticlerical and antienclosure literature. When Calidore discovers the devastation of the shepherd community, he is confronted with a vision of rural depopulation that recalls not only the effects of military conflicts like the Desmond rebellion, which Spenser infamously described in *A View of the Present State of Ireland*, but also accounts of English villages abandoned to enclosure:

> Ne wight he found, to whom he might complaine,
> Ne wight he found, of whom he might inquire;
> . . .
> The woods did nought but echoes vaine rebound;
> The playnes all waste and emptie did appeare[.]
>
> (6.11.26.1–7)

In the earlier English context, it had been sheep and their pastures that silenced the once-active rural community. But in Spenser's vision of Ireland, which in *A View of the Present State of Ireland* pits cattle-herding nomads against an English plantation that included the production of wool, the nightmare of rural depopulation is that of wasted pasturage: "Where wont the shepheards oft their pypes resound, / And feed an hundred flocks, there now not one he found" (6.11.26.8–9). The Brigants' kidnapping of the shepherds matches their waste of the landed infrastructure of wool production. Leaving pastures emptied of people and animals, the Brigants threaten the productive union of land and labor that English settlers like Spenser desired. Fixated on despoiling the population more than anything else, the Brigants resemble those clerics of Skelton's *Collyn Clout* who:

> plucke away and pull
> Theyr fleces of wull.
> Unneth they leve a locke
> Of wolle amongst theyr flocke.
>
> (78–81)

This familiar image of ecclesiastical satire will be pointedly literalized as the poor husbandry of their stolen flock becomes the means of the Brigants' downfall in Calidore's rescue plot.

Spenser activates the long-standing anxieties about enclosure, wage labor, and vagabondage that permeate early Tudor writing about the agrarian crisis in Calidore's plan to rescue Pastorella from the Brigants' lair. Calidore learns what happened to the shepherds and their flocks from Coridon, the only shepherd who escaped from the Brigants during their brawl with the slave traders. Calidore asks Coridon to guide him back to their hiding place, but the terrified shepherd refuses until Calidore plies him with "meed," a word with Langlandian echoes of both bribery and wage (6.11.35.8). The knight and the shepherd then disguise themselves as "poore heardgroomes, the which whylere / Had from their maisters fled, and now sought hyre elswhere" (6.11.39.8–9). The disguise works on the two "euill groomes" (6.11.40.3) who were watching the stolen flocks for the Brigants and who agree to relinquish their duty to these strangers "for litle hyre and chepe" (6.11.40.7). Thus relieved, the two bad shepherds leave Calidore and Coridon to wait nearby the cave until nightfall to attack the Brigants. This prelude to Calidore's violent rescue of Pastorella is laden with images and terms that evoke the deepest worries about enclosure and the related crises of sixteenth-century England: rural depopulation, the rootlessness of wandering wage workers, and the sense that anything—or anyone— might be for sale for the right price (or "meed"), leading to the desertion of a once-profitable and sustainable agrarian political ecology.

Spenser adapts those fears to the perspective of the colonial undertakers, where the ravenous appetites of the greedy landlords and wandering friars of the *Piers Plowman* tradition become the swarming Brigants, whom Calidore slaughters after sneaking into their subterranean dwelling. This accomplished, he comforts Pastorella and then:

> into those theeuish dens he went,
> And thence did all the spoyles and threasures take,
> Which they from many long had robd and rent,
> But fortune now the victors meed did make;
> Of which the best he did his loue betake;
> And also all those flockes, which they before
> Had reft from Meliboe and from his make,
> He did them all to Coridon restore.
>
> (6.11.51.1–8)

The canto ends with a strikingly economic focus on the redistribution of treasure, taking the "victors meed" from the defeated Brigants and giving it to Pastorella and Coridon. The destruction Calidore visits on the Brigants is only the first step in the broader economic and ecological reformation of the shepherd community. Calidore's return of the flocks to pastures that are now under Coridon's control is perhaps the reformation of Eirena's realm that Artegall was unable to complete at the end of book 5, thanks to the release of the Blatant Beast.

The provisional completion of a program of agrarian reform in book 6 underscores the extent to which Colin Clout's presence there is neither just a classicizing pastoral interlude from the chivalric quest nor a clean break from earlier English modes of agrarian poetry. Colin embodies the vatic poet's intermediary status. Like Skelton's Collyn Clout, he sits between a divine font of poetic fury and a disordered political ecology that seems to cry out for correction. Despite the upward pull of poetry's celestial origin, the need to reorder the world according to "degree" and "kynde" entangles the poet in ecological and economic relations and the violence needed to change them. This ambition requires the poet to look up, but not to the ethereal Graces; instead, he addresses the top of the political hierarchy in the hopes of enlisting sovereign force to remake the realm. As Skelton's Collyn discovers, and which Spenser also knew well, acting on such hope is fraught with the danger of attracting the wrong kind of attention from the political elite. Reprising Collyn Clout's intimidated silence at the conclusion of Skelton's poem, the final stanza of book 6 sees the Blatant Beast turning against the very poem that contains it: "Ne may this homely verse, of many meanest, / Hope to escape his venomous despite" (6.12.41.1–2). Alluding to his earlier clashes with the likes of Lord Burghley, Spenser ends book 6 caught between the invocation of sovereign violence as an instrument of reform and the recognition that his verse may be irrelevant or even odious to the agents of such violence. Colin Clout dances with the Graces on Mount Acidale, but he does not accompany Calidore in his descent to the Brigants' lair.

Nevertheless, the view from atop Mount Acidale does not only imply transcendence. Despite its "disdaine" for its surroundings, the mount still "did seeme to ouerlooke the lowly vale" (6.10.8.8)—overlook or, we might say, survey, much like Spenser would do as manorial overseer above the bog besides Kilcolman.[37] In this view, Skelton's *Collyn Clout* ought to be seen as more than just a source for the name of Spenser's pastoral persona; he becomes a kind of figural *ars poetica* that allows Spenser to link the vatic inspiration of the poet to the disorder of the realm he at once surveys and disdains. For both Skelton and Spenser, the figure of the poetic outsider can never actually transcend the political ecology it aims to correct. Instead, it remains entangled in coercive political hierarchies that ultimately override the inspired independence it claims.

Colin Clouts Come Home Againe: The Poet as Agent of Reform

Written shortly after Spenser returned to Ireland from a trip in 1590 with Walter Raleigh to Elizabeth I's court, Spenser revised *Colin Clouts Come Home Againe* before publishing it in 1595. The poem is a thinly veiled account of their journey. In this pastoral epyllion, or "little epic," neoplatonic themes of nature, matter, and mutability—also explored in his 1596 publications *Fowre Hymns* and *The Faerie Queene*—combine with Spenser's most explicit account in verse of the differences between English and Irish ways of life. In *Colin Clouts Come Home Againe*, Ireland is the earthy, violent counterpoint to the higher stages of perfection represented by Cynthia and her realm.[38] By the poem's end, Colin seeks to extend Cynthia's authority to this "barrein soyle."[39] This project becomes in *Colin Clouts Come Home Againe* an assertive fusion of the poet's ability both to shape the landscape and to glorify the sovereign's imperial majesty. For all its emphasis on the elevating power of love, the poem remains focused on the worldly opposition between England and Ireland, which is defined as one between "such wealth" (655) and "cold and care and penury" (657). Only the figure of the effective reformist poet, embodied by Colin in a manner quite different from book 6 of *The Faerie Queene*, can be the true surveyor of Ireland's political ecological disorder and communicate the sovereign's power to correct it.

Spenser signals the poem's attunement to the conditions of Elizabethan Ireland in his dedicatory epistle to Raleigh dated from "my house of Kilcolman the 27. of December. 1591," apologizing for "the meanesse of stile" but defending its fidelity to "the truth in circumstance and matter."[40] This "truth" was Spenser's voyage with Raleigh to England in 1590, which the poem turns into an account of how Colin (Spenser) is visited in Ireland by the Shepherd of the Ocean (Raleigh), who takes him on a voyage to the court of Cynthia (Elizabeth). When the poem begins, Colin has just returned from this trip, and he satisfies the desire of his shepherd companions to hear about his voyage. Colin narrates his journey from Irish pastures to Cynthia's presence, which inspires him to return to Ireland as a prophet of Love and a promoter of Cynthia's power, despite his disillusionment with the courtly striving that goes on around her.

Colin's account of how he came to be invited to join the Shepherd of the Ocean shows Spenser rehearsing one possibility for the poet to alter his material circumstances. By singing the tale of the Bregog and Mulla rivers, Colin so impresses the Shepherd of the Ocean that he secures the latter's

> great lyking to my lore,
> And great dislyking to my lucklesse lot:
> That banisht had my selfe, like wight forlore,
> Into that waste, where I was quite forgot.
>
> (180–83)

Already the poet's art takes a mediating position between "that waste," which supplies the matter for Colin's song about the rivers near Kilcolman, and Cynthia's land of "happie peace and plenteous store" (310). The art enabled by "that waste" allows Colin to leave it behind and to be further inspired in turn to a pitch of "furious insolence" (622) that sends him back to Ireland with an aggressive zeal to make it reflect Cynthia's might. But even in the first part of the poem, where Colin repeats the song of Bregog and Mulla, Spenser rehearses a Crowleyan confidence in the ability of precarious material conditions to inspire poetry that can reach the heights of political power.

The ability of such power to affect Ireland's political ecology is implicit in Colin's tale of how the river Bregog came to flow into the Mulla. In its narrative of rivers seeking to evade containment, Spenser echoes the surveillance and territorial control that define the strategies of colonial domination prescribed in *A View of the Present State of Ireland*.[41] The river "Old father *Mole*" seeks to prevent the river Bregog from "wedding" his daughter, the river Mulla. To evade the watchful Mole, Bregog

> into many parts his streame he shar'd,
> That whilest the one was watcht, the other might
> Passe vnespide to meete her by the way;
> And then besides, those little streames so broken
> He vnder ground so closely did conuay,
> That of their passage doth appeare no token,
> Till they into the *Mullaes* water slide.
>
> (137–44)

But this trick fails when "it was descrie, / And told her father by a shepheards boy" (146–47). Mole gets revenge by rolling stones into the river, dispersing the Bregog's course: "So of a River . . . He none was made, but scattred all to nought" (152–53). The tale reprises themes from *A View of the Present State of Ireland* of secretive movement and the difficulties of surveillance in a "waste" of hilly and riparian landscapes that afford underground hiding places and undetected escape routes.

The personification of Bregog likewise mirrors the riparianization of the Irish population in *A View of the Present State of Ireland*. There, Spenser advocates breaking up the population into small, manageable units (called "Tythinge the polls"), "ffor by this the people are broken into manie smalle partes like little streames that they Cannot easelye come togeather into one heade" (205). This is necessary because rebellions grow large when the "base sorte of people," who otherwise have no interest in revolt, get "carryed awaie with the violence of the streame" (156). In the aftermath of any such rebellion, Irenius recommends that such groups be "dispersed in suche sorte as they shall not Come together nor easelye retorne if they woulde" (157). In a literal register, rivers again signify the threat of unregulated movement when Spenser advocates the construction of bridges over rivers and the destruction of fords so that river crossings would be restricted and easier to regulate (224). Irish topography and its riparian system, which collaborate with and symbolize Irish rebels in *A View of the Present State of Ireland*, become in *Colin Clouts Come Home Againe* the subject of a song that enables its singer eventually to remake that very landscape.

Before he can do so, however, Colin develops the contrast between Ireland and England such that his experience of Cynthia's transcendent greatness motivates his return to a wasteland that needs his inspired intervention. After crossing the Irish Sea, Colin arrives in a land rich in "fruitfull corne, faire trees, fresh herbage . . . / And all things else that liuing creatures need" (298-99). As Colin explains to an amazed Cuddy, this "heauenly" bounty needs to be understood in opposition to Ireland's earthly deficiencies:

> Both heauen and heauenly graces do much more
> (Quoth he) abound in that same land, then this.
> For there all happie peace and plenteous store
> Conspire in one to make contented blisse:
> No wayling there nor wretchednesse is heard,
> No bloodie issues nor no leprosies,
> No griesly famine, nor no raging sweard,
> No nightly bodrags, nor no hue and cries;
> The shepheards there abroad may safely lie,
> On hills and downes, withouten dread or daunger:
> No rauenous wolues the good mans hope destroy,
> Nor outlawes fell affray the forest raunger.
>
> (308-19)

This is one of Spenser's most direct reflections in verse on his Irish experience: wailing and wretchedness, famine, plague, "nightly bodrags" (cattle raids), wolves, and outlaws form a litany of Ireland's wasted political ecology as the environment itself seems to turn against the bodies of its inhabitants, while England's shepherds may rest "on hills and downes, withouten dread or daunger." As Zurcher points out, the only other time Spenser uses the term "hue and cry" in his poetry is when Calidore attacks the Brigants in book 6 of *The Faerie Queene*, further underscoring the Irish reference for that episode.[42] This comparison of England and Ireland turns on the same opposition between earthy violence and celestial peace that structures the pastoral cantos of book 6, but here Colin moves between them rather than staying on the side of elevated poetic making.

In the heavenly realm of England, the light of learning complements its agrarian riches: "There learned arts do florish in great honor, / And Poets wits are had in peerlesse price" (320-21). In a kingdom like this, Spenser's Colin finds a hearing among the powerful that Skelton's Collyn never enjoyed. Thanks to the Shepheard of the Ocean, Colin is introduced "Vnto that Goddesse":

> And to mine oaten pipe enclin'd her eare,
> That she thenceforth therein gan take delight,
> And it desir'd at timely houres to heare,
> All were my notes but rude and roughly dight[.]
>
> (359-63)

Colin moves among the "heauenly graces" of Cynthia's court like he does atop Mount Acidale in book 6 of *The Faerie Queene*, but in *Colin Clouts Come Home Againe* he also directly affects a pastoral landscape threatened by violence.

Here, Colin assumes the role of the reformist poet in its most assertive guise. Like Crowley's Truth or the ideal Sothsegger of the *Mum*-poet, Spenser envisions a direct correlation between a well-ordered agrarian political ecology and the sovereign's receptivity to the poet's truthful report. Of course, Spenser knew as well as Skelton that the reflex of power to such truth telling could be punitive, as the dedicatory epistle to *Colin Clouts Come Home Againe* makes clear with its request that Raleigh "protect against the malice of euill mouthes."[43] Nor is this an uncomplicated celebration of learned poetry's place in Cynthia's court: the catalogue of poets there cannot avoid registering a malicious courtly culture.[44] But Spenser nevertheless airs the fantasy of a sovereign listening to verse "rude and roughly dight" that informs her about the true state of the world.

If we assume that the situation here imagined is a version of Spenser presenting the first three books of *The Faerie Queene* at court, then the pervasive influence of Spenser's Irish experience on that work would no doubt be germane, but so would the fact that, by 1595, when *Colin Clouts Come Home Againe* was printed, Spenser had probably begun composing *A View of the Present State of Ireland* with the intention of circulating it among any contacts he might have in Elizabeth's court when he briefly returned to England in 1596.⁴⁵ This is just one of the ways in which "the discussion begun in *Colin Clouts Come Home Againe* is continued, if not concluded, in *A View*."⁴⁶ This scene of royal reception is a Spenserian continuation of the Tudor "discovery" of Ireland, which, as Christopher Maginn and Steven Ellis put it, "most often occurred on the page" because no Tudor monarch nor any important counselors ever went there.⁴⁷ Colonial tracts like *A View of the Present State of Ireland* were both the textual constructions of Ireland's political ecology and the instruments through which it could be changed. Tudor policy responded to their visions of an Ireland in need of surveillance, with its forests cut, its pastures enclosed, and its arable land settled. For Spenser to imagine, as he brings *Colin Clouts Come Home Againe* to print, a world where Cynthia readily listens to Colin's songs affirms the intermittently articulated hope of the *Piers Plowman* tradition that the true poet is no mere parasite within the realm's political ecology but can direct the sovereign's actions to restore its balance.

Spenser imagines this effectiveness in a decidedly literary figuration of the transformation of the Irish landscape under the sign—or signature—of Cynthia:

> Her name in euery tree I will endosse,
> That as the trees do grow, her name may grow:
> And in the ground each where will it engrosse,
> And fill with stones, that all men may it know.
> The speaking woods and murmuring waters fall,
> Her name Ile teach in knowen terms to frame:
> And eke my lambs when for their dams they call,
> Ile teach to call for *Cynthia* by name.
>
> (632–39)

These lines show Colin fantasizing about the convergence of political ecological and poetic projects in images where writing and remaking the landscape are one and the same. The words "endosse" and "engrosse" are legal terms, the former meaning to sign the back of a document (as today one endorses a check) and the latter meaning to write in large letters appropriate for a legal document.[48] The rhyme links these terms not only aurally but conceptually insofar as they signify the making of legal documents that performatively actualize changes in land use by altering property relations. But the image of Colin pouring stones into ditches that spell Cynthia's name also echoes the tale of Bregog and Mulla.[49] Spenser once again links the filling of an embanked impression in the landscape with stones to the enactment of power over that landscape and its living inhabitants, whether riparian, arboreal, human, or animal. In this way, Colin will "her name recorded . . . leaue for euer" (631). Not merely in the lines of his verse will Elizabeth be remembered but in the living, growing assemblage of forests, pastures, and herds cut, cultivated, and enclosed in perpetuity as a sustainable generator of colonial wealth. The homonym of "engrosse" as a term for writing legal documents and a term for consolidating landholdings is relevant here, as the latter sense shadows the primary metaphor of comparing the Irish land to a document written over with Cynthia's name, linking the textual creation of Elizabeth's dominance to the actual engrossing of Irish lands into New English plantations.

To imagine Elizabethan domination of Ireland as a process of inscription on the land shows Spenser thinking along the same lines that would guide his program for regimenting the landscape and restricting mobility in *A View of the Present State of Ireland*:

> [A]nd firste I wishe that order weare taken for the Cuttinge downe and openinge of all places thoroughe wodes so that a wide waye of the space of C. yardes mighte be laide open in euerye of them for the safetie of trauellers. . . . Next that Bridges weare builte vppon all Riuers and all the fordes marred and spilt so as none mighte passe anie other waye but by those bridges, and euerie bridge to haue a gate and a smalle gatehowse set theareon. whereof this good will Come that no nighte stealthes which are Comonlye driven in by waies and by blinde fordes . . . but that they muste passe by those bridges. . . . Allsoe that in all stretes and narrowe passages as between Two Boggs or thoroughe anie depe forde or vnder anye mountaine side theare shoulde be some litle fortilage or woden Castle set which shoulde kepe and Comaunde that streighte wheareby anie Rebelles that should come into the Countrye mighte be stopped. . . . Moreouer that all highe waies shoulde be fenced and shutt vp on bothe sides . . . wheareby theves and nighte Robbers might be the more easelye pursued and encountred when theare

shalbe no other waie to drive theire stollen Cattell but therein as I formerlye declared.

Further that theare shoulde in sundrie Conveniente places by the highe waies be townes appointed to be builte . . . for theare is nothinge doth soner Cause Civilitye in anye Countrye then manye market Townes. . . . And the Countrymen wilbe allsoe more industrious in Tillage and rearinge all husbandrye Comodities knowinge that they shall haue readye sale for them at these Townes. (224–25)

The carving of Cynthia's name into trees and into soil filled with rocks can be seen as an epitome of Irenius's dream of a land carved to dictate where people move and how they subsist. It distills the essence of a program that enumerates how rivers, bogs, and forests shall be integrated into an infrastructure of bridges, highways, fences, gatehouses, and walled market towns that will spread "Civilitye" by enticing rural dwellers to husband agrarian commodities for sale there. Bruce Avery's reading of Irenius's use of a map in *A View of the Present State of Ireland* is perceptive: "From the contemporary, bird's eye perspective provided by the maps these divisions telescope backward temporally to a medieval system of control and surveillance[.]"[50] But at this later moment in *A View of the Present State of Ireland*, the land itself becomes the site of inscription as the infrastructural transformation of Ireland's political ecology discourages cattle herding and raiding and enables settled agrarian production and the marketing of wool and timber.

The objects of Colin's scriptorial designs on Ireland—trees, ground, water, and lambs—were all essential components of the political ecology of colonial wealth extraction that Spenser and his colleagues pursued: water for transport of commodities through rivers to ports or in powering mills;[51] the ground in all its senses as fertile soil, site of mines, political territory, and legal property; trees for the export of timber and for burning in the production of commodities like iron;[52] and lambs for wool. In teaching them to "call for *Cynthia*," Spenser underscores how much the pastoral ecology he and other New English planters sought to establish was a renewable source of wealth that had as its ultimate destination the figure of the sovereign. Spenser takes the lists of commodities that earlier instances of both the *Piers Plowman* tradition and colonial tracts represent as static resources and makes them dynamic and productive as they grow and reproduce.

Spenser's late pastorals, like Rastell's earlier interlude, look back to late medieval and early Tudor analyses of the interplay of ecology, economy, and royal power in the *Piers Plowman* tradition and extend their insights to new visions of colonial domination of both land and people. Across the sixteenth century, poets from Skelton to Spenser survey the realm's disordered political ecology and imagine poetry's ambiguous power to remake the relationship between land and labor that founds any polity. Spenser's self-consciousness about the poet's place in this process continues to register an awareness of writing's limitations even as he asserts that it is the only thing that will guide the sovereign in how to transform an island she will never see.

By the end of *Colin Clouts Come Home Againe*, Colin becomes the ideal that reformist poets from the *Crede*-poet to Crowley dreamed about: a true visionary and teacher whose inspiration will repair a land defined by waste and violence. While Colin's absence from the defeat of the Brigants and the reformation of the pastoral community in book 6 of *The Faerie Queene* figures an awareness of poetry's potential irrelevance to colonial domination, Colin's overwriting of the Irish landscape in *Colin Clouts Come Home Againe* figures its centrality—as long as the sovereign listens. Spenser's hope that the colonizing monarch might listen to his song is inseparable from the possibility that she will bring to bear direct force on the recalcitrant Ireland. This approach to colonial reform is figured in Calidore's destruction of the Brigants in book 6, which can be read in terms of Spenser's advocacy for the application of martial law in *A View of the Present State of Ireland*.[53] But the other, complementary path of political ecological reform is the indirect application of force by severing the population from its place in the ecological networks that sustain it. As we will see in chapter 6, this logic of coercive deprivation also guides Irenius's plans to subdue the Irish and establish a new political ecological regime of colonial plantations based on the English manorial system in *A View of the Present State of Ireland*.

CHAPTER 6

Colonial Political Ecology and *A View of the Present State of Ireland*

Karl Marx's account of so-called primitive accumulation in England makes clear that it was not only an insular phenomenon, nor does his description of "the expropriation of the worker" only obtain in the sixteenth century.[1] As his brief chapter on "The Modern Theory of Colonization" reveals, Marx's narrative of "the classic form" of primitive accumulation finds its confirmation in colonial power's global extension in his own time. In his critique of E. G. Wakefield's policy of "systematic colonization," Marx describes failed attempts to wrest value from colonies where people could still subsist outside the system of commodity production. This failure revealed that "capital is not a thing, but a social relation between persons which is mediated through things."[2] Creating the conditions for this social relation was an inherently political ecological project because it necessitated changing the social metabolism between humans and nature in places where other ways of subsisting continued. For writers witnessing the domestic side of this process in the sixteenth century, the *Piers Plowman* tradition offered a way to think through the interaction of land, labor, sovereign violence, and hunger in the drive for monetary accumulation. In *A View of the Present State of Ireland* (1596), Edmund Spenser draws from his poetic engagement with this tradition as he articulates a scheme of colonial reform that makes the English plantation the only way to subsist in Elizabethan Ireland.

Even as Spenser strove to be the "new Poete,"[3] he wrestled with questions that animated the vernacular reformist literature and agrarian husbandry manuals of the late Middle Ages and earlier sixteenth century throughout his Irish writings: What is the proper relationship between land and labor? How should toil and its fruits be distributed among a hungry population? And what is to be done with people who threaten the ideal functioning of the social whole? These questions wind through Spenser's attempt to formulate a program of colonial reform in *A View of the Present State of Ireland*, where a dialogue between Eudoxus and Irenius considers how separating Irish rebels from independent sources of subsistence will forcibly integrate them into the circuits of commodity production by driving them to settle in towns and to take up the work of agrarian husbandry.

Spenser's vision for the transformation of Irish political ecology was indelibly marked by the second Desmond rebellion (1579-1583) and the establishment of the Munster plantation, where Spenser eventually settled on his estate at Kilcolman in County Cork. The Desmond rebellions saw the noble FitzGerald family, earls of Desmond, resist the encroachment of English royal control over Ireland. Spenser first came to Ireland as secretary to Arthur, Lord Grey de Wilton, who was appointed lord deputy of Ireland in 1580 to quash the rebellion.[4] He eventually succeeded in 1583, but not before a harsh campaign and resulting famine had inflicted deep casualties in the province of Munster. As Willy Maley observes, "Any study of the Munster plantation has to take as its starting point the reality of its violent induction," which Keith Pluymers describes as "an ecological war" that made Munster no longer supportive of life.[5] The Munster plantation was a scheme for repopulating the devastated region. It worked by distributing the lands of former rebels to English landlords—the so-called New English as opposed to the Old English descendants of the Anglo-Norman nobility that occupied the island after the invasion of Henry II (1171)—and turning those estates to the profitable production of agrarian commodities by settling English and Irish workers on those seigneuries as tenants and wage laborers.[6] Spenser was intimately involved in this project, having served under Grey during the rebellion, and in his subsequent secretarial roles, he was in a position to know when new land titles would become available in Munster, which ultimately allowed him to take possession of the estate at Kilcolman by 1589.[7] By the time Spenser set out to compose *A View of the Present State of Ireland*, he had seen enough problems with the establishment of the English plantation that he wrote a lengthy dialogue to explore the causes of its failures and to propose a scheme of total reform. In its totalizing vision of Irish political ecology, *A View of the Present State of Ireland* describes how colonial primitive accumulation proceeds by using both sovereign force and the biopolitical manipulation of the population's relationship to the environment.

The Political Ecology of *A View of the Present State of Ireland*

A View of the Present State of Ireland begins its dialogue between Irenius and Eudoxus with a lengthy review of traditional Irish social structures, legal culture, and means of subsistence in order to understand why "no purposes whatsoeuer [that] are mente for her good, will, [sic] prosper or take good effecte."[8] In the course of analyzing these faults, Irenius argues that total military defeat of the Irish is the only way to remedy them. But "the sworde" (258), or military force alone, is not the main focus of this strategy. Instead, his vision for the defeat of the Irish is inseparable from his plan for a new political ecological regime based on manorial production for the market. The ultimate aims of any specific reforms were to weaken the decentralized authority of the Old English; to bring the Irish legal system in line with English law; and to turn Ireland into an agrarian economy on the English model of arable farming, established market towns, and exports of wool, timber, and other commodities.[9] In *A View of the Present State of Ireland*, these overarching goals cannot be reached without first intervening in the Irish population's relationship to the ecosystem of upland pastures and woods, because such an intervention would force changes in Irish ways of subsistence so that the Irish people would have to become agrarian laborers.

In the course of their dialogue, Eudoxus and Irenius delve into the history of Ireland's political ecology to understand how the Irish continue to resist English domination. Irenius, the expert who answers Eudoxus's questions, surveys three "evills" that stymie Ireland's pacification— namely, law, "Customes," and religion—in ways that constantly assert the priority of these institutions' relationship to Irish ways of subsistence (45). Irish law, for instance, was never established on a firm footing after Henry II's conquest, he tells Eudoxus, because of Henry's failure to impose a lasting manorial political ecology in Ireland. Henry began the process by installing English landlords there who later received the "pore distressed people of the Irishe . . . such as they thoughte fitt for labour" (56), but it did not take. Unlike John Fitzherbert's account in *Surveying* of the lasting, mutually beneficial relationship between English tenants and their Norman landlords after 1066, who voluntarily turned their vassals into freeholders, in Ireland, according to Irenius, the institution of vassalage only led to a kind of localized tyranny that did not result in the establishment of a stable manorial system rooted in English law (56). The Irish who did not submit as vassals continued to dwell in the mountains living on "white meates" (dairy), only to break out again to reoccupy lands left undefended when the English nobility returned to England to join the fight "between Lancastre and Yorke" for the crown (56–57). As Irenius will later detail, the alternative to manorial toil represented by dairy consumption and nomadic herding continues to trouble English rule in Ireland. The "booley" is the term Irenius uses to describe this pastoral practice, which he is at pains to construct as a sign of Irish backwardness by associating it with legendary "Scythian" origins: "theare is one vse amongest them to kepe theire Cattell and to live themselves the moste parte of the yeare in *Bollyes* pasturinge vppon the mountaine and waste wilde places and removinge still to freshe lande as they haue depastured the former The which appearethe plaine to be the manner of the Scithians" (97). Deriving from the Irish term *buaile*, which describes a seasonal pastureland primarily for dairy cattle, Irenius turns the "booley" into the institution of Irish society that most troubles him because it enables another way of living on the land that ostensibly allows people to eat without working, move about freely, and elude the strictures of hierarchical observation that maintain the manorial economy.[10] It is either the source of or a complement to whatever specific evils Irenius perceives in Irish ways of life because it is an alternative form of subsistence that offers an escape route from the colonial relations of production Spenser wishes to impose.

According to Irenius, the decentralized and mobile lifestyle encouraged by the booley keeps the Irish from enjoying the benefits of settled agrarian civilization: "[T]he people that live thus in these Bollies growe thearby the more Barbarous and live more licentiouslye then they Could in townes vsinge what meanes they liste and practisinge what mischiefs and villanies they will . . .; for theare they thinke themselues haulfe exemted from lawe and obedience" (98). Isolated from the communal life of the town and the kinds of surveillance it enables, the cattle-herding Irish feel free from the strictures of a political ecological regime based on farming arable land. While the target has shifted from clerics to cowherds, the practice of literally rootless subsistence—the exclusively dairy diet of livestock herders—defines the fantasies of wandering idleness that haunt both Spenser's vision of the Irish cattle-herd booleying in the uplands and Barlowe and Roye's vision of the English sheep pasture, populated only by "Pover cilly shepperdes . . ., / Lyvynge on mylke, whyg, and whey" (2812–14). For the Irish of Spenser's *A View of the Present State of Ireland*, the booley not only encourages a life of wandering idleness but also transforms the land from something that can be measured, settled, and used by an accountable population into a grassy waste used only by an indeterminate number of rebels.

In contrast, Eudoxus observes that there is perhaps nothing essentially wrong with Irish ways of subsistence. The booley is not absolutely flawed, he suggests, but rather suits the Irish ecosystem: "[W]hat faulte Cane ye finde with this Custome for thoughe it be an olde Scithian vse yeat it is verye behoofull in this Countrye of Irelande wheare theare are greate mountaines and waste deserts full of grasse that the same shoulde be eaten downe and norishe manye thowsandes of Cattell for the good of the whole realme which Cannot me thinke well be anye other waye then by kepinge those *Bollyes* as theare ye haue shewed" (98). Eudoxus, it seems, is a relativist when it comes to subsistence strategies: the local conditions in Ireland work well with the booley and need not be measured by the standard of England's agrarian economy. Irenius counters this assumption, however, by shifting the priority of the debate. What matters is not the basic ecological suitability of a particular form of subsistence but the social structures that arise from it. As Irenius responds, the boolies are where "loose people . . . which live vppon stealthes and spoile . . . are evermore succored" (98). Without the relief the cattle herd offers, such "loose people" would starve, Irenius asserts: "those Bollies beinge vppon the waste places, wheares els they shoulde be driven shortelye to sterve or to Come downe to the townes to steale reliefe wheare by one meanes or other they woulde sone be Caughte" (98). In a preview of Irenius's proposal to subdue the Irish by driving cattle from their seasonal pastures, he emphasizes the coercive powers of hunger to achieve colonial reform. He is making explicit the priority of transforming ecological conditions before new relations of agrarian production can be established under the control of New English landlords.

The second objection Irenius raises in response to Eudoxus's defense of booleys is that they encourage people to "growe theareby the more

Barbarous and live more licentiouslye then they Could in townes" (98). The allegedly barbarous, lawless life of the booley motivates Irenius's desire to see this way of life destroyed, even though the production of wool as integral to the Munster plantation belies the characterization of all kinds of pasture as "wastes." Similarly, as Pluymers shows of woodlands in Elizabethan Ireland, the political ecology of New English landlords differed from that of the administration in Dublin or London in that the former used them as profitable resources while the latter categorized them as "waste" in their valuations of escheated lands.[11] But Spenser's characterization of the grasslands that support the booley as "waste places" is consistent. As long as they are the home of the booley, they are not integrated into a system of relations that would make them into a source of revenue rather than a source of subsistence. This is why the alleged "Barbarous" life of the booley matters here because it is not the basic interaction of grasslands and herds of animals to which Irenius objects. As Eudoxus has already pointed out, this relationship works insofar as it keeps herds and their human keepers alive. But mere subsistence, Irenius asserts, does not create the conditions that exist within towns, where the wealth of the soil can become monetary wealth thanks to the necessary infrastructural nodes of roads, ports, and markets for exchange.[12] Eudoxus's observation about the "waste deserts" of Ireland being well suited to cattle grazing as a use-value avoids the main issue, as Irenius sees it, which is that the booley, in sustaining allegedly nonlaboring "loose people," prevents their settlement in market towns and their enlistment within the hierarchies of manorial agrarian production and the circulation of exchange value.

The usefulness of pasture alone is not the issue but rather the economic relations in which it is integrated, and this emerges later in the dialogue when Irenius surveys potentially profitable provinces in Ireland. Irenius demonstrates how establishing the right relations of production can make even the most hostile environments into sources of value. Between Dublin and Wexford, for example, he observes that "thoughe the wholle trackt of the Countrie be mountaine and woddye yeat theare are manye goodlie valleis amongst them, fitt for faire habitacion to which those mountaines adioyned wilbe a greate increase of pasturage for that Countrye is a verye great soile of Cattel and verie fit for breede" (189). Irenius recognizes here, as Eudoxus had earlier, that some ecological conditions favor pasturing cattle. Once the right social relations have been established, these mountain pastures will not be "waste wilde places" but an economic boon, enabling "larger penniworthes" to be charged for the rent of these lands because "the widenes of the mountaine pasturage doe recompence the badness of the Soile" (189). Given this optimistic reading of the formerly threatening vista of woods and mountains, Irenius is confident the region "will finde inhabitants and vndertakers enoughe" (189). In these moments, *A View of the Present State of Ireland* exhibits the power of the managerial vision to transform the relationship between the ecology of a given place and the political and economic structures that give it value. This value might be recorded primarily in terms of "penniworthes," but like the *Crede*-poet's assessment of fraternal buildings in terms of "the pris of a plough-lond" (*Pierce the Ploughman's Crede*, 169), assigning a price is another way of signifying the concretion of diffuse economic and ecological relationships. These relationships take on different meanings in different contexts because Irenius performs a new reading of Irish grasslands that translates them from threatening haunts of Irish rebels and their cattle to potentially valuable pastureland for a future English landlord.

But in the present, Irish pasture remains the ecological niche in which unaccountable ways of living outside the circuits of value creation persist. When discussing his desire to limit cattle herding after the defeat of the Irish, Irenius notes that "all Countries that live ... by kepinge of Cattle ... are bothe verie Barbarous and vncivill" (217). A primary reason for this, Irenius implies, is because cattle herding obviates the need for towns and their social and spatial regimes of surveillance and accountability. In towns, the Irish "maye dwell togeather with neighbours and be Conuersante in the viewe of the worlde" (217). Irenius's faith in towns to create conditions where inhabitants become habituated to being "in the viewe of the worlde," thereby disciplining them into new regimes of value accumulation, presages Michel Foucault's description of a town beset by plague in which "the gaze is alert everywhere" in the regimentation of urban space.[13] The regimentation of the town complements the regimentation of the countryside in Irenius's desire to cut roads, break up fords, and build bridges, which was discussed in chapter 5.[14] It is alongside such newly cut and fenced highways that towns will be built, where the population will "daily see and learne Civill manners of the better sorte" (225). For Irenius, cattle herding enables mobility and subsistence outside the relations of wage and market, and it makes rebels invisible to the supervisory attentions of town dwellers. It likewise makes "Civill manners" invisible to the Irish who allegedly resist settlement.

Irenius's invention of the booley as a site of political ecological disorder depends on a particular vision of the past and its persistence in the present of Spenser's vision of Ireland. In *A View of the Present State of Ireland*, the booley becomes knowable to Irenius through a combination of antiquarianism and the surveyor's documentary gaze. Irenius argues that the Irish take many of their cultural characteristics from the groups from which they are descended after successive waves of migration. Their apparent refusal to bring the Irish landscape under cultivation through agrarian labor can be traced to Ireland's earliest settlers, who roamed after cattle from pasture to pasture instead of plowing. The wildness of this "Scithian or Scottishe" practice defines a people who still "live themselves the moste parte of the yeare in Bollyes pasturinge vppon the mountaine and waste wilde places and removinge still to freshe lande as they haue depastured the former" (97). Spenser's presentation of an alleged cultural link between the Scythians, the Scots, and the Irish draws from the methods associated with the Society of Antiquaries, which the research of Laurence Nowell (1530–ca. 1570) and William Lambarde (1536–1601) exemplifies.[15]

Nowell's Old English lexicon in Oxford, Bodleian Library, MS Selden Supra 63, the so-called *Vocabularium saxonicum*, records in the entry for Ireland, "that the Irisshe men & Scottes are but one nation of one tung & nature & maner of liuing."[16] And Nowell's fellow antiquary Lambarde (also a translator of *Walter of Henley*) notes in the margins of his printed copy of his *Perambulation of Kent*, "These Scots (as themselues do write) weare a people of Scythia, that came first into Spaine, then into Ireland, and from thence to the North part of Britaine our Iland, where they yet inhabit."[17] The deployment of an antiquarian reconstruction of the past continues a familiar dynamic from the English Reformation polemics of Simon Fish and Robert Crowley, who each variously describe the threatening persistence of ancient barbarous invaders within England's borders. The booley fills a structurally similar role to the Roman church in these Reformation-era accounts of England's agrarian crisis insofar as Spenser construes it as an institution with roots in some past foreign migration that continues to harbor parasitic idlers and weaken the realm's political ecology.

Spenser's relation of Irish subsistence practices to both land use and history resonates with Nowell's mapping and description of Ireland. In a notebook, now British Library, Cotton MS Domitian A XVIII, Nowell includes among his notes on the "decaye" of Irish culture after the English conquest several detailed maps of Ireland, interspersed with pages describing the inherent "hardiness" of the Irish that makes them so difficult to pacify.[18] As Rebecca Brackmann speculates, Spenser may have met Lambarde through either Walter Raleigh's connection to the Society of Antiquaries or through Thomas Egerton, and Nowell had entrusted this notebook on Ireland to Lambarde, so it is not impossible that Spenser may have seen these pages.[19] It is significant, given Spenser's conception of the poet's role in the process of colonization considered in chapter 5, that within these pages Nowell records a prophecy from "many hundreth yeares ago that Englisshmen shuld conqueare Ireland & keepe it in prosperitie so long as they shuld keepe their owne lawes but falling to Irisshe order they shuld decaye."[20] Nowell claims that, in the distant past, some prophet foresaw what many Tudor writers on Irish reform would note of the present: that "falling to Irisshe order," which is to say adapting to Irish structures of kinship and property ownership, would lead to the decay of English rule. History, ecology, geography, and prophecy are entangled in Nowell's book in a way that sets off Spenser's own understanding of Irish political ecology and its reformation in his poetry and prose of the 1590s. In these works, the meaning of the past and the nature of the future are fought out in Spenser's vision of the Irish population's relationship to its environment.

For Spenser, the booley is a living relic of an earlier mode of pastoralist subsistence that rives Ireland's present political ecology. The closely related forms of social organization known as septency and tanistry likewise stand in the way of Ireland's linear development toward English-style regimes of property and inheritance. Tanistry refers to the practice of nonhereditary selection of rulers of septs, or subgroups of Irish clans. These social and economic structures, in the eyes of English colonial theorists, "seemed designed to foster mobility, encourage violence and disorder, and consolidate power in the hands of the strongest."[21] According to John Perrot, president of Munster from 1571 to 1573 and lord deputy of Ireland from 1584 to 1588, "the corrupt Irishe customes of Saptencie and Tanaist is the roote of all the barbarisme and disordre of this Lande, where if the same were converted to state of inheritance men wolde builde plans and perserve for their posteritie; where nowe no man careth but for his owne time, and herafter spendeth and spoileth—first his owne and then his neighbors."[22] In this view, the type of labor that domesticates the land and makes it fruitful for "posteritie" cannot flourish because there is no system of predictable inheritance. Instead, the Irish seem curiously averse to the kind of labor that would make their wealth accessible to their descendants. One of

Perrot's first observations about the "comodities and discomodities" of Ireland is that "[t]he Soyle is generally fertyle, but little and badlye manured," which is caused not only by septency and tansitry but also because the inhabitants are "geven to a wandringe and Idill life."[23] While the booley enables this "Idill life" by providing food to the allegedly leisured herder, the absence of stable regimes of inheritance likewise allows Irish lords and tenants to avoid long-term investments of labor and capital into their holdings.

As Irenius details, Irish lords only lease their lands year to year, which encourages tenants to leave their freeholds frequently (133). If this were remedied, Irenius believes, the tenant may "builde him selfe some hansome habitacion theareon to ditche and enclose his grounde to mannour and husbande it as good farmers vse" (135). While this evinces the influence of the kind of "improvement" ideology of the husbandry manuals on the promotion of colonial plantations in Ireland, as John Patrick Montaño has argued about Irish reform writing, it also exemplifies a long-standing recognition of the mutual interaction of legal regimes and ecological conditions that undergirds analyses of sovereign and ecclesiastical power in the *Piers Plowman* tradition.[24] Taken together, the booley, the sept, and tanistry represent a political ecology hostile to the English landlords' accumulation of value because these systems, like that of ecclesiastical landlordship in anticlerical polemic, maintain alternative ways of using and consuming the land and its products.

To institute the fundamental reforms that would make the Irish more accountable to the English plantation, Irenius argues that their relationship to the land must be disrupted first. None of the "Civill" benefits of settled life in or near towns can be enjoyed until the booley is definitively destroyed. This demands an aggressive military strategy of stationing permanent garrisons of English troops in Ireland (177). These garrisons would be tasked with remaking the Irish relationship to the land by severing the sustaining link between pasture, cattle, and herders who subsist on dairy products. In this plan, the garrisons would drive cattle away from pastures before they graze for a sufficient time, causing hunger to move from cow to herder, as the harassed cows would no longer produce the milk and cheese that sustain the Irish denizens of the booley, as Irenius construes it. Starvation would eventually function as the coercive instrument that would force the Irish to surrender:

> And these fowre garrisons issuinge forthe at suche Convenient times as they shall haue intelligence or espiall vppon the enemye

will soe drive him from one side to another and tennys him amongest them that he shall finde no wheare safe to kepe his crete [herd] nor hide him selfe but flyinge from the fire into the water and out of one daunger into another that in shorte space his Crete which is his moste sustenaunce shalbe wasted with prayinge or killed with drivinge or starued for wante of pasture in the woodes and he him self broughte so lowe that he shall haue no harte nor habilitye to endure his wretchednes The which will surelie come to passe in verye shorte time, for one winters well followinge of him will so plucke him on his knees that he will neuer be able to stande vp againe. (154)

Irenius strategically follows the chain of human dependence on the biosphere in order to exploit the assumed weakness of the Irish herders, which is their relatively undiversified source of food. Spenser deploys a version of the Irish word *caoraigheacht* to describe the herd of cattle that is gathered in a booley but in so doing erases a distinction between the *buiale* as a regular seasonal pasture ground and the *caoraigheacht* as a group of cattle that is herded from place to place in a more nomadic fashion, without fixed, seasonal sites.[25] This confusion of terms evinces Spenser's "shallow acquaintance" with the Irish language,[26] but it also allows him to conflate all manner of existing practices of transhumance, or the seasonal movement of cattle to different pastures, as unregulated and wasteful, lacking the kind of husbanding of resources that Spenser associates with "good farmers." Flattening the actual practices of cattle herding into the caricature of the booley, Spenser embraces the fantasy that an equally simple interruption of the cattles' grazing will enable a wholesale transformation of Ireland's political ecology. By breaking the link between cattle and pasture, the English garrisons will make the Irish dependent on settled agrarian labor, Irenius asserts.

In detailing how this vicious plan ought to be pursued in winter, Irenius sounds like a reeve advising his dairy manager, recognizing that winter is when the cows "beinge all with Calfe ... will thoroughe muche Chasinge and driving Caste all theire Calfes and lose theire milke" (154), further depleting the food that would sustain the supposedly idle Irish. They would be without sustenance, according to Irenius, because if they killed the cows for meat, they would have no dairy in the summer. As he explains in a way that blames the Irish for their own alleged susceptibility to this scheme of ecological warfare,[27] the Irish would not have any other staples to rely on because they supposedly do not plow: "bread he hathe none[;] he plougheth not in Sommer" (155). In this plan, Irish obedience would be coerced through a famine that Spenser imagines as the justifiable consequence of the supposed lack of labor of those who would suffer starvation's effects.

When Eudoxus asks how long the military phase of Irish reformation would last, Irenius asserts that it would be "verye shorte" because unlike the long delay that might come if every soldier had to be defeated "by the sworde," Irenius's plan of harassing the booley would cause a complete rout: "thus beinge kepte from manurance and theire Cattle ... they woulde quicklye Consume themselues and devour one another" (158).[28] Irenius is confident in this result because he has seen it happen before:

> In Those late wars of mounster, for notwithstandinge that the same was a moste ritche and plentifull Countrye full of Corne and Cattell that ye would haue thoughte they Coulde haue bene able to stande longe yeat ere one yeare and a haulfe they weare brought to soe wonderfull wretchednes as that anie stonie harte would haue rewed the same. Out of euerie Corner of the woods and glinnes they Came Crepinge forthe vppon theire hands for theire Leggs Coulde not beare them, they loked like Anotomies of deathe, they spake like ghostes Crynge out of theire graues, they did eate the dead Carrions, happie wheare they Coulde finde them, Yea and one another sone after, in so much as they verye carcasses they spared not to scrape out of their graves. And if they founde a plotte of water Cresses or Shamarocks theare they flocked as to a feaste for the time, yeat not able longe to Continve thearewithall, that in shorte space theare weare non allmoste lefte and a moste populous and plentifull Countrye sodenlye lefte voide of man or beaste[.] (158)

Munster had been a populated land, full of grain and cattle, but the effects of total war on the agrarian ecology of the region brought about severe famine. In this notorious passage, Irenius describes extreme hunger with a chilling potency that recalls Hunger's assault on Waster, especially in the shared attention to the details of how famine weakens the legs and makes the face resemble the skull underneath. The eating of corpses is an extremity that William Langland never considers, but the desperate consumption of raw greens recalls the litany of vegetables that Langland's workers are obliged to render to Hunger during the "hungry gap" of the harvest year, where only some foraged foods might tide one over to the harvest.[29] More significant than any direct verbal echoes of Langland's Hunger in Spenser's description of the Munster famine is its surrounding argumentative context. Irenius details this brutal scene because he wants to describe how a population that allegedly resists the labor of the plow will be made to join the new political ecological order. He needs to make viscerally clear how it is that "the stoute Rebell" is "driven to the wretchednesse that he is no longer able to houlde vp hande but will Come into anie Condicions" (177). It is an argument about causation and will—about how people's need to eat makes them tractable to political control.

Irenius brings to the fore the latent managerial logic of colonial warfare by channeling the violence of disciplinary deprivation that Langland exposes in his depiction of labor coerced by Hunger. The military violence that causes this famine fades in importance once the initial relationship between people and their sustaining ecosystem has been severed and the defeated rebels have no choice but to seek to live within the new English manorial system. In the absence of the alternative lifeway of the booley, the Irish, Irenius expects, will "applye themselues vnto honest trades of Civilitye" (178). The primary trade for the defeated Irish will be the settled production of crops and crafts under the eye of English landlords, living in towns "sowed and sprincked with englishe" (211), while the Irish themselves are "dispersed wide from theire Acquaintances and scattered farr abroad" (179). Irenius presents this as a matter of military concern—when the Irish live together, they can conspire against their English enemies (179). But Irenius's military strategy is inseparable from the economic and ecological project of compelling the Irish to settle as tenants and urban craftworkers, working the land and making commodities, all in the service of a system designed to enable tenants to pay "a Certaine rente" to English landlords (179). From this, Irenius predicts a transformation in Ireland's religious and literary culture as Spenser finally turns his attention to the relationship between the violent tasks of colonial reform and the "learned arts" (*Colin Clouts Come Home Again*, 320) that likewise occupies his late pastorals.

In Irenius's vision, reform in Irish religion and Irish education will come after the primary political ecological intervention of the English military has ensured the settlement of plantations and towns: "[E]uerye parishe shoulde be forced to kepe one pettie schollmaster adioyninge vnto the parishe Churche . . . whearby they [the children] will in shorte space growe vp to that Civill Conversacion" so that they "will loathe the former rudenes in which they weare bredd" (218). Not just right religion but also the learned arts of civilization will flourish once people are forced to abandon the booley and become farmers. After the rebellious Irish have been "envrde" to the "swetenes" of agrarian toil, it must be "provided that theire Children after them maie be broughte vp likewise in the same and succeed in the romes of theire fathers To which ende theare is a statute in Irelande ... which Comaundeth that all the sonns of husbandmen shalbe trained vp in theire fathers Trade" (216–217). Changing from a pastoral labor regime to an agrarian one will lead to changes in Ireland's human geography as towns follow from the imposition of a system of arable agrarian production that is enforced intergenerationally by law.

Irenius's hope to enforce the practice of husbandry across generations shows Spenser approaching the relationship between agrarian toil and written work from another direction than that of his late pastorals. There, he begins with the figure of the poet, but in *A View of the Present State of Ireland*, he imagines how the conditions for intellectual labor emerge from the enforcement of agrarian labor. Even though Irenius's summary of a social division of labor based on trades that are "manvall, intellectuall and mixed" declares "the intellectuall" to be "the moste principall of them," those "sciences ... Called liberall artes" are secondary and dependent, "bycause by husbandrie which suppliethe vnto vs all things necessarye for foode we Chieflye liue" (215–216). Once he has established this priority, Irenius inventories the virtues of agrarian labor as the foundation of the colonial regime. Irenius begins with the body, cutting mental from physical work as a reason for making "husbandrye" the first thing to establish in a new commonwealth, because "it is the moste easelye to be learned nedinge onelye the labour of the bodye." Next, Irenius moves from the habitation of the individual body to the needs of the population: "because it is moste generall and moste nedefull." And in an efficient condensation of the ideological work of naturalization, Irenius asserts that husbandry must be established "because it is moste naturall" (216). This cannot mean that agrarian husbandry comes naturally, that is, easily and without variation as the universal subsistence practice of any group. The whole of *A View of the Present State of Ireland* up to this point has shown how much work, planning, and violence is needed to make people work as farmers on land that otherwise withholds its fruits. The naturalness of husbandry comes from the view that Irenius shares with the ideologues of toil in the *Piers Plowman* tradition, which is that agrarian work is the innate condition of anyone who is not, by some distinction of birth or learning, called to the tasks of ruling or writing.

Agrarian labor is "moste naturall" not because it is how things are, everywhere and at all times—an idea Fitzherbert tries to affirm in the introduction to his *Boke of Husbandry*. Here, in *A View of the Present State of Ireland*, to state that husbandry is "moste naturall" is to make it a norm that must be imposed. The supposedly "moste naturall" way of life, as the *Piers Plowman* tradition repeatedly attests, requires the most strenuous efforts of regulation and discipline to habituate both land and people to the plow. Theorizing the English plantation in Ireland forces Spenser to expose the mystification of the "natural" order of manorial production in a way that inverts Langland's critique of the coercive power of Hunger by making it the positive engine of historical change. The colonial prism of *A View of the Present State of Ireland* and Spenser's late pastorals brings out the coercive dynamics that had always defined the work ethic of the *Piers Plowman* tradition. *A View of the Present State of Ireland* retrospectively reveals how visions of reform provoke writers to imagine power's insinuation into people's working relationship to agrarian ecosystems. The work of reform is thus the political ecological task of imagining how land and its resources are used in ways that turn humanity's fundamental need to eat into a tool for remaking the world.

Conclusion
Liberatory Dreams and Colonialist Visions

"Great force must be the instrument but famine must be the meane for till Ireland be famished it can not be subdued."[1] This assertion is from the third of a collection of three documents now known as "A Brief Note of Ireland," preserved in the National Archives at Kew, where a later hand has attributed them to Edmund Spenser.[2] According to Andrew Hadfield, this third document bears the strongest case for the Spenserian attribution because it is a series of propositions that distill the main arguments of *A View of the Present State of Ireland*.[3] This proposition about the use of famine to subdue Irish rebels shows what Spenser learned from his experiences of the second Desmond rebellion and the formation of the Munster plantation. As he infamously describes the aftermath of the uprising in *A View of the Present State of Ireland*, the effects of war were such that starved inhabitants of the province fed on wild greens and scraped human corpses from shallow graves to consume. In these two infamous passages from "A Brief Note" and *A View of the Present State of Ireland*, extreme hunger is a consequence of war that is also a brutal way of winning it, as desperate need drives the colonized population to surrender to the regime of the English plantation.

Hunger provokes Spenser to think about how force and need interact to create a vector for colonial power to remake Irish political ecology.

Insofar as hunger makes the links between the individual body and the biosphere urgently felt, it manifests the interplay of humanity's timeless relationship to the earth with the contingent organization of that relationship in quotidian acts of working, growing food, and eating. For Spenser, like other writers in the *Piers Plowman* tradition, hunger could be an instrument for enforcing drastic changes in social organization. The *Piers Plowman* tradition gave writers a way to imagine the transformation of religious, political, and economic conditions through the world-making labors of the agrarian ecosystem. It constructed literary figures for imagining how people could be made to toil by separating them from their means of subsistence.

This book has been an attempt to describe how this feature of the *Piers Plowman* tradition explains its longevity up through Edmund Spenser's colonial poetry and prose. Part of the challenge of seeing the *Piers Plowman* tradition in light of a grim colonial legacy is that it overshadows readings of *Piers Plowman* that attend to its restless critique of things as they are, including its apparent rejection of the utility of Hunger as the basis of a renewed commune. This book has instead tracked readers of *Piers Plowman* for whom the invocation of Hunger in passus 6 is not an ethical dead end but rather an invitation to imagine humanity's need to eat as an instrument of reform. Another challenge of reading the *Piers Plowman* tradition's relationship to colonialist political ecologies is that it subverts the conception of ecology as encoding an inherently progressive, egalitarian social ethos. The theoretical and practical maintenance of the manorial ecosystem, both domestically and in colonized Ireland, necessitates attention to the interconnections among land, labor, and power, but this attention to ecological relations does not lend itself to a real or desired flattening of hierarchical relationships between colonizer and colonized, among classes, or among humans and nonhuman beings. For poets from the *Crede*-poet to Edmund Spenser, the Langlandian idiom proved to be one that enabled a mode of ecological thought that sought to instrumentalize knowledge about the relationship between people and place in order to make both land and workers tractable to an exploitative political and economic hierarchy.

Tracing this literary history has led, against my sympathies and inclinations, away from the legacy of *Piers Plowman* as a poem that challenges the status quo and is linked to the rising of 1381 and the verses of John Ball, who famously asked, "Whan Adam delfe and Eve span / who was then a gentleman?"[4] Scholars from Helen White and Stephen Justice to Katherine C. Little, Mike Rodman Jones, and Karma

Lochrie have traced the egalitarian potential of the *Piers Plowman* tradition, which has likewise marked creative responses to the poem since the nineteenth century.[5] William Morris's *The Dream of John Ball* (1886–1887), as Lochrie argues, exemplifies how the poem could inspire prophetically critical works.[6] This same visionary response to a liberatory *Piers Plowman* informs, in various ways, more recent creative work by Maureen Duffy, Marilynne Robinson, and Keston Sutherland, among others.[7] This *Piers Plowman* tradition might hold out hope for a liberatory vision of communal work and mutual care among humans and the more-than-human world, but it is not the *Piers Plowman* tradition that shapes Edmund Spenser's vision of work, waste, and reform in Tudor Ireland.

The version of the tradition that Spenser continues laments the uneven distribution of work and its products within society, but rather than seeking the redistribution of the burden of toil and its fruits more equitably, it instead seeks to identify and destroy alleged idlers who undermine a rigid social hierarchy. This depressing version of the *Piers Plowman* tradition ignores the restless critical energy of William Langland's ever-unsatisfied original because many of the poem's medieval and early modern readers seem to have been immune to its radical potential. For the strident advocates of a cure to religious corruption and economic disorder in the enforcement of agrarian toil, the plowing of the half acre seems to have offered a congenial way to think about the nature of the manorial ecosystem and its usefulness as both a model and means of enforcing top-down social change.

Poems as early as *Pierce the Ploughman's Crede* and *Mum and the Sothsegger* take *Piers Plowman*'s centering of agrarian labor as a warrant to imagine enforced toil as the basis of a renewed order. In light of this reformist work ethic, the proximity of the *Piers Plowman* tradition to the tradition of Thomas More's *Utopia*—noted since Helen C. White and recently elaborated by Karma Lochrie and Sarah Hogan—underlines the latent colonial potential in the former because the latter offers much more explicit colonialist ramifications due to its island setting informed by recent texts on the New World.[8] While the radical potential of this convergence between *Utopia*'s critique of private property and that found in the *Piers Plowman* tradition inspires Lochrie's perception of a shared "radical rurality at the heart of Utopian politics,"[9] the negative side of their shared celebration of agrarian labor is the deployment of that work ethic against Indigenous people and the supposed "wilderness" they inhabit. Thus, More's brother-in-law John Rastell could celebrate agrarian toil against the idleness of the wealthy in *Gentleness and Nobility*, but the same opposition between labor and leisure defines his depiction of the Indigenous people of North America in *Four Elements* as lacking any kind of culture or cultivation.[10] It is not difficult to see how Spenser deploys similar oppositions between the settled worker and the nomadic Irish in *A View of the Present State of Ireland* and in his late poetry. In these cases, the promise of a just distribution of labor and the proper use of land takes shape around the figure of an Indigenous idler whose land and labor must be disciplined, cultivated, and reformed.

Lest this seem like an account of a misreading of *Piers Plowman* that can be confined to the grim authoritarians of the English Reformation and the Tudor colonization of Ireland, such an understanding of the poem as primarily a celebration of a harsh work ethic in an unequal society also appealed to latter-day imperialists. As Jennifer Jahner and Enid Baxter Ryce note, Theodore Roosevelt read *Piers Plowman* as a paean to the necessity of work in his speech to the Society of the Sons of the American Revolution in Vermont in August 1902, shortly after the official end of the Philippine-American War.[11] "Just this afternoon," Roosevelt begins, "I was reading a wonderful old poem of 'Piers Plowman' of the 14th century in England and it is curious to see how closely the poet, speaking to his fellow countrymen, adheres to the plain common sense rules of morality to which we must adhere now if we are to win."[12] Those "plain common sense rules" are "[t]he need of honesty, the need of resolute purpose to do work well."[13] The honesty and work ethic Roosevelt extols are the ones that strengthen the military extension of imperial American power. The rest of the speech largely celebrates the martial training, morale, and matériel that helped the United States triumph in the Spanish-American War and in the Philippines. For many scholars of *Piers Plowman*, this might seem like a distinctly inapposite context in which to invoke a fourteenth-century dream vision about individual and communal salvation with a socially critical bent. But Roosevelt presses on, following his citation of *Piers Plowman*'s work ethic with an attack on idlers that allows him to sidestep class antagonism by making the divide between worker and waster, rather than between rich and poor, the primary social division:

> A body of men who live only for pleasure, I do not care whether they are rich men or poor men; whether they are the sons of millionaires or whether they are those who are commonly known as

"hoboes," if they do not work, fundamentally they are alike, fundamentally each has shirked his duty. One has shirked the duty of the wage earner, the other has shirked his duty to use the great privileges entrusted to him, but each has also shirked his duty to the State. Each stands on the wrong side in the line of cleavage which divides good citizens from bad citizens, a line of cleavage which runs at right angles to the line that divides wealth and poverty, don't forget that.[14]

Roosevelt seems to transpose readings of the half acre in passus 6 as a spiritual allegory about saved workers and damned idlers into an allegory for the duties each citizen owes to the imperial state. To be idle, whether as a "hobo" or a millionaire, much like the conflation of "sturdy beggars" with wealthy prelates in the *Piers Plowman* tradition, is to be civically damned as a "bad citizen." A celebration of military might that has a veneer of egalitarianism in its seemingly even-handed condemnation of both rich heirs and "hoboes" but that in no way questions the "line that divides wealth and poverty," Roosevelt's speech might seem to be an idiosyncratic reading of *Piers Plowman*. But his embrace of the coercive edge of the poem's vision of agrarian work has a long history that also seeks to join toil to the strength of the state, as in Simon Fish's *A Supplicacyon for the Beggars* or Spenser's *A View of the Present State of Ireland*. It is also a reading of the poem that was shaped by the French ambassador to the United States during Roosevelt's presidency, the medievalist and literary historian J. J. Jusserand.

Roosevelt's reading of *Piers Plowman* is not far off from what he would have learned from Jusserand's *Piers Plowman: A Contribution to the History of English Mysticism*, the first book-length study devoted to the work, first published in French in 1893 and in English translation in 1894. This would have been among the books by Jusserand about which Roosevelt boasted that he was "ready to pass an examination" before meeting the new ambassador.[15] In Jusserand's reading of the plowing of the half acre and the invocation of Hunger in passus 6, he asserts, "Piers Plowman shall feed every one; he is the mainspring of the State."[16] Further on, he explains, "Piers shall feed everyone, except these useless ones.... Langland lets loose upon the indolent, the careless, the busy-bodies who talk much and work little, a foe more terrible and more real than now: Hunger. Piers undertakes the care of all sincere people, and Hunger looks after the rest.... All this part of the Visions is mainly an eloquent declaration of man's duties."[17] This concise reading of the plowing of the half acre as an allegory for working in support of the state, of punishing the "useless ones" who neglect "man's duties," goes a long way toward explaining why Roosevelt felt the poem was an appropriate illustration of the theme of his speech celebrating American military prowess in the Spanish-American and Philippine-American wars, where dutiful work at home enabled victory abroad. In this, both Jusserand and Roosevelt were in the company of readers like Spenser who saw in Langland's Hunger not a baleful threat to which all humans are potentially vulnerable but a means of enforcing work for any idlers who might shirk their most important duty.

This work ethic had an indelibly ecological component for Roosevelt, given his legacy as a conservationist of America's so-called wilderness. His reading of *Piers Plowman* fits within the deeper literary history that this book has traced of writing ideal figures of toil into the colonial project. As William Cronon observes in "The Trouble with Wilderness," Roosevelt's lifelong fascination with and writing about "the wilderness" celebrates the mythos of the frontiersman whose individual labor extends a white, masculine national spirit across the continent's varied ecosystems with genocidal implications for Indigenous peoples.[18] Roosevelt's medievalism supports an imperial political ecology at the dawn of the twentieth century in ways that echo the early colonial appropriations of the vernacular celebration of agrarian toil in the sixteenth century. As Wan-Chuan Kao has shown, medievalism is a central element of contemporary white supremacist groups who co-opt the language of environmental conservation and ecological precarity.[19] As he demonstrates, "The history of nineteenth-century ecomedievalism is inseparable from the history of racialist nativism," which culminates in Theodore Roosevelt's visions of, in the president's words, the "white-skinned, fair-haired, blue-eyed" hunter as founder of the modern European state, whose descendants also subdue the American frontier.[20] Notably, much of the same military leadership that led the war effort in the Philippines also participated in the destruction of the Nez Percé Native Americans, an event indirectly memorialized by Jusserand in his account of attending a reception in Roosevelt's White House that celebrated the US Army and Navy by inviting Chief Joseph of the Nez Percé as a guest.[21]

Instead of an egalitarian vision of communal labor, Roosevelt exemplifies a regard for labor that did not question but rather reinforced preexisting social and economic hierarchies. The division that mattered was between workers and idlers, not rich or poor. The colonial deployment of this figural opposition highlights how much this moralized schema of human action is also a way of advocating for a particular relationship between humans and the earth. Roosevelt's reading of *Piers Plowman* is ecological not because it anticipates care for the more-than-human world but because of its understanding that humans use and exploit the land through labor in ways that are fundamentally inseparable from the ways that society organizes itself. For poets in the *Piers Plowman* tradition, the dense web of mutually shaping, daily interactions between workers and the earth on the manorial estate is not only an image of the ideal form of human activity. It is also a way of thinking about human need and agency as these are shaped and constrained by ecological conditions. Spenser's meditation on how those conditions can be changed to impose a colonial plantation look back to the fantasies of enforced labor that animate the anticlericalism of English Reformation texts and anticipate Theodore Roosevelt's reading of *Piers Plowman* as a poem about doing one's duty to the state.

It is not surprising that *Piers Plowman* could inspire both the egalitarian, democratic visions of a Morris, Duffy, Robinson, or Sutherland and the imperial work ethic of Roosevelt because, as the late medieval and early modern history of the *Piers Plowman* tradition shows, these two ideologies of work sit uncomfortably close to each other. The poignant representation of the impoverished plowman in *Pierce the Ploughman's Crede* gives way to a condemnation of the education of the clergy and a desire to see them sent back to work. The correction to greedy religious figures in Fish's *A Supplicacyon for the Beggars* or Crowley's *Philargyrie of Greate Britayne* at once sympathizes with the plight of poor workers and fantasizes about a strong sovereign forcing idle parasites to toil with a whip or chasing them out with a sword. This ambivalence is there in the plowing of the half acre in passus 6, where a vision of universal cooperative labor ends in the disciplinary starvation of the "wasters," but Langland exacerbates this tension to the point of rupturing the legitimacy of Piers's disciplinary use of hunger. By contrast, Spenser's desire to make alleged idlers work extends Langland's treatment of manorial labor to a vision of colonizing toil, while diverting Langland's self-questioning energy from the ethics of enforced labor to the poetic self-doubt of the artist on the colonial margins.

As each chapter in this book articulates in different ways, the figure of the poet fits uneasily into the coercive triangle of worker, idler, and sovereign. In the paradoxically leisured labor of the poet lies the possibility of another reading of *Piers Plowman*'s liberatory potential. The possibility that nothing is wasted in a holistic system, that excess is part of nature's bounty, that rest and pleasure are also part of life—all these possibilities are implicit in the very existence of poems like *Piers Plowman* or *Collyn Clout* or *The Faerie Queene*. But the difficulty of finding the poet's place in the reformed commonwealth of work points up the difficulty of representation inherent in writing about a political ecological whole. Seeking the proverbial Archimedean point from which to change society's relationship to nature through work leads to inevitable failures of representation, failures that result in writers condemning the very processes of leisured consumption that enable their poetic labors. This is an impasse of both representation and action, in which neither a holistic vision of society nor a clear program for changing it emerge without the construction of figures that must be excluded from the socioecological totality. This goes against the more dynamic recognition, memorably registered in *Wynnere and Wastoure*, that work and waste both materially and semiotically define each other and neither can be banished from the social whole. As we have seen, readers of *Piers Plowman* from the *Crede*-poet to Spenser attempt to construct ideal political ecologies from which idleness and waste have been eliminated. But in so doing, the relational perspective that Langland's allegorical treatment of manorial ecology enables gives way to a perspective that simplifies action to a matter of choice about how individuals or groups relate to their sustaining landscapes. In seeking to grasp the intricate interaction of agency and constraint that still confronts attempts to address the relationship between humans and the biosphere, poems from *Pierce the Ploughman's Crede* to book 6 of *The Faerie Queene* repeatedly succumb to the allure of a binary opposition between work and waste. While a figural poetics can enable a more dialectical recognition of the interaction of labor and consumption, it can also ossify dynamic processes into rigid conflicts between workers and idlers that signify differently when brought to the colonial conflicts of Spenser's Ireland and beyond.

Notes

Introduction

1. A list of foundational books that situate an epochal transition in England in the fourteenth through the sixteenth centuries in political, economic, religious, and literary realms would include Karl Marx, *Capital: A Critique of Political Economy*, vol. 1, trans. Ben Fowkes (London: Penguin, 1990), 873–926; Max Weber, *The Protestant Ethic and the Spirit of Capitalism*, trans. Talcott Parsons (London: Unwin, 1985); R. H. Tawney, *Religion and the Rise of Capitalism* (London: Verso, 2015); Arthur B. Ferguson, *The Articulate Citizen and the English Renaissance* (Durham, NC: Duke University Press, 1965); G. R. Elton, *The Tudor Revolution in Government: Administrative Changes in the Reign of Henry VIII* (Cambridge: Cambridge University Press, 1953); James Simpson, *Reform and Cultural Revolution* (Oxford: Oxford University Press, 2002).

2. Bruce M. S. Campbell, *The Great Transition: Climate, Disease and Society in the Late-Medieval World* (Cambridge: Cambridge University Press, 2016). For accounts of the "strikingly modern environmental crises" that beset Renaissance England, see Ken Hiltner, *What Else Is Pastoral? Renaissance Literature and the Environment* (Ithaca, NY: Cornell University Press, 2011), 9.

3. On the literary continuities between the medieval and the Renaissance in England, see A. C. Spearing, *Medieval to Renaissance in English Poetry* (Cambridge: Cambridge University Press, 1985); on the shared ideas of late medieval and Reformation-era religious reformers, see Anne Hudson, *The Premature Reformation: Wycliffite Texts and Lollard History* (Oxford: Clarendon, 1988). For a defense of "Trans-Reformation Studies" as the pursuit of previously obscured continuities between the medieval and the early modern, see James Simpson, "Trans-Reformation English Literary History," in *Early Modern Histories of Time: The Periodizations of Sixteenth- and Seventeenth-Century England*, ed. Kristen Poole and Owen Williams (Philadelphia: University of Pennsylvania Press, 2019), 88–101.

4. Among the most thorough studies of this relationship are Judith Anderson, *The Growth of a Personal Voice: "Piers Plowman" and "The Faerie Queene"* (New Haven, CT: Yale University Press, 1976); John N. King, *English Reformation Literature: The Tudor Origins of the Protestant Tradition* (Princeton, NJ: Princeton University Press, 1982), 445–49; John N. King, *Spenser's Poetry and the Reformation Tradition* (Princeton, NJ: Princeton University Press, 1990); Katherine C. Little, *Transforming Work: Early Modern Pastoral and Late Medieval Poetry* (Notre Dame, IN: University of Notre Dame Press, 2013), 13–14, 143–93.

5. I use the term "ecology" throughout in keeping with most work in the environmental humanities and because of the term's implication of knowledge production. For a persuasive defense of "ecosystemic" as preferable to "ecological" on the etymological grounds that "ecosystem" enables perception of "the complex network of living and nonliving things that constitutes the habitable world," see Eleanor Johnson, *Waste and the Wasters: Poetry and Ecosystemic Thought in Medieval England* (Chicago: University of Chicago Press, 2023), 1.

6. The articles from the discipline of human geography that have most informed my understanding of political ecology are Eric Wolf, "Ownership and Political Ecology," *Anthropological Quarterly* 45, no. 3 (1972): 201–5; David Harvey, "The Nature of the Environment: The Dialectics of Social and Environmental Change," *Socialist Register* 29 (1993): 1–51; Joshua Muldavin, "The Time and Place for Political Ecology: An Introduction to the Articles Honoring the Life-Work of Piers Blaikie," *Geoforum* 39 (2008): 687–97. I have also found the following works of environmental history to be especially useful developments of the concept: Keith Pluymers, *No Wood, No Kingdom: Political Ecology in the English Atlantic* (Philadelphia: University of Pennsylvania Press, 2021); Gabriel de Avilez Rocha, "Maroons in the *Montes*: Toward a Political Ecology of Marronage in the Sixteenth-Century Caribbean," in *Early Modern Black Diaspora Studies: A Critical Anthology*, ed. Cassander L. Smith, Nicholas R. Jones, and Miles P. Grier (Cham, Switzerland: Palgrave Macmillan, 2018), 15–36. Articles from medieval and early modern literary studies that inform my usage here are Alexis K. Becker, "Sustainability Romance: *Havelok the Dane*'s Political Ecology," *New Medieval Literatures* 16 (2016): 83–108; and Emily Shortslef and Bryan Lowrance, "Renaissance Political Ecologies," *Journal for Early Modern Cultural Studies* 13, no. 3 (2013): 1–6. For Latour's and Bennett's influential formulations, see Bruno Latour, *We Have Never Been Modern*, trans. Catherine Porter (Cambridge, MA: Harvard University Press, 1993); Bruno Latour, "To Modernise or to Ecologise?," in *Remaking Reality*, ed. Bruce Braun and Noel Castree (New York: Routledge, 1998), 220–41; Jane Bennett, *Vibrant Matter: A Political Ecology of Things* (Durham, NC: Duke University Press, 2010).

7. See, for example, Bennett, *Vibrant Matter*, xiii.

8. Richard Halpern, *The Poetics of Primitive Accumulation: English Renaissance Culture and the Genealogy of Capital* (Ithaca, NY: Cornell University Press, 1991), 6. Halpern's book is foundational for my approach to the interplay of Marxian and Foucauldian paradigms in late medieval and early modern England, but so is recent theoretical work by Leerom Medovoi, Christopher Chitty, and Søren Mau on the intersections of Marx's and Foucault's thought. Leerom Medovoi, "The Biopolitical Unconscious: Toward an Eco-Marxist Literary Theory," *Mediations* 24, no. 2 (2009): 122–39; Christopher Chitty, *Sexual Hegemony: Statecraft, Sodomy, and Capital in the Rise of the World System* (Durham, NC: Duke University Press, 2020); Søren Mau, *Mute Compulsion: A Marxist Theory of the Economic Power of Capital* (London: Verso, 2023).

9. Michel Foucault, *Society Must Be Defended: Lectures at the Collège de France 1975–1976*, trans. David Macey (New York: Picador, 2003), 244–45.

10. For key debates among Marxist historians and their critics about the transition from feudalism to capitalism, see Rodney Hilton, ed., *The Transition from Feudalism to Capitalism* (London: New Left Books, 1976); and T. H. Aston and C. H. E. Philpin, eds., *The Brenner Debate: Agrarian Class Structure and Economic Development in Pre-industrial Europe* (Cambridge: Cambridge University Press, 1985). For a review and contribution to the debate, see Ellen Meiksins Wood, *The Origin of Capitalism: A Longer View* (London: Verso, 2002). For more recent surveys of agrarian and economic history in the fourteenth to the sixteenth centuries as transitional but that depart from the framework of the transition debate, see Bruce M. S. Campbell, *English Seigniorial Agriculture, 1250–1450*, Cambridge Studies in Historical Geography 31 (Cambridge: Cambridge University Press, 2000); Christopher Dyer, *An Age of Transition? Economy and Society in England in the Later Middle Ages* (Oxford: Oxford University Press, 2005).

11. For a critique of the construction of "feudalism" and its role in periodizing claims for modernity, see Kathleen Davis, *Periodization and Sovereignty: How Ideas of Feudalism and Secularization Govern the Politics of Time* (Philadelphia: University of Pennsylvania Press, 2008).

12. Marx, *Capital*, 1:876. As Julianne Werlin points out, this "rather ambiguous formulation" has prompted generations of scholars to debate whether England was an outlier or representative of broader shifts in Europe. Julianne Werlin, *Writing at the Origin of Capitalism: Literary Circulation and Social Change in Early Modern England* (Oxford: Oxford University Press, 2021), 7.

13. Marx, *Capital*, 1:900.

14. Marx, *Capital*, 1:878–79.

15. The elaborations of Marx's ecological thought that have most informed this study are John Bellamy Foster, *Marx's Ecology: Materialism and Nature* (New York: Monthly Review Press, 2000); Kohei Saito, *Karl Marx's Ecosocialism: Capital, Nature, and the Unfinished Critique of Political Economy* (New York: Monthly Review Press, 2017); Harvey, "The Nature of the Environment"; Andreas Malm, *The Progress of This Storm: Nature and Society in a Warming World* (London: Verso, 2018); Jason W. Moore, *Capitalism in the Web of Life: Ecology and the Accumulation of Capital* (London: Verso, 2015).

16. Marx, *Capital*, 1:290.

17. Michel Foucault, *The History of Sexuality*, vol. 1, *An Introduction*, trans. Robert Hurley (New York: Vintage, 1990), 136.

18. Foucault, *The History of Sexuality*, 1:140; Michel Foucault, *Discipline and Punish: The Birth of the Prison*, trans. Alan Sheridan (New York: Vintage, 1977), 137.

19. Foucault, *The History of Sexuality*, 1:140–41.

20. Foucault, *The History of Sexuality*, 1:141–42.

21. My understanding of the interaction of sovereignty and biopolitics in the Middle Ages, notwithstanding Foucault's strong periodization of the two, has benefited from Randy P. Schiff and Joseph Taylor, "Introduction," in *The Politics of Ecology: Land, Life, and Law in Medieval Britain*, ed. Randy P. Schiff and

Joseph Taylor (Columbus: Ohio State University Press, 2016), 1–30; and Karl Steel, "Biopolitics in the Forest," in Randy P. Schiff and Joseph Taylor, *The Politics of Ecology: Land, Life, and Law in Medieval Britain*, ed. Randy P. Schiff and Joseph Taylor (Columbus: Ohio State University Press, 2016), 37–43. I have similarly benefited from the accounts of sovereignty and biopolitics in early modernity in Joseph Campana, "Introduction: After Sovereignty," *Studies in English Literature 1500–1900* 58, no. 1 (2018): 1–21; and Ben Parris, *Vital Strife: Sleep, Insomnia, and the Early Modern Ethics of Care* (Ithaca, NY: Cornell University Press, 2022), especially 11–22.

22. Søren Mau offers a compelling account of Marx's and Foucault's complementary approaches to power in Mau, *Mute Compulsion*, 35–36.

23. William Langland, *The Vision of Piers Plowman: A Critical Edition of the B-Text*, ed. A. V. C. Schmitt (London: Dent, 1991), 1.17–18, 23–25. All subsequent citations from *Piers Plowman* will be from this edition, denoted B., and given in text by passus and line number.

24. John Fitzherbert, *The Boke of Husbandry* (London, 1533), STC 10995.5, A2^r.

25. Fitzherbert, *The Boke of Husbandry*, A2^r.

26. Richard Harvey was the brother of Gabriel Harvey, Spenser's friend whose correspondence with the poet was published in 1580. Richard Harvey owned and annotated a copy of Rogers's edition, now at Yale University, Beinecke Library, ID L 26 550F. For a brief description, see Lawrence Warner, "Owen Rogers and *Piers Plowman's Crede*, 1561: A Census of STC 19908," in *Later Middle English Literature, Materiality, and Culture: Essays in Honor of James M. Dean*, ed. Brian Gastle and Erick Kelemen (Newark: University of Delaware Press, 2018), 211. For a longer description and a reading of Harvey's annotations in terms of "the light they shed on Spenser's milieu," see Barbara A. Johnson, *Reading "Piers Plowman" and "The Pilgrim's Progress": Reception and the Protestant Reader* (Carbondale: Southern Illinois University Press, 1992), 153–55.

27. For influential readings that emphasize the episode's spiritual significance but nevertheless recognize its investment in worldly conflicts, see Robert Worth Frank Jr., *Piers Plowman and the Scheme of Salvation* (New Haven, CT: Yale University Press, 1957; repr., New Haven: Archon, 1969), 23. Citation refers to the Archon edition. See also J. A. Burrow, "The Action of Langland's Second Vision," in *Essays on Medieval Literature* (Oxford: Clarendon, 1984), 79–101. My approach to personification in the plowing of the half acre is especially informed by Kathleen Hewett-Smith, "Allegory on the Half-Acre: The Demands of History," *Yearbook of Langland Studies* 10 (1996): 1–22; Larry Scanlon, "Penance and Personification," *Yearbook of Langland Studies* 21 (2007): 2; Julie Orlemanski, "Langland's Poetics of Animation: Body, Soul, Personification," *Yearbook of Langland Studies* 33 (2019): 167–71; Katharine Breen, *Machines of the Mind: Personification in Medieval Literature* (Chicago: University of Chicago Press, 2021).

28. Wendy Scase describes annotations to the plowing of the half acre in the context of disputes about clerical poverty and idle begging. See Wendy Scase, *Piers Plowman and the New Anticlericalism* (Cambridge: Cambridge University Press, 1989), 78.

29. Sebastian Sobecki's article traces the links between a poacher on the estate of Richard Holdych in 1381 who called himself "William Longewille" after the author-persona hinted at in B.15.152 and whose resistance to knightly authority echoes the inefficacy of the knight in passus 6. Sebastian Sobecki, "Hares, Rabbits, Pheasants: *Piers Plowman* and William Longewille, a Norfolk Rebel in 1381," *Review of English Studies* 69, no. 289 (2018): 216-36.

30. Sarah Wood, *"Piers Plowman" and Its Manuscript Tradition* (York: York Medieval Press, 2022), 2-5.

31. For the annotation to British Library, Add. MS 35157, see Carl James Grindley, "Reading *Piers Plowman* C-Text Annotations: Notes toward the Classification of Printed and Written Marginalia in Texts from the British Isles, 1300-1641," in *The Medieval Professional Reader at Work: Evidence from Manuscripts of Chaucer, Langland, Kempe, and Gower*, ed. Kathryn Kerby-Fulton and Maidie Hilmo (Victoria, British Columbia: University of Victoria Press, 2001), 89. For the Crowley annotation, see William Langland, *The vision of Pierce Plowman now fyrste imprinted by Roberte Crowley* (London, 1550), STC 19906, Iii^r.

32. For the "prophecie" annotations in the *p*-group manuscripts, see Wood, *"Piers Plowman" and Its Manuscript Tradition*, 164-65. Sharon L. Jansen describes its excerpting as prophecy in British Library, Sloane MS 2578, a collection of political prophecies circa 1553, in Sharon L. Jansen, "Politics, Protest, and a New *Piers Plowman* Fragment: The Voice of the Past in Tudor England," *Review of English Studies* 40, no. 157 (1989): 93-99. For an account of Churchyard's poem, its reception, and its influence on Spenser, see Scott Lucas, "Diggon Davie and Davy Dicar: Edmund Spenser, Thomas Churchyard, and the Poetics of Public Protest," *Spenser Studies* 16 (2002): 151-65. Wendy Scase assesses the possible importance of the *Dauy Dycar* controversy for Crowley's editions of *Piers Plowman*, positing an earlier publication date of 1547 than John King's of 1551 or 1552 in *"Dauy Dycars Dreame* and Robert Crowley's Prints of *Piers Plowman*," *Yearbook of Langland Studies* 21 (2007): 171-98.

33. Helen Barr, ed., *The "Piers Plowman" Tradition: A Critical Edition of "Pierce the Ploughman's Crede," "Richard the Redeless," "Mum and the Sothsegger," and "The Crowned King"* (London: J. M. Dent, 1993).

34. The overviews of this more diffuse tradition of late medieval and early modern *Piers Plowman* literature that have most informed my approach are Helen C. White, *Social Criticism in the Popular Religious Literature of the Sixteenth Century* (New York: Macmillan, 1944), 1-40; King, *English Reformation Literature*, 319-57; Little, *Transforming Work*; and Mike Rodman Jones, *Radical Pastoral, 1381-1594: Appropriation and the Writing of Religious Controversy* (Farnham, Surrey: Ashgate, 2011), 133-60.

35. Edmund Spenser, *The Shorter Poems*, ed. Richard A. McCabe (New York: Penguin, 1999), 29. For an overview of Spenser's poetic affinities with early Tudor verse, see Little, *Transforming Work*, 143-45. For a similar account that includes Skelton and Spenserian resonances with Crowley, see King, *Spenser's Poetry and the Reformation Tradition*, 25-26, 51, 57. David Lee Miller develops a reading of Spenser's engagement with Skelton in *The Poem's Two Bodies: The Poetics of the 1590 "Faerie Queene"* (Princeton, NJ: Princeton University Press,

1988), 44–49. See also Kreg Segall, "Skeltonic Anxiety and Rumination in *The Shepherds Calender*," *Studies in English Literature 1500–1900* 47, no. 1 (2007): 29–56.

36. Edmund Spenser, *The Faerie Queene*, 2nd ed., ed. A. C. Hamilton (Harlow, Essex: Longman, 2007), 4.2.32.8. All subsequent citations of *The Faerie Queene* will be from this edition and given in text by book, canto, stanza, and line number.

37. A. C. Hamilton, "Spenser and Langland," *Studies in Philology* 55, no. 4 (1958): 535–36.

38. Anderson, *The Growth of a Personal Voice*, 75.

39. For Batman's influence on *The Faerie Queene*, see Anne Lake Prescott, "Spenser's Chivalric Restoration: From Bateman's *Travayled Pylgrime* to the Redcrosse Knight," *Studies in Philology* 86, no. 2 (1989): 166–97. For Batman's addition of the prophetic lines at B.6.327–31 to a manuscript of the A-text, see Simon Horobin, "Stephan Batman and His Manuscripts of *Piers Plowman*," *Review of English Studies* 62, no. 255 (2010): 362–63.

40. For accounts of the centrality of prophecy to *Piers Plowman*'s reception and circulation that have informed my approach to a confessionally diverse sixteenth-century *Piers Plowman* tradition, see Jansen, "Politics, Protest Protest, and a New *Piers Plowman* Fragment"; Lawrence Warner, *The Myth of "Piers Plowman": Constructing a Medieval Literary Archive* (Cambridge: Cambridge University Press, 2014), 72–86; Eric Weiskott, "A Sixteenth-Century Political Prophecy Inspired by *Piers Plowman*," *Notes and Queries* 66, no. 2 (2019): 217–19; Eric Weiskott, "Prophetic *Piers Plowman*: New Sixteenth-Century Excerpts," *Review of English Studies* 67, no. 278 (2016): 21–41; Eric Weiskott, "More Prophetic *Piers Plowman*," *ANQ* 30, no. 3 (2017): 21–41. But the poem's reception as prophetic was complicated by events like Kett's Rebellion so that even as Crowley wrote in a prophetic mode, his annotations of *Piers Plowman* attempt to downplay its status as prophecy. See Mike Rodman Jones, "'This Is No Prophecy': Robert Crowley, 'Piers Plowman,' and Kett's Rebellion," *Sixteenth Century Journal* 42, no. 1 (2011): 37–55.

41. For readings of personification in *Piers Plowman* that emphasize its facility with mixing abstraction and corporeality, individual and collective, see Katharine Breen, "Introduction," in *Yearbook of Langland Studies* 33 (2019): 156; and Orlemanski, "Langland's Poetics of Animation," 181.

42. Shannon Gayk, "Apocalyptic Ecologies: Eschatologies, Ethics of Care, and the Fifteen Signs of the Doom in Early England," *Speculum* 96, no. 1 (2021): 1–37; Eric Weiskott, "Political Prophecy and the Form of *Piers Plowman*," *Viator* 50, no. 1 (2019): 207–47.

43. For the argument that *Wynnere and Wastoure* "manifestly influenced" *Piers Plowman*, see Breen, *Machines of the Mind*, 253. See also Katharine Breen, "The Need for Allegory: *Wynnere and Wastoure* as an *Ars Poetica*," *Yearbook of Langland Studies* 26 (2012): 222–23; Weiskott, "Political Prophecy and the Form of *Piers Plowman*," 222. On the dating of the poem's composition, see *Wynnere and Wastoure*, ed. Stephanie Trigg, Early English Text Society 297 (Oxford: Oxford University Press, 1990), xxii–xxvii. Trigg sets the date at 1352

to circa 1370. For the most recent overview and support of the later dates of the 1350s or 1360s, see W. Mark Ormrod, *"Winner and Waster" and Its Contexts: Chivalry, Law and Economics in Fourteenth-Century England* (Cambridge: Brewer, 2021), 6–11.

44. *Wynnere and Wastoure*, lines 11–15. All subsequent quotations of the poem will be from Trigg's edition and cited in text by line number.

45. For an account of the poem's engagement with political prophecy, see Victoria Flood, "*Wynnere and Wastoure* and the Influence of Political Prophecy," *Chaucer Review* 49, no. 4 (2015): 427–48; and Weiskott, "Political Prophecy and the Form of *Piers Plowman*," 219–22.

46. On the poem as a work of political economic analysis, see D. Vance Smith, "*Piers Plowman* and the National Noetic of Edward III," in *Imagining a Medieval English Nation*, ed. Kathy Lavezzo (Minneapolis: University of Minnesota Press, 2004), 235. Breen notes how the poem "allow[s] vernacular readers to gain conceptual purchase on economic phenomena and their social, moral, and even emotional repercussions long before the development of a specialized economic vocabulary." Breen, *Machines of the Mind*, 237.

47. Johnson, *Waste and the Wasters*, 76.

48. For a reading of the appeal of husbandry manuals to lordly readers because of the pleasures afforded by an orderly literary presentation of a manorial estate, see Alexis K. Becker, "Practical Georgics: Managing the Land in Medieval Britain" (PhD diss., Harvard University, 2015), 45–46.

49. Becker, "Practical Georgics," 32; Dorothea Oschinsky, "Introduction," in *Walter of Henley and Other Treatises on Estate Management and Accounting*, ed. Dorothea Oschinsky (Oxford: Clarendon, 1971), 129–30; Alexandra Da Costa, *Marketing English Books, 1476–1550* (Oxford: Oxford University Press, 2020), 206–8.

50. Da Costa, *Marketing English Books*, 219.

51. On the statute's impact on the composition of the estate management treatises, see Oschinsky, "Introduction," 72–74.

52. Oschinsky, "Introduction," 67–72.

53. Oschinsky, "Introduction," 66–67.

54. Campbell, *English Seigniorial Agriculture*, 3–10.

55. Campbell, *English Seigniorial Agriculture*, 3.

56. Oschinsky, "Introduction," 70.

57. Oschinsky, "Introduction," 3.

58. For a description of this abstract model of the three estates, see Andrew Cole, "Trifunctionality and the Tree of Charity: Literary and Social Practice in *Piers Plowman*," *ELH* 62, no. 1 (1995): 5–8. The classic study of the estates model and Middle English literature is Jill Mann, *Chaucer and Medieval Estates Satire: The Literature of Social Classes and the "General Prologue" to the "Canterbury Tales"* (Cambridge: Cambridge University Press, 1973).

59. Martin Jay, *Marxism and Totality: The Adventures of a Concept from Lukács to Habermas* (Berkeley: University of California Press, 1984), 24–80.

60. Jay cites Joachim of Fiore as a conduit of totalizing historical thought in the Middle Ages. Jay, *Marxism and Totality*, 26. Joachim of Fiore is also a

central figure in Morton Bloomfield's and Kathryn Kerby-Fulton's readings of *Piers Plowman*'s apocalypticism. Morton W. Bloomfield, *"Piers Plowman" as a Fourteenth-Century Apocalypse* (New Brunswick, NJ: Rutgers University Press, 1962); Kathryn Kerby-Fulton, *Books under Suspicion: Censorship and Tolerance of Revelatory Writing in Late Medieval England* (Notre Dame, IN: University of Notre Dame Press, 2006).

61. Christopher Maginn and Steven G. Ellis, *The Tudor Discovery of Ireland* (Dublin: Four Courts, 2015), 13–23; William J. Smyth, *Map-Making, Landscapes and Memory: A Geography of Colonial and Early Modern Ireland c. 1530–1750* (Notre Dame, IN: University of Notre Dame Press, 2006), 21–102; Jason Ross Rozumalski, "Lords of All They Survey: The Social and Economic Origins of the English State, c. 1520–1620" (PhD diss., University of California, Berkeley, 2017); John Patrick Montaño, *The Roots of English Colonialism in Ireland* (Cambridge: Cambridge University Press, 2011), 154–212.

62. Moore, *Capitalism in the Web of Life*, 59.

63. Cedric Robinson, *Black Marxism: The Making of the Black Radical Tradition* (Chapel Hill: University of North Carolina Press, 2000), 24; Silvia Federici, *Caliban and the Witch* (Brooklyn, NY: Autonomedia, 2004).

64. Michael MacCarthy-Morrogh, *The Munster Plantation: English Migration to Southern Ireland, 1583–1641* (Oxford: Clarendon, 1986), 4–38, 56–67; Pluymers, *No Wood, No Kingdom*, 61–75.

65. MacCarthy-Morrogh, *The Munster Plantation*, 26.

1. Manorial Political Ecology and Passus 6 of *Piers Plowman*

1. For descriptions of both manuscripts and transcriptions of their annotations, see C. David Benson and Lynne S. Blanchfield, *The Manuscripts of "Piers Plowman": The B-Version* (Cambridge: Brewer, 1997), 44–48, 86–90, 137–49, 198–202. For a digital facsimile and complete edition of O, see *The "Piers Plowman" Electronic Archive*, vol. 3, *Oxford, Oriel College, MS 79 (O)*, ed. Katherine Heinrichs, SEENET Series A.5, online edition updated April 24, 2017, http://piers.chass.ncsu.edu/texts/O. The electronic version of C^2 is in preparation.

2. William Langland, *The Vision of Piers Plowman: A Critical Edition of the B-Text*, ed. A. V. C. Schmitt (London: Dent, 1991), B.prologue.18–19. All subsequent citations from *Piers Plowman* will be from this edition, denoted B., and given in text by passus and line number.

3. As evidenced, for example, by the variety of proverbs along the lines of "No castle so strong that hunger will not win," "Hunger breaks the stone wall," "Hunger chases the wolf out of the wood," or "Hunger fights within and may overcome without iron." See Bartlett Jere Whiting, *Proverbs, Sentences, and Proverbial Phrases from English Writings Mainly before 1500* (Cambridge, MA: Harvard University Press, 1968), 72, 300.

4. For readings of this legislation, see Anthony Musson, "Reconstructing English Labor Laws: A Medieval Perspective," in *The Middle Ages at Work: Practicing Labor in Late Medieval England*, ed. Kellie Robertson and Michael Uebel (New York: Palgrave Macmillan, 2004), 113–32; Kellie Robertson, *The Laborer's Two*

Bodies: Literary and Legal Productions in Britain, 1350–1500 (New York: Palgrave Macmillan, 2006).

5. He goes on to note: "Such matters would have been part of the experience of many clerics who received some training in compiling manorial documents and who worked at least occasionally for lords, stewards, or reeves writing court rolls or annual accounts." Christopher Dyer, "Piers Plowman and Plowmen: A Historical Perspective," *Yearbook of Langland Studies* 8 (1994): 156.

6. Michel Foucault, *Discipline and Punish: The Birth of the Prison*, trans. Alan Sheridan (New York: Vintage, 1977), 170. The full quotation on the "political technology of the body" is suggestive of how Foucault's otherwise non-Marxist approach is at least partially coincident with Marxian idioms of forces and relations of production: "This political investment of the body is bound up, in accordance with complex reciprocal relations, with its economic use; it is largely as a force of production that the body is invested with relations of power and domination; but, on the other hand, its constitution as labor power is possible only if it is caught up in a system of subjection (in which need is also a political instrument meticulously prepared, calculated, and used); the body becomes a useful force only if it is both a productive body and a subjected body.... [T]here may be a 'knowledge' of the body that is not exactly the science of its functioning, and a mastery of its forces that is more than the ability to conquer them: this knowledge and this mastery constitute what might be called the political technology of the body" (Foucault, *Discipline and Punish*, 26).

7. Michel Foucault, *Society Must Be Defended: Lectures at the Collège de France 1975–1976*, trans. David Macey (New York: Picador, 2003), 244–45. See the introduction to this book.

8. Karl Marx, *Capital: A Critique of Political Economy*, vol. 1, trans. Ben Fowkes (London: Penguin, 1990), 899.

9. *Seneschaucy*, *Walter of Henley*, and Grosseteste's *Rules* were the most widely circulated husbandry manuals in late medieval England, surviving in fifteen, thirty-five, and fourteen manuscripts, respectively. Dorothea Oschinsky, "Introduction," in *Walter of Henley and Other Treatises on Estate Management and Accounting*, ed. Dorothea Oschinsky (Oxford: Clarendon, 1971), 4, 11. On the manuscripts themselves, see Oschinsky, "Introduction," 10–58. For the related tradition of classical Latin agrarian writers in late medieval Europe, see G. E. Fussell, "The Classical Tradition in West-European Farming: The Fourteenth and Fifteenth Centuries," *Agricultural History Review* 17, no. 1 (1969): 1–8; Mauro Ambrosoli, *The Wild and the Sown: Botany and Agriculture in Western Europe: 1350–1850*, trans. Mary McCann Salvatorelli (Cambridge: Cambridge University Press, 1997).

10. Bruce M. S. Campbell estimates about 30 percent of arable production was on the manorial demesne and about 70 percent was peasant production ("between two-thirds and three-quarters"). Bruce M. S. Campbell, "Ecology versus Economics in Late Thirteenth- and Early Fourteenth-Century English Agriculture," in *Agriculture in the Middle Ages: Technology, Practice, and Representation*, ed. Del Sweeney (Philadelphia: University of Pennsylvania Press, 1995), 81, 90.

11. For an overview of these changes in population, prices, and wages across the fourteenth century, see David L. Farmer, "Prices and Wages, 1350–1500," in *The Agrarian History of England and Wales*, ed. Joan Thirsk, vol. 3, *1348–1500*, ed. Edward Miller (Cambridge: Cambridge University Press, 1991), 436–43.

12. Bruce M. S. Campbell, *English Seigniorial Agriculture, 1250–1450*, Cambridge Studies in Historical Geography 31 (Cambridge: Cambridge University Press, 2000), 1–3, 55–60. On the interplay between workers on the seigneurial demesne and the practices of the broader peasant sector, see Mavis Mate, "Medieval Agrarian Practices: Determining Factors?," *Agricultural History Review* 33, no. 1 (1985): 22–31. See also Del Sweeney, "Introduction," in *Agriculture in the Middle Ages: Technology, Practice, and Representation*, ed. Del Sweeney (Philadelphia: University of Pennsylvania Press, 1995), 4–5.

13. Oschinsky, "Introduction," 61–74, especially 72–73. For the text of the statute, see Statute of Westminster II (1285), in Great Britain, *The Statutes of the Realm: Printed by Command of His Majesty King George the Third, in Pursuance of an Address of the House of Commons of Great Britain. From Original Records and Authentic Manuscripts*, vol. 1 (London, 1810; repr., London: Dawsons, 1963), 80, https://babel.hathitrust.org/cgi/pt?id=pst.000017915496&view=1up&seq=260.

14. Oschinsky, "Introduction," 60.

15. Oschinsky, "Introduction," 61–67.

16. Oschinsky, "Introduction," 67.

17. *Walter of Henley*, in *Walter of Henley and Other Treatises on Estate Management and Accounting*, ed. Dorothea Oschinsky (Oxford: Clarendon, 1971), 308.

18. Oschinsky, "Introduction," 67–68.

19. *Walter of Henley*, 312. Throughout, I will quote both William Lambarde's sixteenth-century translation and the Anglo-French original presented in Oshchinsky's edition. This signals the continuous early modern interest in earlier estate management texts while registering the linguistic changes that also mark this period of literary history.

20. *Walter of Henley*, 309.

21. The evolving legal discourse of "waste" likewise participates in a growing emphasis on estate management and the monetary valuation of land, as Eleanor Johnson shows. Eleanor Johnson, *Waste and the Wasters: Poetry and Ecosystemic Thought in Medieval England* (Chicago: University of Chicago Press, 2023), 45, 49–50.

22. Oschinsky, "Introduction," 73.

23. *Seneschaucy*, in *Walter of Henley and Other Treatises on Estate Management and Accounting*, ed. Dorothea Oschinsky (Oxford: Clarendon, 1971), 264–65. I quote Oschinsky's modern English translation alongside the Anglo-French of the *Seneschaucy*, unless otherwise noted.

24. *Seneschaucy*, 264–67.

25. *Walter of Henley*, 326–27.

26. *Walter of Henley*, 326–27.

27. *Walter of Henley*, 324–25.

28. *Seneschaucy*, 274–75.

29. *Walter of Henley*, 336–37.

30. *Seneschaucy*, 266–67, 268–69.

31. *Walter of Henley*, 316–17.
32. *Seneschaucy*, 276–77, 286–89.
33. *Seneschaucy*, 286–87.
34. *Seneschaucy*, 292–93. I modify Oschinsky's translation of "peche" from "trespass" to "sin."
35. Oschinsky, "Introduction," 73.
36. Foucault, *Discipline and Punish*, 27–28.
37. Steven Justice, *Writing and Rebellion: England in 1381* (Berkeley: University of California Press, 1994), 124.
38. Andrew Cole, "Scribal Hermeneutics and the Genres of Social Organization in *Piers Plowman*," in *The Middle Ages at Work: Practicing Labor in Late Medieval England*, ed. Kellie Robertson and Michael Uebel (New York: Palgrave Macmillan, 2004), 179–206; Emily Steiner, *Documentary Culture and the Making of Medieval English Literature* (Cambridge: Cambridge University Press, 2003); Ellen K. Rentz, *Imagining the Parish in Late Medieval England* (Columbus: Ohio State University Press, 2015); Justice, *Writing and Rebellion*.
39. Dyer, "Piers Plowman and Plowmen," 162.
40. *Seneschaucy*, 275–76.
41. *Walter of Henley*, 340–41.
42. Dyer, "Piers Plowman and Plowmen," 157.
43. Oschinsky, "Introduction," 145, 175, 181, 184.
44. For a full consideration of the importance of textile work as gendered labor in *Piers Plowman*, see A. Robin Hoffman, "Sewing and Weaving in *Piers Plowman*," *Women's Studies* 35 (2006): 431–52.
45. On similar treatments of mutual support for the benefit of Christian community around images of agrarian labor, see Andrew Cole, "Trifunctionality and the Tree of Charity: Literary and Social Practice in *Piers Plowman*," *ELH* 62, no. 1 (1995): 1–27.
46. S. A. Mileson, *Parks in Medieval England* (Oxford: Oxford University Press, 2009), 158.
47. On such conflicts, see Mileson, *Parks in Medieval England*, 177.
48. Marc Liddell, ed., *The Middle-English Translation of Palladius "De re rustica"* (Berlin: Ebering, 1896), book 1, lines 827–987.
49. Dyer notes, "While the local justices enforced the labour laws, a 'seigneurial reaction' was being mounted in the manors. Manorial courts had always provided useful profits, but after the Black Death their revenues increased, a remarkable development as the number of tenants had fallen drastically.... On some manors each peasant was paying on average twice as much to the courts as his predecessors had done before 1348." Christopher Dyer, *Making a Living in the Middle Ages: The People of Britain, 850–1520* (New Haven, CT: Yale University Press, 2002), 285.
50. Sebastian Sobecki, "Hares, Rabbits, Pheasants: *Piers Plowman* and William Longewille, a Norfolk Rebel in 1381," *Review of English Studies* 69, no. 289 (2018): 226–28.
51. David Aers, *Chaucer, Langland, and the Creative Imagination* (London: Routledge and Kegan Paul, 1980), 18; Cole, "Trifunctionality and the Tree of Charity," 9.

52. Johnson, *Waste and the Wasters*, 91.

53. On the social and ecological critique of hunting implicit in the portrayal of the knight, see Karl Steel, "The Rules of the Game: Wolf-Hunting and the Usefulness of Knights in *Piers Plowman*," *Yearbook of Langland Studies* 36 (2022): 123–36.

54. Aers, *Chaucer, Langland, and the Creative Imagination*, 17–18.

55. Britton Harwood, "The Plot of *Piers Plowman* and the Contradictions of Feudalism," in *Speaking Two Languages: Traditional Disciplines and Contemporary Theory in Medieval Studies*, ed. Allen J. Frantzen (Albany: State University of New York Press, 1991), 111.

56. Kathleen Hewett-Smith, "Allegory on the Half-Acre: The Demands of History," *Yearbook of Langland Studies* 10 (1996): 19. Hewett-Smith writes, "He [Piers] cannot reconcile his experience of actual hunger and distress with this easy intellectualization of the propriety of need." See also David Aers, *Beyond Reformation? An Essay on William Langland's "Piers Plowman" and the End of Constantinian Christianity* (Notre Dame, IN: University of Notre Dame Press, 2015), 27, where he observes that Piers confronts in this episode "the problem with coercive jurisdiction . . . [which] goes against the grain of Christian discipleship."

57. On "the potential for ethical catastrophe" in the denial of charity that causes Piers such anxiety here, see Kate Crassons, *The Claims of Poverty: Literature, Culture, and Ideology in Late Medieval England* (Notre Dame, IN: Notre Dame University Press, 2010), 14.

58. Rebecca Davis, *"Piers Plowman" and the Books of Nature* (Oxford: Oxford University Press, 2016), 189.

59. Robert Worth Frank Jr., "The 'Hungry Gap,' Crop Failure, and Famine: The Fourteenth-Century Agricultural Crisis and *Piers Plowman*," *Yearbook of Langland Studies* 4 (1990): 90.

60. On the poetics of lists, see James Simpson and Eva von Contzen, eds., *Enlistment: Lists in Medieval and Early Modern Literature* (Columbus: Ohio State University Press, 2022). As M. T. Clanchy notes, "The book called *Husbandry* recommends the bailiff in the autumn to list everything that remains on the manor, such as tools and horseshoes, great and small, so that he will know what to buy for the coming year." M. T. Clanchy, *From Memory to Written Record: England 1066–1307*, 3rd ed. (Malden, MA: Wiley-Blackwell, 2013), 49.

61. Johnson, *Waste and the Wasters*, 94.

62. For an overview of interpretations of Need and an argument for Need's centrality to the poem's theology of salvation, see Jill Mann, "The Nature of Need Revisited," *Yearbook of Langland Studies* 18 (2004): 3–29.

2. Ecologies of Antifraternalism in *Pierce the Ploughman's Crede*

1. For an account of how this tradition emerged in Middle English scholarship and a convincing defense of its legitimacy, see Helen Barr, *Signes and Sothe: Language in the "Piers Plowman" Tradition* (Cambridge: Brewer, 1994), 1–22.

2. According to Christina von Nolcken, for example, the *Crede*-poet "invit[es] his reader to try to peer through the temporal to the archetypal," eliminating

Piers Plowman's self-questioning attunement to the difficulties of negotiating specific encounters with representatives of the church. Christina von Nolcken, "*Piers Plowman*, the Wycliffites, and *Pierce the Plowman's Crede*," *Yearbook of Langland Studies* 2 (1988): 92.

3. Penn R. Szittya, *The Antifraternal Tradition in Medieval Literature* (Princeton, NJ: Princeton University Press, 1986), 6.

4. On the possible origins of this acrostic, see Margaret Aston, "'Caim's Castles': Politics, Poverty, and Disendowment," in *The Church, Politics, and Patronage in the Fifteenth Century*, ed. Barrie Dobson (New York: St. Martin's, 1984), 47.

5. Aston, "Caim's Castles," 46.

6. John V. Fleming, "The Friars and Medieval English Literature," in *The Cambridge History of Medieval English Literature*, ed. David Wallace (Cambridge: Cambridge University Press, 1999), 374.

7. Von Nolcken, "*Piers Plowman*, the Wycliffites," 91.

8. See Helen Barr, "Introduction," in *The "Piers Plowman" Tradition: A Critical Edition of "Pierce the Ploughman's Crede," "Richard the Redeless," "Mum and the Sothsegger," and "The Crowned King*," ed. Helen Barr (London: Dent, 1993), 8–10; Lawrence Warner, "Owen Rogers and *Piers Plowman's Crede*, 1561: A Census of STC 19908," in *Later Middle English Literature, Materiality, and Culture: Essays in Honor of James M. Dean*, ed. Brian Gastle and Erick Kelemen (Newark: University of Delaware Press, 2018), 189–218.

9. For an account of the poem as a quintessential Wycliffite text, see von Nolcken, "*Piers Plowman*, the Wycliffites," 90–97. For a study that situates the *Crede* within a longer tradition of both Wycliffite and orthodox antifraternalism, see Szittya, *The Antifraternal Tradition*, 197–98, 204, 207.

10. *Pierce the Ploughman's Crede*, in *The "Piers Plowman" Tradition: A Critical Edition of "Pierce the Ploughman's Crede," "Richard the Redeless," "Mum and the Sothsegger," and "The Crowned King*," ed. Helen Barr (London: Dent, 1993), line 213. All subsequent citations of the poem will be from this edition and given in text by line number.

11. Kate Crassons, *The Claims of Poverty: Literature, Culture, and Ideology in Late Medieval England* (Notre Dame, IN: Notre Dame University Press, 2010), 99.

12. I. A. Doyle, "An Unrecognized Piece of *Pierce the Ploughman's Crede* and Other Works by Its Scribe," *Speculum* 34, no. 3 (1959): 434.

13. Jens Röhrkasten, *The Mendicant Houses of Medieval London, 1221–1539* (Münster: Lit Verlag, 2004), 239–41.

14. Röhrkasten, *The Mendicant Houses*, 260–61.

15. Barr, *The "Piers Plowman" Tradition*, 221.

16. Crassons, *The Claims of Poverty*, 100.

17. Röhrkasten, *The Mendicant Houses*, 148.

18. Karl Marx, *Capital: A Critique of Political Economy*, vol. 1, trans. Ben Fowkes (London: Penguin, 1990), 199, 229.

19. Marx, *Capital*, 1:198.

20. Marx, *Capital*, 1:198, 199.

21. Marx, *Capital*, 1:199.

22. Anne Müller, "Presenting Identity in the Cloister: Remarks on Benedictine and Mendicant Concepts of Space," in *Self-Representation of Medieval*

Religious Communities: The British Isles in Context, ed. Anne Müller and Karen Stöber (Berlin: Lit Verlag, 2009), 183.

23. Müller, "Presenting Identity in the Cloister," 186.

24. For a reading of the poem's ekphrastic attention to visual display as an effect of its poetic artfulness, see Bruce Holsinger, "Lollard Ekphrasis: Situated Aesthetics and Literary History," *Journal of Medieval and Early Modern Studies* 35, no. 1 (2005): 67–89.

25. John Bellamy Foster, *Marx's Ecology: Materialism and Nature* (New York: Monthly Review Press, 2000), 155–77.

26. "Fen" (n1, n2), in *Middle English Dictionary*, ed. Robert E. Lewis et al. (Ann Arbor: University of Michigan Press, 1952–2001), online ed. in *Middle English Compendium*, ed. Frances McSparran et al. (Ann Arbor: University of Michigan Library, 2000–2018), http://quod.lib.umich.edu/m/middle-english-dictionary/.

27. Helen Barr, *Socioliterary Practice in Late Medieval England* (Oxford: Oxford University Press, 2001), 131.

28. See Helen Barr's gloss on lines 438–39; David Lampe, "The Satiric Strategy of *Peres the Ploughmans Crede*," in *The Alliterative Tradition in the Fourteenth Century*, ed. Bernard S. Levy and Paul E. Szarmach (Kent, OH: Kent State University Press, 1981), 75.

29. Röhrkasten, *The Mendicant Houses*, 152.

30. Geoffrey Chaucer, "The Summoner's Prologue," in *The Riverside Chaucer*, ed. Larry D. Benson (Boston: Houghton Mifflin, 1987), lines 1693–96.

31. John Scattergood, *The Lost Tradition: Essays on Middle English Alliterative Poetry* (Dublin: Four Courts Press, 2000), 178.

32. Fleming, "The Friars and Medieval English Literature," 375.

33. Holsinger, "Lollard Ekphrasis," 74.

34. Barr, *Signes and Sothe*, 49.

3. The Drone and the Sovereign

1. For example, the parliament of rats and mice episode or the topical treatment of Mede as Alice Perrers; see Elizaveta Strakhov, "Political Animals: Form and the Animal Fable in Langland's Rodent Parliament and Chaucer's *Nun's Priest's Tale*," *Yearbook of Langland Studies* 32 (2018): 289–313; Matthew Giancarlo, *Parliament and Literature in Late Medieval England* (Cambridge: Cambridge University Press, 2007), 179–208; Stephanie Trigg, "The Traffic in Medieval Women: Alice Perrers, Feminist Criticism, and *Piers Plowman*," *Yearbook of Langland Studies* 12 (1998): 5–29.

2. *Mum and the Sothsegger*, in *The "Piers Plowman" Tradition: A Critical Edition of "Pierce the Ploughman's Crede," "Richard the Redeless," "Mum and the Sothsegger," and "The Crowned King,"* ed. Helen Barr (London: Dent, 1993), line 1637. All subsequent citations of the poem are from this edition and given in text by line number.

3. See Ruth Mohl, "Theories of Monarchy in *Mum and the Sothsegger*," *PMLA* 59, no. 1 (1944): 26–44; Arthur B. Ferguson, *The Articulate Citizen and the English Renaissance* (Durham, NC: Duke University Press, 1965), 75–85.

4. On fraternal correction, see Edwin Craun, *Ethics and Power in Medieval English Reformist Writing* (Cambridge: Cambridge University Press, 2010), 125–31. On parliamentary petitions, see Giancarlo, *Parliament and Literature*, 218–54. On legal and documentary culture in *Mum and the Sothsegger*, see Helen Barr, *Signes and Sothe: Language in the "Piers Plowman" Tradition* (Cambridge: Brewer, 1994), 139–66; Frank Grady, "The Generation of 1399," in *The Letter of the Law: Legal Practice and Literary Production in Medieval England*, ed. Emily Steiner and Candace Barrington (Ithaca, NY: Cornell University Press, 2002), especially 222–29; Richard Firth Green, *A Crisis of Truth: Literature and Law in Ricardian England* (Philadelphia: University of Pennsylvania Press, 1999), 280–81; Emily Steiner, *Documentary Culture and the Making of Medieval English Literature* (Cambridge: Cambridge University Press, 2003), 177–90; Stephen Yeager, *From Lawmen to Plowmen: Anglo-Saxon Legal Tradition and the School of Langland* (Toronto: University of Toronto Press, 2014), 183–204.

5. Alexis K. Becker, "Practical Georgics: Managing the Land in Medieval Britain" (PhD diss., Harvard University, 2015); Kathleen Biddick, *The Other Economy: Pastoral Husbandry on a Medieval Estate* (Berkeley: University of California Press, 1989); Randy P. Schiff and Joseph Taylor, eds., *The Politics of Ecology: Land, Life, and Law in Medieval Britain* (Columbus: Ohio State University Press, 2016). See also Yeager's remarks about the combined legal and agrarian meanings of the Middle English term "plough," in Yeager, *From Lawmen to Plowmen*, 150–51. For a relevant discussion of the interaction of law, literacy, and land in Old English contexts, see Scott T. Smith, *Land and Book: Literature and Land Tenure in Anglo-Saxon England* (Toronto: University of Toronto Press, 2012).

6. This is analogous to the function of depictions of artisanal labor in the speculum principium tradition, as Lisa H. Cooper describes them. These call attention to the capacity of literature to inform a ruler who otherwise remains isolated from the material making that supports his rule. Lisa H. Cooper, *Artisans and Narrative Craft in Late Medieval England* (Cambridge: Cambridge University Press, 2011), 146–87.

7. *The Crowned King*, in *The "Piers Plowman" Tradition: A Critical Edition of "Pierce the Ploughman's Crede," "Richard the Redeless," "Mum and the Sothsegger," and "The Crowned King,"* ed. Helen Barr (London: Dent, 1993), lines 65–74. All subsequent citations of the poem are from this edition and given in text by line number.

8. Judith Ferster, *Fictions of Advice: The Literature and Politics of Counsel in Late Medieval England* (Philadelphia: University of Pennsylvania Press, 1996), 49, 53–54.

9. Georges Bataille, *The Accursed Share: An Essay on General Economy*, vol. 3, *Sovereignty*, trans. Robert Hurley (New York: Zone, 1991), especially 202: "To know is always to strive, to work; it is always a servile operation, indefinitely resumed, indefinitely repeated. Knowledge is never sovereign: to be *sovereign* it would have to occur in a moment."

10. As Karl Steel observes, "The paired concerns of the medieval English forest, namely its attempt to monopolize legitimate violence and to oversee cervid wellbeing, frustrates attempts to seal off medieval and modern forms

of governmentality and, indeed, sovereignty and biopolitics from each other, because in England, at least, the birth of the sovereign is also simultaneously the birth of biopolitics." Karl Steel, "Biopolitics in the Forest," in *The Politics of Ecology: Land, Life, and Law in Medieval Britain*, ed. Randy P. Schiff and Joseph Taylor (Columbus: Ohio State University Press, 2016), 38.

11. See Helen Barr's gloss on line 604.

12. See Helen Barr's gloss on lines 613–16.

13. "Link," definition 1, in *Middle English Dictionary*, ed. Robert E. Lewis et al. (Ann Arbor: University of Michigan Press, 1952–2001), online ed. in *Middle English Compendium*, ed. Frances McSparran et al. (Ann Arbor: University of Michigan Library, 2000–2018), http://quod.lib.umich.edu/m/middle-english-dictionary/.

14. On "the co-constitution of the legal and the biological in an acutely law-saturated medieval West," see Randy P. Schiff and Joseph Taylor, "Introduction," in *The Politics of Ecology: Land, Life, and Law in Medieval Britain*, ed. Randy P. Schiff and Jospeh Taylor (Columbus: Ohio State University Press, 2016), 2.

15. Grady, "The Generation of 1399," 212.

16. As Henrik Specht notes of this passage in relation to the lavish entertainments of Chaucer's Franklin described in "The General Prologue." Henrik Specht, *Chaucer's Franklin in the Canterbury Tales: The Social and Literary Background of a Chaucerian Character* (Copenhagen: Akademisk Forlag, 1981), 71–72.

17. Giancarlo, *Parliament and Literature*, 244.

18. Yeager, *From Lawmen to Plowmen*, 192–93.

19. John G. Fitch, "Introduction," in *"The Work of Farming" (Opus agriculturae) and "Poem on Grafting,"* by Palladius, trans. John G. Fitch (Totnes, Devon: Prospect, 2013), 17–18.

20. Lisa H. Cooper, "Agronomy and Affect in Duke Humfrey's *On Husbondrie*," *Speculum* 95, no. 1 (2020): 45. As Cooper observes, "*On Husbondrie*'s affective intimations do not come anywhere close to acknowledging . . . the real physical hardships of farming."

21. Lynn Staley, *Languages of Power in the Age of Richard II* (University Park: Pennsylvania State University Press, 2005), 265–303.

22. As Lynn Staley observes, the franklin complements the poet, insofar as *Mum and the Sothsegger* imagines each as sharing "duties . . . to preserve the harmony of the whole." Staley, *Languages of Power*, 324.

23. Johnson, *Waste and the Wasters*, 155–56.

24. Barr believes the quotation to be "authorial." Helen Barr, *Socioliterary Practice in Late Medieval England* (Oxford: Oxford University Press, 2001), 166.

25. William of Saint-Amour, the most influential antifraternal Paris exegete, influenced by Augustine's commentary on the same verses from 2 Thessalonians in *De Opere Monachorum*, makes much of these lines in his case against mendicancy. See Penn R. Szittya, *The Antifraternal Tradition in Medieval Literature* (Princeton, NJ: Princeton University Press, 1986), 48.

26. Barr, *Socioliterary Practice*, 166.

27. Bartholomaeus Anglicus, *On the Properties of Things: John Trevisa's Translation of Bartholomaeus Anglicus' "De proprietatibus rerum,"* ed. M. C. Seymour, 3 vols. (Oxford: Clarendon, 1975), 1:612, lines 13–16.

28. Giancarlo, *Parliament and Literature*, 246.

29. Katharine Breen, *Machines of the Mind: Personification in Medieval Literature* (Chicago: University of Chicago Press, 2021), 23–24.

30. Michel Foucault discusses "power-knowledge relations" as an aspect of "the political technology of the body" in which violence is only one part of a wider field that can be thought of as environmental, insofar as it "pit[s] force against force, bearing on material elements, and yet without involving violence." Michel Foucault, *Discipline and Punish: The Birth of the Prison*, trans. Alan Sheridan (New York: Vintage, 1977), 26. This way of thinking of power's insinuation into the physical environment by altering certain ecological conditions marks a possible convergence of Foucault's approach to biopower and Karl Marx's conception of the "silent compulsion" of economic power, as Søren Mau argues. Søren Mau, *Mute Compulsion: A Marxist Theory of the Economic Power of Capital* (London: Verso, 2023), 145.

31. On how in the poem "thingness itself becomes a figure for counsel poetry," see Steiner, *Documentary Culture*, 185.

32. On the origins of the metaphor, see E. R. Curtius, *European Literature and the Latin Middle Ages*, trans. Willard R. Trask (Princeton, NJ: Princeton University Press, 1990), 313–14. For an extensive bibliography on this tradition, see Cooper, "Agronomy and Affect," 40n15.

33. Green, *A Crisis of Truth*, 281.

34. Giancarlo, *Parliament and Literature*, 248–49.

35. Ferguson, *The Articulate Citizen*, 75–86; Andrew Wawn, "Truth-Telling and the Tradition of *Mum and the Sothsegger*," *Yearbook of English Studies* 13 (1983): 27–87; Giancarlo, *Parliament and Literature*, 249.

36. "Surrender and regrant" is defined by Christopher Maginn as "the process whereby Gaelic chiefs and English lords acknowledged royal authority and, in return, received a feudal charter to hold their lands of the crown." Christopher Maginn, "'Surrender and Regrant' in the Historiography of Sixteenth-Century Ireland," *Sixteenth Century Journal* 38, no. 4 (2007): 955.

4. The Political Ecology of Primitive Accumulation in English Reformation Literature

1. A. R. Heiserman notes, for example, the similarities in denotation and treatment of John Skelton's "bowge" in *Bowge of Court* and Langland's "mede" in *Piers Plowman*. A. R. Heiserman, *Skelton and Satire* (Chicago: University of Chicago Press, 1961), 19, 42–49. John Scattergood situates *Collyn Clout* in a longer lineage of Middle English literary history that encompasses *Wynnere and Wastoure*, *Piers Plowman*, *Pierce the Ploughman's Crede*, and *Mum and the Sothsegger*, all of which feature wandering, truth-seeking narrators of some sort. John Scattergood, *John Skelton: The Career of an Early Tudor Poet* (Dublin: Four Courts Press, 2014), 303–4. Scattergood also identifies specific verbal echoes (like the "mayden Meed" of *Ware the Hauke*) in *John Skelton*, 120, 124, 156, 177. Elizabeth Fowler analyzes the Langlandian nature of Skelton's grasp of economic personhood in *Literary Character: The Human Figure in Early English Writing* (Ithaca, NY: Cornell University Press, 2003), 140–41. David R. Carlson surveys much of this

scholarship in his argument for Skelton's Langlandian affinities in "Protestant Skelton: The Satires of 1519–1523 and the *Piers Plowman* Tradition," in *John Skelton and Early Modern Culture: Papers Honoring Robert S. Kinsman*, ed. David R. Carlson (Tempe: Arizona Center for Medieval and Renaissance Studies, 2008), 227–31.

2. Douglas H. Parker, "Introduction," in *Rede Me and Be Nott Wroth*, by Jerome Barlowe and William Roye, ed. Douglas H. Parker (Toronto: University of Toronto Press, 1992), 28. Scattergood notes specific borrowings from *Collyn Clout* in *Rede Me*. Scattergood, *John Skelton*, 318, 320.

3. Parker, "Introduction," 34. Rainer Pineas, *Thomas More and Tudor Polemics* (Bloomington: Indiana University Press, 1968), 152.

4. For a brief background on *A Supplicacyon* and a reading of More's response, see Pineas, *Thomas More and Tudor Polemics*, 152–72. Frederick J. Furnivall reprints Foxe's account of *A Supplicacyon*'s origins in his introduction to *Four Supplications: 1529–1553*, ed. J. Meadows Cowper (London: Early English Texts Society, 1871), vi–xi. On its popularity, see William A. Clebsch, *England's Earlier Protestants, 1520–1535* (New Haven, CT: Yale University Press, 1964), 241–42. On its English printing in 1546, see Wendy Scase, *Literature and Complaint in England, 1272–1553* (Oxford: Oxford University Press, 2007), 158.

5. A manuscript excerpt of *Collyn Clout*, lines 462–80, in British Library, Lansdowne MS 762, describes a passage that seems to predict Wolsey's downfall as "The profecy of Skylton, 1529." Greg Walker, *John Skelton and the Politics of the 1520s* (Cambridge: Cambridge University Press, 1988), 153. For a full transcription of the excerpt in British Library, Lansdowne MS 762, see John Skelton, *The Poetical Works of John Skelton*, ed. Alexander Dyce, vol. 1 (London: Thomas Rodd, 1843), 329. For a description of this manuscript's collection of political prophecies, see Sharon L. Jansen, "The Paston Family, 'Hogan the Prophet,' and Sixteenth-Century Political Prophecy," *Manuscripta* 39 (1995): 140–41. Crowley's edition of *Piers Plowman* worries over its prophetic passages, which likewise circulated as manuscript excerpts in the sixteenth century. My understanding of the centrality of prophecy to William Langland's sixteenth-century reception has been shaped by Sharon L. Jansen, "Politics, Protest, and a New *Piers Plowman* Fragment: The Voice of the Past in Tudor England," *Review of English Studies* 40, no. 157 (1989): 93–99; Thomas A. Prendergast, "The Work of Robert Langland," in *Renaissance Retrospections: Tudor Views of the Middle Ages*, ed. Sarah A. Kelen (Kalamazoo, MI: Medieval Institute Publications, 2013), 82–83; Sarah A. Kelen, *Langland's Early Modern Identities* (New York: Palgrave Macmillan, 2007), 33–38; Lawrence Warner, *The Myth of "Piers Plowman": Constructing a Medieval Literary Archive* (Cambridge: Cambridge University Press, 2014), 72–86; Eric Weiskott, "A Sixteenth-Century Political Prophecy Inspired by *Piers Plowman*," *Notes and Queries* 66, no. 2 (2019): 217–19; Eric Weiskott, "Prophetic *Piers Plowman*: New Sixteenth-Century Excerpts," *Review of English Studies* 67, no. 278 (2016): 21–41; Eric Weiskott, "More Prophetic *Piers Plowman*," *ANQ* 30, no. 3 (2017): 133–36. For a reading of Crowley's delicate handling of these prophetic passages in his edition, see Mike Rodman Jones, "'This Is No Prophecy': Robert Crowley, 'Piers Plowman,' and Kett's Rebellion," *Sixteenth Century Journal* 42, no. 1 (2011): 37–55. In Thomas Betteridge's view, "Crowley adopted

a prophetic poetic voice, identical to that to which John Skelton aspired, in order to comment on the state of the polity and country." Thomas Betteridge, *Literature and Politics in the English Reformation* (Manchester: Manchester University Press, 2004), 105. For persuasive readings of Crowley's edition that situates it as a response to mid-Tudor upheavals, see Michael Johnston, "From Edward III to Edward VI: *The Vision of Piers Plowman* and Early Modern England," *Reformation* 11, no. 1 (2006); Larry Scanlon, "Langland, Apocalypse, and the Early Modern Editor," in *Reading the Medieval in Early Modern England*, ed. David Matthews and Gordon McMullan (Cambridge: Cambridge University Press, 2007), 51–73.

6. King describes the similarities between Spenser's Archimago and Crowley's Hypocrisy (from *Philargyrie*) in John N. King, *Spenser's Poetry and the Reformation Tradition* (Princeton, NJ: Princeton University Press, 1990), 51. Spenser's close knowledge of *Piers Plowman* would have come via Crowley's editorial work (even if he read Rogers's edition, which copies Crowley's text). A. C. Hamilton notes this in his account of how Spenser's reference to "the Pilgrim that the Ploughman playde awhile" in *The Shepheards Calender* is a reading of *Piers Plowman*. A. C. Hamilton, "The Visions of *Piers Plowman* and *The Faerie Queene*," in *Form and Convention in the Poetry of Edmund Spenser*, ed. William Nelson (New York: Columbia University Press, 1961), 2–4. Paul McLane and David Lee Miller fill out the depths of Spenser's engagement with Skelton in *The Shepheardes Calender*: Paul E. McLane, "Skelton's *Colyn Cloute* and Spenser's *Shepheardes Calender*," *Studies in Philology* 70, no. 2 (1973): 141–59; David Lee Miller, *The Poem's Two Bodies: The Poetics of the 1590 "Faerie Queene"* (Princeton, NJ: Princeton University Press, 1988), 44–49.

7. Alexandra Da Costa, *Marketing English Books, 1476–1550* (Oxford: Oxford University Press, 2020), 219. Andrew McRae, "Husbandry Manuals and the Language of Agrarian Improvement," in *Culture and Cultivation in Early Modern England: Writing the Land*, ed. Michael Leslie and Timothy Raylor (Leicester: Leicester University Press, 1992), 37.

8. The classic critical account of this crisis is R. H. Tawney, *The Agrarian Problem in the Sixteenth Century* (New York: Harper Torchbooks, 1967). For a comprehensive overview, see Joan Thirsk, "Enclosing and Engrossing," in *The Agrarian History of England and Wales*, vol. 4, *1500–1640*, ed. Joan Thirsk (Cambridge: Cambridge University Press, 1967). For a summary of its contours, see Mike Rodman Jones, *Radical Pastoral, 1381–1594: Appropriation and the Writing of Religious Controversy* (Farnham, Surrey: Ashgate, 2011), 112–17; Katherine C. Little, *Transforming Work: Early Modern Pastoral and Late Medieval Poetry* (Notre Dame, IN: University of Notre Dame Press, 2013), 87–89.

9. R. H. Tawney and Eileen Power, eds., *Tudor Economic Documents*, vol. 1 (New York: Longmans, 1924), 4–6.

10. John Fitzherbert, *The Boke of Husbandrye* (London, 1530), STC 10995, A2^r.

11. John Fitzherbert, *Surveying* (London, 1523), STC 11005, b1^v–b2^r. Throughout, I have changed the forward slashes in the text to commas and silently expanded abbreviations.

12. Fitzherbert, *Surveying*, b1^v.

13. Fitzherbert, *Surveying*, g1^r–g1^v.

14. Andrew McRae, "To Know One's Own: Estate Surveying and the Representation of Land in Early Modern England," *Huntington Library Quarterly* 56, no. 4 (1993): 339.

15. McRae, "To Know One's Own," 340, 349.

16. Fitzherbert, *Husbandry* (1533), E2^v.

17. Fitzherbert, *Husbandry*, j8^r–j8^v.

18. Fitzherbert, *Surveying*, b2^r.

19. Fitzherbert, *Surveying*, b2^v.

20. Fitzherbert, *Surveying*, b2^v–b3^r.

21. Acknowledging this tension between what new surveying techniques enable and the social structures they disrupt proves to be an enduring characteristic of surveyors' manuals as the genre developed across the sixteenth and seventeenth centuries. McRae, "To Know One's Own," 341–42.

22. Jason W. Moore, *Capitalism in the Web of Life: Ecology and the Accumulation of Capital* (London: Verso, 2015), 174.

23. On surveying and state formation, see Jasons Ross Rozumalski, "Lords of All They Survey: The Social and Economic Origins of the English State, c. 1520–1620" (PhD diss., University of California, Berkeley, 2017). On surveying, maps, colonization, and the early modern state, see William J. Smyth, *Map-Making, Landscapes and Memory: A Geography of Colonial and Early Modern Ireland c. 1530–1750* (Notre Dame, IN: University of Notre Dame Press, 2006), 21–53; Keith Pluymers, *No Wood, No Kingdom: Political Ecology in the English Atlantic* (Philadelphia: University of Pennsylvania Press, 2021), 64–76.

24. Karl Marx, *Capital: A Critique of Political Economy*, vol. 1, trans. Ben Fowkes (London: Penguin, 1990), 638.

25. Karl Marx, *Capital: A Critique of Political Economy*, vol. 3, trans. David Fernbach (London: Penguin, 1991), 949–50.

26. John Bellamy Foster, *Marx's Ecology: Materialism and Nature* (New York: Monthly Review Press, 2000), 149–56.

27. Marx, *Capital*, 1:879.

28. These terms are from Richard Halpern, *The Poetics of Primitive Accumulation: English Renaissance Culture and the Genealogy of Capital* (Ithaca, NY: Cornell University Press, 1991), 73.

29. Eric Weiskott, *Meter and Modernity in English Verse, 1350–1650* (Philadelphia: University of Pennsylvania Press, 2021), 204–5.

30. Eric Weiskott, *English Alliterative Verse: Poetic Tradition and Literary History* (Cambridge: Cambridge University Press, 2016), 165–66.

31. For an account of Skelton's construction of a Middle English literary tradition centered on Chaucer, Gower, and Lydgate in the *Garlande of Laurell*, see R. D. Perry, *Coterie Poetics and the Beginnings of the English Literary Tradition from Chaucer to Spenser* (Philadelphia: University of Pennsylvania Press, 2024), 188.

32. For the "ragged farmer" reading of Collyn's name, see James Simpson, *Reform and Cultural Revolution* (Oxford: Oxford University Press, 2002), 381; Jane Griffiths, *John Skelton and Poetic Authority: Defining the Liberty to Speak* (Oxford: Oxford University Press, 2006), 136. Stanley Fish notes use of personification in the poem in Stanley Fish, *John Skelton's Poetry* (New Haven, CT: Yale

University Press, 1965), 183. On prophecy in *Collyn Clout* and *Piers Plowman*, see Heiserman, *Skelton and Satire*, 216.

33. For overviews of this literature that minimize the Langland connection, see Anne Hudson, "Epilogue: The Legacy of Piers Plowman," in *A Companion to "Piers Plowman,"* ed. J. A. Alford (Berkeley: University of California Press, 1988), 251–66. For a consideration of this literature in closer connection to Langland, see Kelen, who usefully sums up the complex literary genealogy thus: "The sixteenth-century reception of *Piers Plowman* (the poem) intersects with, but is not identical to, the reception of Piers Plowman (the character)." Kelen, *Langland's Early Modern Identities*, 70–71.

34. Skelton's relationship to dissident religious poetry from before and after the Reformation has been well studied. See John N. King, *English Reformation Literature: The Tudor Origins of the Protestant Tradition* (Princeton, NJ: Princeton University Press, 1982), 255; David R. Carlson, "Protestant Skelton: The Satires of 1519–1523 and the *Piers Plowman* Tradition," in *John Skelton and Early Modern Culture: Papers Honoring Robert S. Kinsman* ed. David R. Carlson (Tempe: Arizona Center for Medieval and Renaissance Studies, 2008), 215–38.

35. Scattergood, *John Skelton*, 318.

36. For a summary account of Skelton's vatic ambitions, see Scattergood, *John Skelton*, 29–33.

37. For formulations of this ambivalence, see Fish, *John Skelton's Poetry*, 194–95; W. Scott Blanchard, "Skelton's Critique of Wealth and the Autonomy of the Early Modern Intellectual," in *John Skelton and Early Modern Culture: Papers Honoring Robert S. Kinsman* ed. David R. Carlson (Tempe: Arizona Center for Medieval and Renaissance Studies, 2008), 45; Mishtooni Bose, "Useless Mouths: Reformist Poetics in Audelay and Skelton," in *Form and Reform: Reading across the Fifteenth Century*, ed. Shannon Gayk and Kathleen Tonry (Columbus: Ohio State University Press, 2011), 159.

38. John Fitzherbert, *Fitzharberts booke of husbandrie Deuided into foure seuerall bookes, very necessary and profitable for all sorts of people. And now newlie corrected, amended, and reduced, into a more pleasing forme of English then before* (London: 1598), STC 11004, B1r.

39. John Skelton, *The Complete English Poems*, ed. John Scattergood, rev. ed. (Liverpool: Liverpool University Press, 2015), lines 47–58. All subsequent citations of the poem will be from this edition and given in text by line number.

40. As Scattergood notes in relation to Douglas Gray's speculation about Skelton's possible familiarity with the earlier work. See Skelton, *Complete English Poems*, 440–41; Scattergood, *John Skelton*, 304. See also Douglas Gray, *The Phoenix and the Parrott: Skelton and the Language of Satire*, Otago Studies in English 10 (Dunedin, New Zealand: University of Otago, 2012), 81. Helen Barr and Kate Ward-Perkins also fruitfully compare *Mum* and Skelton's *Bowge of Court* in Helen Barr and Kate Ward-Perkins, "'Spekyng for One's Sustenance': The Rhetoric of Counsel in *Mum and the Sothsegger*, Skelton's *Bowge of Court*, and Elyot's *Pasquil the Playne*," in *The Long Fifteenth Century: Essays for Douglas Gray*, ed. Helen Cooper and Sally Mapstone (Oxford: Clarendon, 1997), 249–72.

41. On *copia* in Skelton, see Gray, *The Phoenix and the Parrot*, 159–62.

42. The spuriously Chaucerian *Plowman's Tale* likewise accuses monks of forsaking the true asceticism of worldly labor out of pride:

> To pryde and ease have hem take;
> Thys religion is yvell besette.
> Had they ben out of religioun,
> They must have honged at the plowe,
> Threshynge and dykynge fro towne to towne,
> With sory mete, and not halfe ynowe.

The Plowman's Tale, in *Six Ecclesiastical Satires*, ed. James M. Dean (Kalamazoo, MI: Medieval Institute Publications, 1991), lines 1039–44.

43. Griffiths, *John Skelton and Poetic Authority*, 162–64.

44. Skelton's claims for vatic authority are one of the most commented upon aspects of his works. See Vincent Gillespie, "Justification by Faith: Skelton's *Replycacion*," in *The Long Fifteenth Century: Essays for Douglas Gray*, ed. Hellen Cooper and Sally Mapstone (Oxford: Clarendon, 1997), 273–311; Scattergood, *John Skelton*, 29–33; Griffiths, *John Skelton and Poetic Authority*, 11, 34–37; Gray, *The Phoenix and the Parrot*, 8–9, 191, 250–51; Robert J. Meyer-Lee, "Conception Is a Blessing: Marian Devotion, Heresy, and the Literary in Skelton's *A Replycacion*," in *Form and Reform: Reading across the Fifteenth Century*, ed. Shannon Gayk and Kathleen Tonry (Columbus: Ohio State University Press, 2011), 149–54; Bose, "Useless Mouths," 175–76; Jason Peters, "The Trouble with Authority in Skelton's *Replycacion*," *Philological Quarterly* 101, no. 1-2 (2022): 23–45. For a more general account of the *vates* across the fifteenth century, culminating with Skelton, see Lois A. Ebin, *Illuminator, Makar, Vates: Visions of Poetry in the Fifteenth Century* (Lincoln: University of Nebraska Press, 1988).

45. Scattergood's translation, see Skelton, *The Complete English Poems*, 481.

46. Robert S. Kinsman, "The Voices of Dissonance: Pattern in Skelton's *Colyn Cloute*," *Huntington Library Quarterly* 26, no. 4 (1963): 302-3.

47. Parker, "Introduction," 30–34.

48. Parker, "Introduction," 28.

49. Parker, "Introduction," 35.

50. Jerome Barlowe and William Roye, in *Rede Me and Be Nott Wroth*, ed. Douglas H. Parker, (Toronto: University of Toronto Press, 1992), lines 3–4. All citations of the poem will be from this edition and given in text by line number.

51. Scase, *Literature and Complaint in England*, 152.

52. Pineas, *Thomas More and Tudor Polemics*, 154.

53. Simon Fish, *A Supplicacyon for the Beggars*, ed. F. J. Furnivall, in *Four Supplications: 1529–1553*, ed. J. Meadows Cowper (London: Early English Texts Society, 1871), 1–2.

54. Fish, *A Supplicacyon for the Beggars*, 2.

55. Fish, *A Supplicacyon for the Beggars*, 3–4.

56. Fish, *A Supplicacyon for the Beggars*, 4.

57. Pineas, *Thomas More and Tudor Polemics*, 155.

58. Fish, *A Supplicacyon for the Beggars*, 8.

59. As Lynn Staley observes, Simon Fish's account of the Catholic clergy's occupation and consumption of England reprises Bede's description of the

Saxon invasion and seizure of all the fertile land, which required the surviving Britons to "ek[e] out a wretched and fearful existence among the mountains, forests, and crags, ever on the alert for danger." Lynn Staley, *The Island Garden: England's Language of Nation from Gildas to Marvell* (Notre Dame, IN: University of Notre Dame Press, 2012), 64.

60. Fish, *A Supplicacyon for the Beggars*, 14.

61. Fish, *A Supplicacyon for the Beggars*, 14–15.

62. A number of scholars have modified King's assertion in *English Reformation Literature*, 322, that Crowley "kidnapped" the poem. For a more appreciative account of Crowley's practice as an editor that still sees the project as largely motivated by a desire to reinforce English Protestantism, see R. Carter Hailey, "'Geuyng Light to the Reader': Robert Crowley's Editions of *Piers Plowman* (1550)," *Papers of the Bibliographic Society of America* 95, no. 4 (2001). For an extension of this view to Crowley's construction of the poem's author as Robert Langland, see Prendergast, "The Work of Robert Langland," 70–71. To round out a more nuanced picture of Crowley's reformist but historically sensitive approach to *Piers Plowman*, see Scanlon, "Langland, Apocalypse, and the Early Modern Editor"; Jones, "This Is No Prophecy."

63. Langland, *Vision of Pierce Plowman* (1550), I1^v, I2^r.

64. On the nature of Crowley's political economic critique in relation to older discourses of economic morality and Protestant theology, see Christopher Warley, "Reforming the Reformers: Robert Crowley and Nicholas Udall," in *The Oxford Handbook of Tudor Literature: 1485–1603*, ed. Mike Pincombe and Cathy Shrank (Oxford: Oxford University Press, 2012), 273–90; James Holstun on "literary commonwealthmen" in "The Giant's Faction: Spenser, Heywood, and the Mid-Tudor Crisis," *Journal of Medieval and Early Modern Studies* 37, no. 2 (2007): 363; McRae on Crowley's moral critique of surveying in "To Know One's Own," 334–35; Kenneth J. E. Graham, "Distributive Measures: Theology and Economics in the Writings of Robert Crowley," *Criticism* 47, no. 2 (2005): 152. For an appreciation of *Philargyrie*'s politics as "radical and incisive," see Betteridge, *Literature and Politics*, 110.

65. Tawney and Power, *Tudor Economic Documents*, 1:150.

66. R. Carew, *Survey of Cornwall and an Epistle Concerning the Excellencies of the English Tongue*, new ed. (London: E. Law, 1769), 110, quoted in Hugh Wilmott, *The Dissolution of the Monasteries in England and Wales*, Studies in the Archaeology of Medieval Europe (Sheffield: Equinox, 2020), 49.

67. Wilmott, *The Dissolution of the Monasteries*, 51–58.

68. Scanlon, "Langland, Apocalypse, and the Early Modern Editor," 65.

69. G. J. Piccope, ed., *Lancashire and Cheshire Wills and Inventories from the Ecclesiastical Court, Chester*, vol. 2 (Manchester: Chetham Society, 1857), 107, quoted in Wilmott, *The Dissolution of the Monasteries*, 58.

70. Wilmott, *The Dissolution of the Monasteries*, 67–69.

71. Wilmott, *The Dissolution of the Monasteries*, 93–96.

72. Robert Crowley, *Philargyrie of greate Britayne*, ed. John N. King, *English Literary Renaissance* 10, no. 1 (1980), lines 34, 60. All subsequent citations of the poem are from this edition and given in text by line number.

73. Warley, "Reforming the Reformers," 276.

74. Mike Rodman Jones notes Philargyrie's similarity to Hunger in Jones, *Radical Pastoral*, 43.

75. For a consideration of the Foucauldian dimensions of this move as a biopolitical operation of extending power through care for the population's health, see William Rhodes, "Personification, Power, and the Body in Late Medieval and Early Modern English Poetry," in *Personification: Embodying Meaning and Emotion*, ed. B. A. M. Ramakers and Walter S. Melion (Leiden: Brill, 2016), 95–120.

76. Betteridge argues that "the end of *Philargyrie* strongly suggests that poets like Crowley were fundamental to the reform of the commonwealth." Betteridge, *Literature and Politics*, 112.

5. Why Colin Clout Came to Ireland

1. On the authorship of *Gentleness and Nobility*, see E. J. Devereux, *A Bibliography of John Rastell* (Montreal: McGill-Queen's University Press, 1999), 125–26; James Holstun, "The Giant's Faction: Spenser, Heywood, and the Mid-Tudor Crisis," *Journal of Medieval and Early Modern Studies* 37, no. 2 (2007): 347; Greg Walker, *John Heywood: Comedy and Survival in Tudor England* (Oxford: Oxford University Press, 2020), 61–62. For readings of the interlude that emphasize its radical class critique of private property, see Mike Rodman Jones, *Radical Pastoral, 1381–1594: Appropriation and the Writing of Religious Controversy* (Farnham: Ashgate, 2011), 89–93; Karma Lochrie, *Nowhere in the Middle Ages* (Philadelphia: University of Pennsylvania Press, 2016), 200–211; Sarah Hogan, *Other Englands: Utopia, Capital, and Empire in an Age of Transition* (Stanford, CA: Stanford University Press, 2018), 44–45.

2. John Rastell, *Gentleness and Nobility*, in *Three Rastell Plays*, ed. Richard Axton (Cambridge: Brewer, 1979), line 98. All subsequent citations of the play are from this edition and given in text by line number.

3. David Bevington, *Tudor Drama and Politics: A Critical Approach to Topical Meaning* (Cambridge, MA: Harvard University Press, 1968), 79.

4. Devereux, *A Bibliography of John Rastell*, 134–37.

5. John Rastell may also have printed Skelton's *Magnyficence* in 1530, according to Devereux, *A Bibliography of John Rastell*, 177. For the text and accounts of *A New Boke of Purgatory*, see John Rastell, *"The Pastyme of People" and "A New Boke of Purgatory,"* ed. Albert J. Geritz (New York: Garland, 1985). On *A New Boke of Purgatory* and its role in bringing about Rastell's embrace of Protestant views, see Albert J. Geritz and Amos Lee Laine, *John Rastell* (Boston: Twayne, 1983), 81–91.

6. Devereux, *A Bibliography of John Rastell*, 106. For an overview of Rastell's career that covers his innovative printing of music and playing cards as well as influential legal texts, see Kathleen Tonry, *Agency and Intention in English Print, 1476–1526* (Turnhout, Belgium: Brepols, 2016), 54–59.

7. Devereux, *A Bibliography of John Rastell*, 9–10.

8. Devereux, *A Bibliography of John Rastell*, 106.

9. Devereux, *A Bibliography of John Rastell*, 107–8.

10. John Rastell, *Four Elements*, in *Three Rastell Plays*, lines 68–69. All subsequent citations are from this edition and given in text by line number.

11. For an account of Henrician writing about Ireland and the wished-for "reform" of England's limited control over the island during the early part of his reign, see David Heffernan, *Debating Tudor Policy in Sixteenth-Century Ireland: "Reform" Treatises and Political Discourse* (Manchester: Manchester University Press, 2018), 26–56.

12. The introductory epistle to *The Shepheardes Calender* describes pastoral as best for poets "at the first to trye theyr habilities." Edmund Spenser, *The Shorter Poems*, ed. Richard A. McCabe (New York: Penguin, 1999), 29.

13. Reencountering Colin Clout in book 6 of *The Faerie Queene*, according to Richard A. McCabe, is "as if Virgil's Tityrus were to reappear in the sixth book of the *Aeneid*." Richard A. McCabe, *Spenser's Monstrous Regiment: Elizabethan Ireland and the Poetics of Difference* (Oxford: Oxford University Press, 2002), 233. *Colin Clouts Come Home Againe* appears, in Patrick Cheney's words, as one of "Spenser's veerings." Patrick Cheney, *Spenser's Famous Flight: A Renaissance Idea of a Literary Career* (Toronto: University of Toronto Press, 1993), 47. Richard Helgerson reads book 6 as a major break from the epic moral project of *The Faerie Queene* in Richard Helgerson, *Self-Crowned Laureates: Spenser, Jonson, Milton, and the Literary System* (Berkeley: University of California Press, 1993), 90–100. Paul Alpers describes the late pastorals as "alternatives" to "heroic poetry." Paul Alpers, "Spenser's Late Pastorals," *ELH* 56, no. 4 (1989): 797. For a similar argument about pastoral as an alternative career, see Sue Petitt Starke, "British Knight or Irish Bard? Spenser's Pastoral Persona and the Epic Project in *A View of the Present State of Ireland* and *Colin Clouts Come Home Againe*," *Spenser Studies* 12 (1998): 133–50. For arguments in favor of the primarily Virgilian model of Spenser's career, as well as considerations of other classical and modern models like Ovid, Cicero, Torquato Tasso, and Clément Marot, see David Scott Wilson-Okamura, "Problems in the Virgilian Career," *Spenser Studies* 26 (2011): 1–30; David Lee Miller, "Spenser's Vocation, Spenser's Career," *ELH* 50, no. 2 (1983): 197–231; Patrick Cheney, "The Old Poet Presents Himself: *Prothalamion* as a Defense of Spenser's Career," *Spenser Studies* 8 (1990): 211–38.

14. On the distinction in English Renaissance pastoral between a courtly continental and classical tradition and a demotic insular tradition, see Katherine C. Little, *Transforming Work: Early Modern Pastoral and Late Medieval Poetry* (Notre Dame, IN: University of Notre Dame Press, 2013), 1–17; David Norbrook, *Poetry and Politics in the English Renaissance* (Oxford: Oxford University Press, 2002), 53–96; Helen Cooper, *Pastoral: Medieval into Renaissance* (Ipswich, Suffolk: Brewer, 1977), 144–45.

15. Edmund Spenser, *The Shepheardes Calender*, in *Shorter Poems*, lines 9–10, of the envoy. All subsequent citations are from this edition and given by line number in text.

16. David Lee Miller, *The Poem's Two Bodies: The Poetics of the 1590 "Faerie Queene"* (Princeton, NJ: Princeton University Press, 1988), 44–49; Roland Greene, "Calling Colin Clout," *Spenser Studies* 10 (1989): 229–44; Paul E. McLane, "Skelton's *Colyn Cloute* and Spenser's *Shepheardes Calender*," *Studies in Philology* 70, no. 2 (1973): 141–59. On the Skeltonic source for the name in the *Calender*, see Robert Lane, *Shepheards Devises: Edmund Spenser's "Shepheardes Calender" and the Institutions of Elizabethan Society* (Athens: University of Georgia Press, 1993),

85; Kreg Segall, "The Precarious Poet in *Colin Clouts Come Home Againe*," *Studies in English Literature 1500–1900* 53, no. 1 (2013): 31–51. For the other potential source of the name in the work of Clément Marot, see Annabel Patterson, "Re-Opening the Green Cabinet: Clément Marot and Edmund Spenser," *English Literary Renaissance* 16, no. 1 (1986): 44–70.

17. As John King makes clear, book 6 of *The Faerie Queene* continues Spenser's pervasive responsiveness to the apocalyptic and satirical texts of English Reformation literature, even though he confines the Skeltonic resonance of Colin Clout to his reading of the *Calender*. For the reference to Skelton (and Marot) in the name Colin Clout, see John N. King, *Spenser's Poetry and the Reformation Tradition* (Princeton, NJ: Princeton University Press, 1990), 25–26. For King's reading of book 6 in terms of English Reformation religious satire more broadly, see King, *Spenser's Poetry and the Reformation Tradition*, 89–91, 108–9, 206. See also John N. King, *English Reformation Literature: The Tudor Origins of the Protestant Tradition* (Princeton, NJ: Princeton University Press, 1982), 444–48; Norbrook, *Poetry and Politics in the English Renaissance*, 53–81; Lane, *Shepheards Devises*, 86–88; Andrew McRae, *God Speed the Plough: The Representation of Agrarian England, 1500–1660* (Cambridge: Cambridge University Press, 1996), 270–73; Jones, *Radical Pastoral*, 137.

18. Andrew Hadfield, *Edmund Spenser: A Life* (Oxford: Oxford University Press, 2012), 201.

19. Thomas Herron, *Spenser's Irish Work: Poetry, Plantation, and Colonial Reformation* (Aldershot: Ashgate, 2007), 38–39.

20. Karl Marx, *Capital: A Critique of Political Economy*, vol. 1, trans. Ben Fowkes (London: Penguin, 1990), 876. As Iyko Day argues, colonial dispossession up to the present suggests that "we can approach primitive accumulation as both structure *and* stage of capital accumulation." Iyko Day, "Eco-Criticism and Primitive Accumulation in Indigenous Studies," in *After Marx: Literature, Theory, and Value in the Twenty-First Century*, ed. Colleen Lye and Christopher Nealon (Cambridge: Cambridge University Press, 2022), 47.

21. William J. Smyth, *Map-Making, Landscapes and Memory: A Geography of Colonial and Early Modern Ireland c. 1530–1750* (Notre Dame, IN: University of Notre Dame Press, 2006), 346.

22. Keith Pluymers, *No Wood, No Kingdom: Political Ecology in the English Atlantic* (Philadelphia: University of Pennsylvania Press, 2021), 61.

23. Herron, *Spenser's Irish Work*, 210–16.

24. Edmund Spenser, "Letter to Raleigh," *The Faerie Queene*, 2nd ed., ed. A. C. Hamilton (Harlow, Essex: Longman, 2007), 715.

25. On the continuity of book 5 with book 6, see Herron, *Spenser's Irish Work*, 186; Benjamin P. Myers, "The Green and Golden World: Spenser's Rewriting of the Munster Plantation," *ELH* 76, no. 2 (2009): 473. Douglas A. Northrop summarizes these geopolitical personifications. See Douglas A. Northrop, "The Uncertainty of Courtesy in Book VI of *The Faerie Queene*," *Spenser Studies* 14 (2000): 215. Andrew Hadfield sees book 5's Grantorto as "an enemy within," representing Catholic Irish resistance, in addition to Spain as representative of international Catholic rivalry with English rule. Andrew Hadfield, *Spenser's Irish Experience: Wilde Fruit and Salvage Soyl* (Oxford: Clarendon, 1997), 155. See also Herron, *Spenser's Irish Work*, 95.

26. McCabe, *Spenser's Monstrous Regiment*, 241.

27. Andrew Zurcher, *Spenser's Legal Language: Law and Poetry in Early Modern England* (Cambridge: Brewer, 2007), 176.

28. Edmund Spenser, *A View of the Present State of Ireland*, in *The Works of Edmund Spenser: A Variorum Edition*, ed. Edwin Almiron Greenlaw et al., vol. 10, *The Prose Works*, ed. Rudolf Gottfriend (Baltimore, MD: Johns Hopkins University Press, 1949), 157. All subsequent citations are from this edition and cited in text by page number.

29. Spenser, *The Faerie Queene*, 6.4.13.5-9. All subsequent citations of the poem will be from Hamilton's edition and given in text by book, canto, stanza, and line numbers.

30. Thomas Herron, "Irish Den of Thieves: Souterrains (and a Crannog?) in Books V and VI of Spenser's *Faerie Queene*," *Spenser Studies* 14 (2000): 303-17.

31. Judith Anderson, *The Growth of a Personal Voice: "Piers Plowman" and "The Faerie Queene"* (New Haven, CT: Yale University Press, 1976), 158.

32. Richard A. McCabe, "Edmund Spenser, Poet of Exile," *Proceedings of the British Academy* 80 (1993): 75.

33. As Herron notes, "Calidore in his chase thereby hints at (in reverse order) an agrarian economy that collected goods from 'open fields,' processed them in 'private farmes' and shipped them to market in 'towns' . . ., which in turn sent their wholesale goods to the 'cities,' whose revenue and loyalty ultimately support 'court' rule." Herron, *Spenser's Irish Work*, 203. Benjamin Myers notes how the compatibility of sheepherding and arable farming was key to both this pastoral vision and the economic aims of Tudor colonists like Spenser. Myers, "The Green and Golden World," 478.

34. Little, *Transforming Work*, 185-86.

35. For the importance of this episode in early modern race making, see Urvashi Chakravarty, "Slavery and White Womanhood in Early Modern England," *Renaissance Quarterly* 75, no. 4 (2022): 1170-74. See also Katherine C. Little's consideration of the generic and social liabilities of the relationship between classical *otium* and slavery within pastoral in Little, *Transforming Work*, 185-90.

36. Maureen Quilligan, "On the Renaissance Epic: Spenser and Slavery," *South Atlantic Quarterly* 100, no. 1 (2001): 26.

37. Tadhg O'Keeffe, "Kilcolman Castle, Co. Cork: A New Interpretation of Edmund Spenser's Residence in Plantation Munster," *International Journal of Historical Archaeology* 21, no. 1 (2017): 228.

38. For an account of Spenser's relationship to Irish earth as a kind of archaeology that seeks to efface its traces of violence, see Philip Schwyzer, "Exhumation and Ethnic Conflict: From *St. Erkenwald* to Spenser in Ireland," *Representations* 95, no. 1 (2006): 1-26.

39. Edmund Spenser, *Colin Clouts Come Home Again*, in *Shorter Poems*, line 656. All subsequent citations of the poem are from this edition and given in text by line number.

40. Spenser, *Shorter Poems*, 344.

41. Courtney Druzak shows that Spenser not only imaginatively dominates Irish waterscapes with this narrative but also enlists Fenian mythology in his

rewriting of the landscape that surrounds his home at Kilcolman. Courtney Druzak, "'Scattred All to Nought': Feminine Waters, Irish Sources, and Colonialism in Spenser's River Mulla," *English* 68, no. 262 (2019): 213–34.

42. Zurcher, *Spenser's Legal Language*, 177.

43. Spenser, *Shorter Poems*, 344. On the Skeltonic resonance of Spenser's need to find a middle way between silence and punishable speech, see Segall, "The Precarious Poet," 41.

44. McCabe, *Spenser's Monstrous Regiment*, 174–76.

45. Hadfield, *Edmund Spenser*, 334–35, 339–41.

46. McCabe, *Spenser's Monstrous Regiment*, 176.

47. Christopher Maginn and Steven G. Ellis, *The Tudor Discovery of Ireland* (Dublin: Four Courts Press, 2015), 15.

48. Thomas Herron, "Love's 'Emperye': Raleigh's 'Ocean to Scinthia,' Spenser's 'Colin Clouts Come Home Againe' and *The Faerie Queene* IV.vii in Colonial Context," in *Literary and Visual Ralegh*, ed. Christopher M. Armitage (Manchester: Manchester University Press, 2013), 122.

49. Starke, "British Knight or Irish Bard?," 146–47.

50. Bruce Avery, "Mapping the Irish Other: Spenser's *A View of the Present State of Ireland*," *ELH* 57, no. 2 (1990): 274.

51. On the usefulness of rivers for New English planters, see Thomas Herron, "Native Irish Property and Propriety in the Faunus Episode and *Colin Clouts Come Home Againe*," in *Celebrating Mutabilitie: Essays on Edmund Spenser's Mutabilitie Cantos*, ed. Jane Grogan (Manchester: Manchester University Press, 2010), 163.

52. On the burning of wood for iron production on the Munster plantation, see Michael MacCarthy-Morrogh, *The Munster Plantation: English Migration to Southern Ireland, 1583–1641* (Oxford: Clarendon, 1986), 224–25. For the centrality of forestry for the estate management schemes of English planters in Munster like Raleigh, as opposed to the Elizabethan administration's treatment of Irish woods as common wastes, see Pluymers, *No Wood, No Kingdom*, 74.

53. Zurcher, *Spenser's Legal Language*, 180; Starke, "British Knight or Irish Bard?," 145.

6. Colonial Political Ecology and *A View of the Present State of Ireland*

1. Karl Marx, *Capital: A Critique of Political Economy*, vol. 1, trans. Ben Fowkes (London: Penguin, 1990), 940.

2. Marx, *Capital*, 1:932–33.

3. Edmund Spenser, *The Shorter Poems*, ed. Richard A. McCabe (New York: Penguin, 1999), 29.

4. Andrew Hadfield, *Edmund Spenser: A Life* (Oxford: Oxford University Press, 2012), 153.

5. Willy Maley, *Salvaging Spenser: Colonialism, Culture, Identity* (London: Macmillan, 1997), 61; Keith Pluymers, *No Wood, No Kingdom: Political Ecology in the English Atlantic* (Philadelphia: University of Pennsylvania Press, 2021), 61.

6. Michael MacCarthy-Morrogh, *The Munster Plantation: English Migration to Southern Ireland, 1583–1641* (Oxford: Clarendon, 1986), 28–38.

7. Hadfield, *Edmund Spenser*, 186–89, 200–201; Thomas Herron, *Spenser's Irish Work: Poetry, Plantation, and Colonial Reformation* (Aldershot: Ashgate, 2007), 37.

8. Edmund Spenser, *A View of the Present State of Ireland*, in *The Works of Edmund Spenser: A Variorum Edition*, ed. Edwin Almiron Greenlaw et al., vol. 10, *The Prose Works*, ed. Rudolf Gottfriend (Baltimore, MD: Johns Hopkins University Press, 1949), 43. All subsequent citations are from this edition and cited in text by page number.

9. For an account of the material and mercantile means and ends of Tudor policy in Ireland, see Steven G. Ellis, *Ireland in the Age of the Tudors, 1447–1603: English Expansion and the End of Gaelic Rule* (London: Longman, 1998), 31–50; R. Gillespie, "Explorers, Exploiters and Entrepreneurs: Early Modern Ireland and Its Context, 1500–1700," in *An Historical Geography of Ireland*, ed. B. J. Graham and L. J. Proudfoot (London: Academic Press, 1993), 123–52.

10. Eugene Costello, *Transhumance and the Making of Ireland's Uplands, 1550–1900* (Woodbridge, Suffolk: Boydell and Brewer, 2020), 1–2; Patricia Palmer, *Language and Culture in Early Modern Ireland: English Renaissance Literature and Elizabethan Imperial Expansion* (Cambridge: Cambridge University Press, 2001), 217.

11. Pluymers, *No Wood, No Kingdom*, 60.

12. As Thomas Herron points out, towns were central to the economic life of Munster even as Spenser arrived amid the devastation of the Desmond rebellions, and coastal towns like Cork were essential for the export of wool from Munster. See Herron, *Spenser's Irish Work*, 40.

13. Michel Foucault, *Discipline and Punish: The Birth of the Prison*, trans. Alan Sheridan (New York: Vintage, 1977), 195.

14. Tamsin Badcoe notes of the passage on cutting roads and building bridges how the impetus to "lay things bare in clear sight is juxtaposed with a need for the protections made available by enclosure and fortification." Tamsin Badcoe, *Edmund Spenser and the Romance of Space* (Manchester: Manchester University Press, 2019), 232.

15. Bart van Es lays out the connections between *A View of the Present State of Ireland* and the antiquarian method pioneered by the likes of William Lambarde and William Camden in Bart van Es, "Discourses of Conquest: *The Faerie Queene*, the Society of Antiquaries, and *A View of the Present State of Ireland*," *English Literary Renaissance* 32, no. 1 (2002): 118–51. Rebecca Brackmann outlines the many similarities between Laurence Nowell's and Edmund Spenser's approaches to the history of Ireland in Rebecca Brackmann, *The Elizabethan Invention of Anglo-Saxon England: Laurence Nowell, William Lambarde, and the Study of Old English* (Cambridge: Brewer, 2012), 178–85.

16. Laurence Nowell, *Vocabularium saxonicum*, ca. 1565, MS Selden Supra 63, Bodleian Library, Oxford, 87^r.

17. William Lambarde, *A Perambulation of Kent*, London, 1576, 4° Rawlinson 263, Bodleian Library, A1^v. On the connections between Nowell's lexical

research and Lambarde's work, see Albert H. Marckwardt, "The Sources of Laurence Nowell's 'Vocabularium Saxonicum,'" *Studies in Philology* 45 (1948): 21–36.

18. Laurence Nowell, notebook, ca. 1564, Cotton MS Domitian A XVIII, British Library, London, 93^r, 96^v. Robin Flower has suggested 1564 as a date for this collection of maps and Irish historical material. Robin Flower, "Laurence Nowell and the Discovery of England in Tudor Times," *Proceedings of the British Academy* 21 (1935): 61.

19. Brackmann, *The Elizabethan Invention of Anglo-Saxon England*, 184–85.

20. Laurence Nowell, notebook, ca. 1564, Cotton MS Domitian A XVIII, British Library, London, 97^v.

21. John Patrick Montaño, *The Roots of English Colonialism in Ireland* (Cambridge: Cambridge University Press, 2011), 15.

22. John Perrot, "A letter to the Lords of the Cownsell," 1584–86, MS Perrot 1, Bodleian Library, 42^v. For his career, see *Oxford Dictionary of National Biography*, s.v. "Perrot, Sir John," by Roger Turvey, last updated October 8, 2009, https://doi.org/10.1093/ref:odnb/21986.

23. John Perrot, "The lengthe, breadthe and situation of that Countrye, the comodities and discomodities with the nature of the people, and the manner of their goverment before the Conqueste," 1584–88, MS Additional C. 39, Bodleian Library, 1^r.

24. Montaño, *The Roots of English Colonialism in Ireland*, 58.

25. Costello, *Transhumance and the Making of Ireland's Uplands*, 31.

26. Palmer, *Language and Culture in Early Modern Ireland*, 79.

27. As Andrew Hadfield notes of the passage describing the famine quoted below, the Irish are cast in *A View of the Present State of Ireland* as if they were caught "in a seemingly endless cycle of *self-destruction*." Andrew Hadfield, *Spenser's Irish Experience: Wilde Fruit and Salvage Soyl* (Oxford: Clarendon, 1997), 67.

28. For an account of this passage that contrasts it with accounts of cannibalism in the New World, see Robert Viking O'Brien, "Cannibalism in Edmund Spenser's *Faerie Queene*, Ireland, and the Americas," in *Eating Their Words: Cannibalism and the Boundaries of Cultural Identity*, ed. Kristen Guest (Albany: State University of New York Press, 2001), 35–56.

29. Robert Worth Frank Jr., "The 'Hungry Gap,' Crop Failure, and Famine: The Fourteenth-Century Agricultural Crisis and *Piers Plowman*," *Yearbook of Langland Studies* 4 (1990): 90.

Conclusion

1. Edmund Spenser, "A Brief Note of Ireland," in *The Works of Edmund Spenser: A Variorum Edition*, ed. Edwin Almiron Greenlaw, Charles Grosvenor Osgood, Frederick Morgan Padelford, and Ray Heffner, vol. 10, *The Prose Works*, ed. Rudolf Gottfriend (Baltimore, MD: Johns Hopkins University Press, 1949), 10:244.

2. The documents are catalogued as National Archives, SP 63/202. See "A Note on the Text," in Spenser, *Works*, 10:233.

3. Andrew Hadfield, *Edmund Spenser: A Life* (Oxford: Oxford University Press, 2012), 389.

4. Steven Justice, *Writing and Rebellion: England in 1381* (Berkeley: University of California Press, 1994), 102–39.

5. Helen C. White, *Social Criticism in the Popular Religious Literature of the Sixteenth Century* (New York: Macmillan, 1944); Justice, *Writing and Rebellion*; Katherine C. Little, *Transforming Work: Early Modern Pastoral and Late Medieval Poetry* (Notre Dame, IN: University of Notre Dame Press, 2013); Mike Rodman Jones, *Radical Pastoral, 1381–1594: Appropriation and the Writing of Religious Controversy* (Farnham, Surrey: Ashgate, 2011); Karma Lochrie, *Nowhere in the Middle Ages* (Philadelphia: University of Pennsylvania Press, 2016).

6. Lochrie, *Nowhere in the Middle Ages*, 176–79.

7. See Michael Johnston and Lawrence Warner, "'The Pure and Perfect Book': Marilynne Robinson, Maureen Duffy, and the Heirs of *Piers Plowman*," *Yearbook of Langland Studies* 35 (2021): 61–104; Keston Sutherland, untitled poem, plenary presented at the International *Piers Plowman* Society conference, London, July 6, 2023.

8. White, *Social Criticism*, 41–81, especially 42: "Like the *Piers Plowman* literature it [More's *Utopia*] may be regarded as a bridge over which some of the most stimulating ideas of the past carry into a new age." On this connection between *Piers Plowman* and utopianism more broadly, see Lochrie, *Nowhere in the Middle Ages*, 132–79. On *Utopia*'s colonial implications, see Sarah Hogan, *Other Englands: Utopia, Capital, and Empire in an Age of Transition* (Stanford, CA: Stanford University Press, 2018), 27–70, especially 52–59.

9. Lochrie, *Nowhere in the Middle Ages*, 212.

10. See chapter 5 in this book. On John Rastell's *Gentleness and Nobility* in relation to both More and the *Piers Plowman* tradition, see Lochrie, *Nowhere in the Middle Ages*, 200–205.

11. Jennifer Jahner and Enid Baxter Ryce, "Unsettling the Half-Acre: *Piers Plowman* in the Making of Modern California," *Yearbook of Langland Studies* 38 (2024): 243–62; Jennifer Jahner, "*Piers Plowman* and the Unmaking of the American Acre," paper presented at the International *Piers Plowman* Society conference, London, July 8, 2023.

12. Theodore Roosevelt, "Remarks to the Society of the Sons of the American Revolution in Montpelier, Vermont," August 30, 1902, *The American Presidency Project*, ed. Gerhard Peters and John T. Woolley (University of California, Santa Barbara), https://www.presidency.ucsb.edu/node/343502.

13. Roosevelt, "Remarks to the Society of the Sons of the American Revolution."

14. Roosevelt, "Remarks to the Society of the Sons of the American Revolution."

15. J. J. Jusserand, *What Me Befell: The Reminiscences of J. J. Jusserand* (Boston: Houghton Mifflin, 1934), 221.

16. J. J. Jusserand, *"Piers Plowman": A Contribution to the History of English Mysticism*, trans. M. E. R. (London: T. Fisher Unwin, 1894), 118.

17. Jusserand, *"Piers Plowman,"* 119–20.

18. William Cronon, "The Trouble with Wilderness: Or, Getting Back to the Wrong Nature," *Environmental History* 1, no. 1 (1996): 14–15.

19. Wan-Chuan Kao, "Identitarian Politics, Precarious Sovereignty," *postmedieval* 11 (2020): 371–83.

20. Theodore Roosevelt, foreword, *The Master of Game* (New York: Duffield, 1909), xxi, quoted in Kao, "Identitarian Politics, Precarious Sovereignty," 377.

21. On the connections between the war in the Philippines and the "Indian wars," including the campaign against Chief Joseph and the Nez Percé, see Roxanne Dunbar-Ortiz, *An Indigenous Peoples' History of the United States* (Boston: Beacon, 2014), 161–62. For Jusserand's account of seeing Chief Joseph at the White House reception, see Jusserand, *What Me Befell*, 221.

Bibliography

Primary Texts

Barlowe, Jerome, and William Roye. *Rede Me and Be Nott Wroth*. Edited by Douglas H. Parker. Toronto: University of Toronto Press, 1992.

Barr, Helen, ed. *The "Piers Plowman" Tradition: A Critical Edition of "Pierce the Ploughman's Crede," "Richard the Redeless," "Mum and the Sothsegger," and "The Crowned King."* London: Dent, 1993.

Bartholomaeus Anglicus. *On the Properties of Things: John Trevisa's Translation of Bartholomaeus Anglicus' "De proprietatibus rerum."* 3 vols. Edited by M. C. Seymour. Oxford: Clarendon, 1975.

Chaucer, Geoffrey. *The Riverside Chaucer*. Edited by Larry D. Benson. Boston: Houghton Mifflin, 1987.

Crowley, Robert. *Philargyrie of greate Britayne*. Edited by John N. King. *English Literary Renaissance* 10, no. 1 (1980): 47–75.

The Crowned King. In *The "Piers Plowman" Tradition: A Critical Edition of "Pierce the Ploughman's Crede," "Richard the Redeless," "Mum and the Sothsegger," and "The Crowned King,"* edited by Helen Barr, 203–10. London: Dent, 1993.

Fish, Simon. *A Supplicacyon for the Beggers*. Edited by F. J. Furnivall. In *Four Supplications: 1529–1553*, edited by J. Meadows Cowper, 1–18. London: Early English Texts Society, 1871.

Fitzherbert, John. *The Boke of Husbandrye*. London, 1530. STC 10995.

Fitzherbert, John. *The Boke of Husbandry*. London, 1533. STC 10995.5.

Fitzherbert, John. *Fitzharberts booke of husbandrie Deuided into foure seuerall bookes, very necessary and profitable for all sorts of people. And now newlie corrected, amended, and reduced, into a more pleasing forme of English then before*. London, 1598. STC 11004.

Fitzherbert, John. *Surveying*. London, 1523. STC 11005.

Lambarde, William. *A Perambulation of Kent*. London, 1576. 4° Rawlinson 263. Bodleian Library, Oxford.

Langland, William. *The vision of Pierce Plowman now fyrste imprynted by Roberte Crowley*. London, 1550. STC 19906.

Langland, William. *The Vision of Piers Plowman: A Critical Edition of the B-Text*. Edited by A. V. C. Schmitt. London: Dent, 1991.

Liddell, Marc, ed. *The Middle English Translation of Palladius "De re rustica."* Berlin: Ebering, 1896.

Mum and the Sothsegger. In *The "Piers Plowman" Tradition: A Critical Edition of "Pierce the Ploughman's Crede," "Richard the Redeless," "Mum and the Sothsegger," and "The Crowned King,"* edited by Helen Barr, 135–202. London: Dent, 1993.

Nowell, Laurence. Notebook, ca. 1564. Cotton MS Domitian A XVIII. British Library, London.

Nowell, Laurence. *Vocabularium saxonicum*, ca. 1565. MS Selden Supra 63. Bodleian Library, Oxford.

Perrot, John. "The lengthe, breadthe and situation of that Countrye, the comodities and discomodities with the nature of the people, and the manner of their goverment before the Conqueste," 1584-88. MS Additional C. 39. Bodleian Library, Oxford.

Perrot, John. "A letter to the Lords of the Cownsell," 1584-86. MS Perrot 1. Bodleian Library, Oxford.

Pierce the Ploughman's Crede. In *The "Piers Plowman" Tradition: A Critical Edition of "Pierce the Ploughman's Crede," "Richard the Redeless," "Mum and the Sothsegger," and "The Crowned King,"* edited by Helen Barr, 60-97. London: Dent, 1993.

The "Piers Plowman" Electronic Archive. Vol. 3, *Oxford, Oriel College, MS 79 (O)*, edited by Katherine Heinrichs. SEENET series A.5. Web ed. Updated April 24, 2017. http://piers.chass.ncsu.edu/texts/O.

The Plowman's Tale. In *Six Ecclesiastical Satires*, edited by James M. Dean, 58-114. Kalamazoo, MI: Medieval Institute Publications, 1991.

Rastell, John. *"The Pastyme of People" and "A New Boke of Purgatory."* Edited by Albert J. Geritz. New York: Garland, 1985.

Rastell, John. *Three Rastell Plays*. Edited by Richard Axton. Cambridge: Brewer, 1979.

Roosevelt, Theodore. "Remarks to the Society of the Sons of the American Revolution in Montpelier, Vermont," August 30, 1902. *The American Presidency Project*, edited by Gerhard Peters and John T. Woolley. University of California, Santa Barbara. https://www.presidency.ucsb.edu/node/343502.

Seneschaucy. In *Walter of Henley and Other Treatises on Estate Management and Accounting*. Edited by Dorothea Oschinsky, 261-305. Oxford: Clarendon, 1971.

Skelton, John. *The Complete English Poems*. Rev. ed. Edited by John Scattergood. Liverpool: Liverpool University Press, 2015.

Skelton, John. *The Poetical Works of John Skelton*. Vol. 1. Edited by Alexander Dyce. London: Thomas Rodd, 1843.

Spenser, Edmund. *The Faerie Queene*. 2nd ed. Edited by A. C. Hamilton. Harlow, Essex: Longman, 2007.

Spenser, Edmund. *The Shorter Poems*. Edited by Richard A. McCabe. New York: Penguin, 1999.

Spenser, Edmund. *The Works of Edmund Spenser: A Variorum Edition*. Edited by Edwin Almiron Greenlaw, Charles Grosvenor Osgood, Frederick Morgan Padelford, and Ray Heffner. Vol. 10, *The Prose Works*. Edited by Rudolf Gottfriend. Baltimore, MD: Johns Hopkins University Press, 1949.

Statute of Westminster II (1285). In Great Britain, *The Statutes of the Realm: Printed by Command of His Majesty King George the Third, in Pursuance of an Address of the House of Commons of Great Britain. From Original Records and Authentic Manuscripts*. Vol. 1, 80-81. London, 1810. Repr., London: Dawsons, 1963. https://babel.hathitrust.org/cgi/pt?id=pst.000017915496&view=1up&seq=260.

Sutherland, Keston. Untitled poem. Plenary presented at the International *Piers Plowman* Society Conference, London, July 6, 2023.
Tawney, R. H., and Eileen Power, eds. *Tudor Economic Documents*. Vol. 1. New York: Longmans, 1924.
Walter of Henley. In *Walter of Henley and Other Treatises on Estate Management and Accounting*, edited by Dorothea Oschinsky, 307-85. Oxford: Clarendon, 1971.
Walter of Henley and Other Treatises on Estate Management and Accounting. Edited by Dorothea Oschinsky. Oxford: Clarendon, 1971.
Wynnere and Wastoure. Edited by Stephanie Trigg. Early English Text Society 297. Oxford: Oxford University Press, 1990.

Secondary Texts

Aers, David. *Beyond Reformation? An Essay on William Langland's "Piers Plowman" and the End of Constantinian Christianity*. Notre Dame, IN: University of Notre Dame Press, 2015.
Aers, David. *Chaucer, Langland, and the Creative Imagination*. London: Routledge and Kegan Paul, 1980.
Alpers, Paul. "Spenser's Late Pastorals." *ELH* 56, no. 4 (1989): 797–817.
Ambrosoli, Mauro. *The Wild and the Sown: Botany and Agriculture in Western Europe: 1350–1850*. Translated by Mary McCann Salvatorelli. Cambridge: Cambridge University Press, 1997.
Anderson, Judith. *The Growth of a Personal Voice: "Piers Plowman" and "The Faerie Queene."* New Haven, CT: Yale University Press, 1976.
Aston, Margaret. "'Caim's Castles': Politics, Poverty, and Disendowment." In *The Church, Politics, and Patronage in the Fifteenth Century*, edited by Barrie Dobson, 45-81. New York: St. Martin's, 1984.
Aston, T. H., and C. H. E. Philpin, eds. *The Brenner Debate: Agrarian Class Structure and Economic Development in Pre-industrial Europe*. Cambridge: Cambridge University Press, 1985.
Avery, Bruce. "Mapping the Irish Other: Spenser's *A View of the Present State of Ireland*." *ELH* 57, no. 2 (1990): 263–79.
Badcoe, Tamsin. *Edmund Spenser and the Romance of Space*. Manchester: Manchester University Press, 2019.
Barr, Helen. "Introduction," in *The "Piers Plowman" Tradition: A Critical Edition of "Pierce the Ploughman's Crede," "Richard the Redeless," "Mum and the Sothsegger," and "The Crowned King,"* edited by Helen Barr, 1-45. London: Dent, 1993.
Barr, Helen. *Signes and Sothe: Language in the "Piers Plowman" Tradition*. Cambridge: Brewer, 1994.
Barr, Helen. *Socioliterary Practice in Late Medieval England*. Oxford: Oxford University Press, 2001.
Barr, Helen, and Kate Ward-Perkins. "'Spekyng for One's Sustenance': The Rhetoric of Counsel in *Mum and the Sothsegger*, Skelton's *Bowge of Court*, and Elyot's *Pasquil the Playne*." In *The Long Fifteenth Century: Essays for Douglas Gray*, edited by Helen Cooper and Sally Mapstone, 249-72. Oxford: Clarendon, 1997.

Bataille, Georges. *The Accursed Share: An Essay on General Economy*. Vol. 3, *Sovereignty*, translated by Robert Hurley. New York: Zone, 1991.

Becker, Alexis K. "Practical Georgics: Managing the Land in Medieval Britain." PhD diss., Harvard University, 2015.

Becker, Alexis K. "Sustainability Romance: *Havelok the Dane*'s Political Ecology." *New Medieval Literatures* 16 (2016): 83–108.

Bennett, Jane. *Vibrant Matter: A Political Ecology of Things*. Durham, NC: Duke University Press, 2010.

Benson, C. David, and Lynne S. Blanchfield. *The Manuscripts of "Piers Plowman": The B-Version*. Cambridge: Brewer, 1997.

Betteridge, Thomas. *Literature and Politics in the English Reformation*. Manchester: Manchester University Press, 2004.

Bevington, David. *Tudor Drama and Politics: A Critical Approach to Topical Meaning*. Cambridge, MA: Harvard University Press, 1968.

Biddick, Kathleen. *The Other Economy: Pastoral Husbandry on a Medieval Estate*. Berkeley: University of California Press, 1989.

Blanchard, W. Scott. "Skelton's Critique of Wealth and the Autonomy of the Early Modern Intellectual." In *John Skelton and Early Modern Culture: Papers Honoring Robert S. Kinsman*, edited by David R. Carlson, 45–62. Tempe: Arizona Center for Medieval and Renaissance Studies, 2008.

Bloomfield, Morton W. *"Piers Plowman" as a Fourteenth-Century Apocalypse*. New Brunswick, NJ: Rutgers University Press, 1962.

Bose, Mishtooni. "Useless Mouths: Reformist Poetics in Audelay and Skelton." In *Form and Reform: Reading across the Fifteenth Century*, edited by Shannon Gayk and Kathleen Tonry, 159–79. Columbus: Ohio State University Press, 2011.

Brackmann, Rebecca. *The Elizabethan Invention of Anglo-Saxon England: Laurence Nowell, William Lambarde, and the Study of Old English*. Cambridge: Brewer, 2012.

Bradshaw, Brendan. *The Irish Constitutional Revolution of the Sixteenth Century*. Cambridge: Cambridge University Press, 1979.

Brady, Ciaran. "The Road to the *View*: On the Decline of Reform Thought in Tudor Ireland." In *Spenser and Ireland: An Interdisciplinary Perspective*, edited by Patricia Coughlan, 25–45. Cork: Cork University Press, 1989.

Breen, Katharine. "Introduction," in *The Yearbook of Langland Studies* 33 (2019): 145–58.

Breen, Katharine. *Machines of the Mind: Personification in Medieval Literature*. Chicago: University of Chicago Press, 2021.

Breen, Katharine. "The Need for Allegory: *Wynnere and Wastoure* as an Ars Poetica." *Yearbook of Langland Studies* 26 (2012): 187–229.

Burrow, J. A. "The Action of Langland's Second Vision." In *Essays on Medieval Literature*, 79–101. Oxford: Clarendon, 1984.

Campana, Joseph. "Introduction: After Sovereignty." *Studies in English Literature 1500–1900* 58, no. 1 (2018): 1–21.

Campbell, Bruce M. S. "Ecology versus Economics in Late Thirteenth- and Early Fourteenth-Century English Agriculture." In *Agriculture in the Middle Ages:*

Technology, Practice, and Representation, edited by Del Sweeney, 76–108. Philadelphia: University of Pennsylvania Press, 1995.

Campbell, Bruce M. S. *English Seigniorial Agriculture, 1250–1450*. Cambridge Studies in Historical Geography 31. Cambridge: Cambridge University Press, 2000.

Campbell, Bruce M. S. *The Great Transition: Climate, Disease and Society in the Late-Medieval World*. Cambridge: Cambridge University Press, 2016.

Canny, Nicholas. "Introduction: Spenser and the Reform of Ireland." In *Spenser and Ireland: An Interdisciplinary Perspective*, edited by Patricia Coughlan, 9–24. Cork: Cork University Press, 1989.

Carlson, David R., ed. *John Skelton and Early Modern Culture: Papers Honoring Robert S. Kinsman*. Tempe: Arizona Center for Medieval and Renaissance Studies, 2008.

Carlson, David R. "Protestant Skelton: The Satires of 1519–1523 and the *Piers Plowman* Tradition." In *John Skelton and Early Modern Culture: Papers Honoring Robert S. Kinsman*, edited by David R. Carlson, 215–38. Tempe: Arizona Center for Medieval and Renaissance Studies, 2008.

Chakravarty, Urvashi. "Slavery and White Womanhood in Early Modern England." *Renaissance Quarterly* 75, no. 4 (2022): 1144–79.

Cheney, Patrick. "The Old Poet Presents Himself: *Prothalamion* as a Defense of Spenser's Career." *Spenser Studies* 8 (1990): 211–38.

Cheney, Patrick. *Spenser's Famous Flight: A Renaissance Idea of a Literary Career*. Toronto: University of Toronto Press, 1993.

Chitty, Christopher. *Sexual Hegemony: Statecraft, Sodomy, and Capital in the Rise of the World System*. Durham, NC: Duke University Press, 2020.

Clanchy, M. T. *From Memory to Written Record: England 1066–1307*. 3rd ed. Malden, MA: Wiley-Blackwell, 2013.

Clebsch, William A. *England's Earlier Protestants, 1520–1535*. New Haven, CT: Yale University Press, 1964.

Cole, Andrew. "Scribal Hermeneutics and the Genres of Social Organization in *Piers Plowman*." In *The Middle Ages at Work: Practicing Labor in Late Medieval England*, edited by Kelllie Robertson and Michael Uebel, 179–206. New York: Palgrave Macmillan, 2004.

Cole, Andrew. "Trifunctionality and the Tree of Charity: Literary and Social Practice in *Piers Plowman*." *ELH* 62, no. 1 (1995): 1–27.

Cooper, Helen. *Pastoral: Medieval into Renaissance*. Ipswich: Brewer, 1977.

Cooper, Helen, and Sally Mapstone, eds. *The Long Fifteenth Century: Essays for Douglas Gray*. Oxford: Clarendon, 1997.

Cooper, Lisa H. "Agronomy and Affect in Duke Humfrey's *On Husbondrie*." *Speculum* 95, no. 1 (2020): 36–88.

Cooper, Lisa H. *Artisans and Narrative Craft in Late Medieval England*. Cambridge: Cambridge University Press, 2011.

Costello, Eugene. *Transhumance and the Making of Ireland's Uplands, 1550–1900*. Woodbridge: Boydell and Brewer, 2020.

Coughlan, Patricia, ed. *Spenser and Ireland: An Interdisciplinary Perspective*. Cork: Cork University Press, 1989.

Crassons, Kate. *The Claims of Poverty: Literature, Culture, and Ideology in Late Medieval England*. Notre Dame, IN: Notre Dame University Press, 2010.

Craun, Edwin. *Ethics and Power in Medieval English Reformist Writing*. Cambridge: Cambridge University Press, 2010.
Cronon, William. "The Trouble with Wilderness: Or, Getting Back to the Wrong Nature." *Environmental History* 1, no. 1 (1996): 7–28.
Curtius, E. R. *European Literature and the Latin Middle Ages*. Translated by Willard R. Trask. Princeton, NJ: Princeton University Press, 1990.
Da Costa, Alexandra. *Marketing English Books, 1476–1550*. Oxford: Oxford University Press, 2020.
Davis, Kathleen. *Periodization and Sovereignty: How Ideas of Feudalism and Secularization Govern the Politics of Time*. Philadelphia: University of Pennsylvania Press, 2008.
Davis, Rebecca. *"Piers Plowman" and the Books of Nature*. Oxford: Oxford University Press, 2016.
Day, Iyko. "Eco-Criticism and Primitive Accumulation in Indigenous Studies." In *After Marx: Literature, Theory, and Value in the Twenty-First Century*, edited by Colleen Lye and Christopher Nealon, 40–54. Cambridge: Cambridge University Press, 2022.
Devereux, E. J. *A Bibliography of John Rastell*. Montreal: McGill-Queen's University Press, 1999.
Doyle, I. A. "An Unrecognized Piece of *Pierce the Ploughman's Crede* and Other Works by Its Scribe." *Speculum* 34, no. 3 (1959): 428–36.
Druzak, Courtney. "'Scattred All to Nought': Feminine Waters, Irish Sources, and Colonialism in Spenser's River Mulla." *English* 68, no. 262 (2019): 213–34.
Dunbar-Ortiz, Roxanne. *An Indigenous Peoples' History of the United States*. Boston: Beacon, 2014.
Dyer, Christopher. *An Age of Transition? Economy and Society in England in the Later Middle Ages*. Oxford: Oxford University Press, 2005.
Dyer, Christopher. *Making a Living in the Middle Ages: The People of Britain, 850–1520*. New Haven, CT: Yale University Press, 2002.
Dyer, Christopher. "Piers Plowman and Plowmen: A Historical Perspective." *Yearbook of Langland Studies* 8 (1994): 155–76.
Ebin, Lois A. *Illuminator, Makar, Vates: Visions of Poetry in the Fifteenth Century*. Lincoln: University of Nebraska Press, 1988.
Ellis, Steven G. *Ireland in the Age of the Tudors, 1447–1603: English Expansion and the End of Gaelic Rule*. London: Longman, 1998.
Elton, G. R. *The Tudor Revolution in Government: Administrative Changes in the Reign of Henry VIII*. Cambridge: Cambridge University Press, 1953.
Farmer, David L. "Prices and Wages, 1350–1500." In *The Agrarian History of England and Wales*, edited by Joan Thirsk, vol. 3, *1348–1500*, edited by Edward Miller, 431–525. Cambridge: Cambridge University Press, 1991.
Federici, Silvia. *Caliban and the Witch*. Brooklyn, NY: Autonomedia, 2004.
Ferguson, Arthur B. *The Articulate Citizen and the English Renaissance*. Durham, NC: Duke University Press, 1965.
Ferster, Judith. *Fictions of Advice: The Literature and Politics of Counsel in Late Medieval England*. Philadelphia: University of Pennsylvania Press, 1996.

Fish, Stanley. *John Skelton's Poetry*. New Haven, CT: Yale University Press, 1965.
Fitch, John G. "Introduction," in *"The Work of Farming" (Opus agriculturae) and "Poem on Grafting,"* by Palladius, translated by John G. Fitch, 11–28. Totnes, Devon: Prospect, 2013.
Fleming, John V. "The Friars and Medieval English Literature." In *The Cambridge History of Medieval English Literature*, edited by David Wallace, 349–75. Cambridge: Cambridge University Press, 1999.
Flood, Victoria. *"Wynnere and Wastoure* and the Influence of Political Prophecy." *Chaucer Review* 49, no. 4 (2015): 427–48.
Flower, Robin. "Laurence Nowell and the Discovery of England in Tudor Times." *Proceedings of the British Academy* 21 (1935): 47–73.
Foster, John Bellamy. *Marx's Ecology: Materialism and Nature*. New York: Monthly Review Press, 2000.
Foucault, Michel. *Discipline and Punish: The Birth of the Prison*. Translated by Alan Sheridan. New York: Vintage, 1977.
Foucault, Michel. *The History of Sexuality*. Vol. 1, *An Introduction*, translated by Robert Hurley. New York: Vintage, 1990.
Foucault, Michel. *Society Must Be Defended: Lectures at the Collège de France 1975–1976*. Translated by David Macey. New York: Picador, 2003.
Fowler, Elizabeth. *Literary Character: The Human Figure in Early English Writing*. Ithaca, NY: Cornell University Press, 2003.
Frank, Robert Worth, Jr. "The 'Hungry Gap,' Crop Failure, and Famine: The Fourteenth-Century Agricultural Crisis and *Piers Plowman*." *Yearbook of Langland Studies* 4 (1990): 87–104.
Frank, Robert Worth, Jr. *"Piers Plowman" and the Scheme of Salvation*. New Haven, CT: Yale University Press, 1957. Repr., New Haven, CT: Archon, 1969.
Furnivall, Frederick J. "Introduction," in *Four Supplications: 1529–1553*, edited by J. Meadows Cowper, v–xiv. London: Early English Texts Society, 1871.
Fussell, G. E. "The Classical Tradition in West-European Farming: The Fourteenth and Fifteenth Centuries." *Agricultural History Review* 17, no. 1 (1969): 1–8.
Gayk, Shannon. "Apocalyptic Ecologies: Eschatologies, Ethics of Care, and the Fifteen Signs of the Doom in Early England." *Speculum* 96, no. 1 (2021): 1–37.
Gayk, Shannon, and Kathleen Tonry, eds. *Form and Reform: Reading across the Fifteenth Century*. Columbus: Ohio State University Press, 2011.
Geritz, Albert J., and Amos Lee Laine. *John Rastell*. Boston: Twayne, 1983.
Giancarlo, Matthew. *Parliament and Literature in Late Medieval England*. Cambridge: Cambridge University Press, 2007.
Gillespie, R. "Explorers, Exploiters and Entrepreneurs: Early Modern Ireland and Its Context, 1500–1700." In *An Historical Geography of Ireland*, edited by B. J. Graham and L. J. Proudfoot, 123–52. London: Academic Press, 1993.
Gillespie, Vincent. "Justification by Faith: Skelton's *Replycacion*." In *The Long Fifteenth Century: Essays for Douglas Gray*, edited by Helen Cooper and Sally Mapstone, 273–311. Oxford: Clarendon, 1997.

Grady, Frank. "The Generation of 1399." In *The Letter of the Law: Legal Practice and Literary Production in Medieval England*, edited by Emily Steiner and Candace Barrington, 202–29. Ithaca, NY: Cornell University Press, 2002.

Graham, Kenneth J. E. "Distributive Measures: Theology and Economics in the Writings of Robert Crowley." *Criticism* 47, no. 2 (2005): 137–58.

Gray, Douglas. *The Phoenix and the Parrott: Skelton and the Language of Satire*. Otago Studies in English 10. Dunedin, New Zealand: University of Otago, 2012.

Green, Richard Firth. *A Crisis of Truth: Literature and Law in Ricardian England*. Philadelphia: University of Pennsylvania Press, 1999.

Greene, Roland. "Calling Colin Clout." *Spenser Studies* 10 (1989): 229–44.

Griffiths, Jane. *John Skelton and Poetic Authority: Defining the Liberty to Speak*. Oxford: Oxford University Press, 2006.

Grindley, Carl James. "Reading *Piers Plowman* C-Text Annotations: Notes toward the Classification of Printed and Written Marginalia in Texts from the British Isles, 1300–1641." In *The Medieval Professional Reader at Work: Evidence from Manuscripts of Chaucer, Langland, Kempe, and Gower*, edited by Kathryn Kerby-Fulton and Maidie Hilmo, 73–142. Victoria, British Columbia: University of Victoria Press, 2001.

Hadfield, Andrew. *Edmund Spenser: A Life*. Oxford: Oxford University Press, 2012.

Hadfield, Andrew. *Spenser's Irish Experience: Wilde Fruit and Salvage Soyl*. Oxford: Clarendon, 1997.

Hailey, R. Carter. "'Geuyng Light to the Reader': Robert Crowley's Editions of *Piers Plowman* (1550)." *Papers of the Bibliographic Society of America* 95, no. 4 (2001): 483–502.

Halpern, Richard. *The Poetics of Primitive Accumulation: English Renaissance Culture and the Genealogy of Capital*. Ithaca, NY: Cornell University Press, 1991.

Hamilton, A. C. "Spenser and Langland." *Studies in Philology* 55, no. 4 (1958): 533–48.

Hamilton, A. C. "The Visions of *Piers Plowman* and *The Faerie Queene*." In *Form and Convention in the Poetry of Edmund Spenser*, edited by William Nelson, 1–34. New York: Columbia University Press, 1961.

Harvey, David. "The Nature of the Environment: The Dialectics of Social and Environmental Change." *Socialist Register* 29 (1993): 1–51.

Harwood, Britton. "The Plot of *Piers Plowman* and the Contradictions of Feudalism." In *Speaking Two Languages: Traditional Disciplines and Contemporary Theory in Medieval Studies*, edited by Allen J. Frantzen, 91–114. Albany: State University of New York Press, 1991.

Heffernan, David. *Debating Tudor Policy in Sixteenth-Century Ireland: "Reform" Treatises and Political Discourse*. Manchester: Manchester University Press, 2018.

Heiserman, A. R. *Skelton and Satire*. Chicago: University of Chicago Press, 1961.

Helgerson, Richard. *Self-Crowned Laureates: Spenser, Jonson, Milton, and the Literary System*. Berkeley: University of California Press, 1993.

Herron, Thomas. "Irish Den of Thieves: Souterrains (and a Crannog?) in Books V and VI of Spenser's *Faerie Queene*." *Spenser Studies* 14 (2000): 303–17.

Herron, Thomas. "Love's 'Emperye': Raleigh's 'Ocean to Scinthia,' Spenser's 'Colin Clouts Come Home Againe' and *The Faerie Queene* IV.vii in Colonial

Context." In *Literary and Visual Ralegh*, edited by Christopher M. Armitage, 100–139. Manchester: Manchester University Press, 2013.

Herron, Thomas. "Native Irish Property and Propriety in the Faunus Episode and *Colin Clouts Come Home Againe*." In *Celebrating Mutabilitie: Essays on Edmund Spenser's Mutabilitie Cantos*, edited by Jane Grogan, 136–77. Manchester: Manchester University Press, 2010.

Herron, Thomas. *Spenser's Irish Work: Poetry, Plantation, and Colonial Reformation*. Aldershot: Ashgate, 2007.

Hewett-Smith, Kathleen. "Allegory on the Half-Acre: The Demands of History." *Yearbook of Langland Studies* 10 (1996): 1–22.

Hiltner, Ken. *What Else is Pastoral? Renaissance Literature and the Environment*. Ithaca, NY: Cornell University Press, 2011.

Hilton, Rodney, ed. *The Transition from Feudalism to Capitalism*. London: New Left Books, 1976.

Hoffman, A. Robin. "Sewing and Weaving in *Piers Plowman*." *Women's Studies* 35 (2006): 431–52.

Hogan, Sarah. *Other Englands: Utopia, Capital, and Empire in an Age of Transition*. Stanford, CA: Stanford University Press, 2018.

Holsinger, Bruce. "Lollard Ekphrasis: Situated Aesthetics and Literary History." *Journal of Medieval and Early Modern Studies* 35, no. 1 (2005): 67–89.

Holstun, James. "The Giant's Faction: Spenser, Heywood, and the Mid-Tudor Crisis." *Journal of Medieval and Early Modern Studies* 37, no. 2 (2007): 335–71.

Horobin, Simon. "Stephan Batman and His Manuscripts of *Piers Plowman*." *Review of English Studies* 62, no. 255 (2010): 358–72.

Hudson, Anne. "Epilogue: The Legacy of *Piers Plowman*." In *A Companion to "Piers Plowman,"* edited by J. A. Alford, 251–66. Berkeley: University of California Press, 1988.

Hudson, Anne. *The Premature Reformation: Wycliffite Texts and Lollard History*. Oxford: Clarendon, 1988.

Jahner, Jennifer. "*Piers Plowman* and the Unmaking of the American Acre." Paper presented at the International *Piers Plowman* Society Conference, London, July 8, 2023.

Jahner, Jennifer, and Enid Baxter Ryce. "Unsettling the Half-Acre: *Piers Plowman* in the Making of Modern California." *Yearbook of Langland Studies* 38 (2024): 243–62.

Jansen, Sharon L. "The Paston Family, 'Hogan the Prophet,' and Sixteenth-Century Political Prophecy." *Manuscripta* 39 (1995): 137–47.

Jansen, Sharon L. "Politics, Protest, and a New *Piers Plowman* Fragment: The Voice of the Past in Tudor England." *Review of English Studies* 40, no. 157 (1989): 93–99.

Jay, Martin. *Marxism and Totality: The Adventures of a Concept from Lukács to Habermas*. Berkeley: University of California Press, 1984.

Johnson, Barbara A. *Reading "Piers Plowman" and "The Pilgrim's Progress": Reception and the Protestant Reader*. Carbondale: Southern Illinois University Press, 1992.

Johnson, Eleanor. *Waste and the Wasters: Poetry and Ecosystemic Thought in Medieval England*. Chicago: University of Chicago Press, 2023.

Johnston, Michael. "From Edward III to Edward VI: *The Vision of Piers Plowman* and Early Modern England." *Reformation* 11, no. 1 (2006): 47-78.

Johnston, Michael, and Lawrence Warner. "'The Pure and Perfect Book': Marilynne Robinson, Maureen Duffy, and the Heirs of *Piers Plowman*." *Yearbook of Langland Studies* 35 (2021): 61-104.

Jones, Mike Rodman. *Radical Pastoral, 1381-1594: Appropriation and the Writing of Religious Controversy*. Farnham: Ashgate, 2011.

Jones, Mike Rodman. "'This Is No Prophecy': Robert Crowley, 'Piers Plowman,' and Kett's Rebellion." *Sixteenth Century Journal* 42, no. 1 (2011): 37-55.

Jusserand, J. J. *"Piers Plowman": A Contribution to the History of English Mysticism*. Translated by M. E. R. London: Fisher Unwin, 1894.

Jusserand, J. J. *What Me Befell: The Reminiscences of J. J. Jusserand*. Boston: Houghton Mifflin, 1934.

Justice, Steven. *Writing and Rebellion: England in 1381*. Berkeley: University of California Press, 1994.

Kao, Wan-Chuan. "Identitarian Politics, Precarious Sovereignty." *postmedieval* 11 (2020): 371-83.

Kelen, Sarah A. *Langland's Early Modern Identities*. New York: Palgrave Macmillan, 2007.

Kerby-Fulton, Kathryn. *Books under Suspicion: Censorship and Tolerance of Revelatory Writing in Late Medieval England*. Notre Dame, IN: University of Notre Dame Press, 2006.

King, John N. *English Reformation Literature: The Tudor Origins of the Protestant Tradition*. Princeton, NJ: Princeton University Press, 1982.

King, John N. *Spenser's Poetry and the Reformation Tradition*. Princeton, NJ: Princeton University Press, 1990.

Kinsman, Robert S. "The Voices of Dissonance: Pattern in Skelton's *Colyn Cloute*." *Huntington Library Quarterly* 26, no. 4 (1963): 291-313.

Lampe, David. "The Satiric Strategy of *Peres the Ploughmans Crede*." In *The Alliterative Tradition in the Fourteenth Century*, edited by Bernard S. Levy and Paul E. Szarmach, 69-80. Kent, OH: Kent State University Press, 1981.

Lane, Robert. *Shepheards Devises: Edmund Spenser's "Shepheardes Calender" and the Institutions of Elizabethan Society*. Athens: University of Georgia Press, 1993.

Latour, Bruno. "To Modernise or to Ecologise?" In *Remaking Reality*, edited by Bruce Braun and Noel Castree, 220-41. New York: Routledge, 1998.

Latour, Bruno. *We Have Never Been Modern*. Translated by Catherine Porter. Cambridge, MA: Harvard University Press, 1993.

Little, Katherine C. *Transforming Work: Early Modern Pastoral and Late Medieval Poetry*. Notre Dame, IN: University of Notre Dame Press, 2013.

Lochrie, Karma. *Nowhere in the Middle Ages*. Philadelphia: University of Pennsylvania Press, 2016.

Lucas, Scott. "Diggon Davie and Davy Dicar: Edmund Spenser, Thomas Churchyard, and the Poetics of Public Protest." *Spenser Studies* 16 (2002): 151-65.

MacCarthy-Morrogh, Michael. *The Munster Plantation: English Migration to Southern Ireland, 1583-1641*. Oxford: Clarendon, 1986.

Maginn, Christopher. "'Surrender and Regrant' in the Historiography of Sixteenth-Century Ireland." *Sixteenth Century Journal* 38, no. 4 (2007): 955-74.

Maginn, Christopher, and Steven G. Ellis. *The Tudor Discovery of Ireland*. Dublin: Four Courts Press, 2015.

Maley, Willy. *Salvaging Spenser: Colonialism, Culture, Identity*. London: Macmillan, 1997.

Malm, Andreas. *The Progress of This Storm: Nature and Society in a Warming World*. London: Verso, 2018.

Mann, Jill. *Chaucer and Medieval Estates Satire: The Literature of Social Classes and the "General Prologue" to the "Canterbury Tales."* Cambridge: Cambridge University Press, 1973.

Mann, Jill. "The Nature of Need Revisited." *Yearbook of Langland Studies* 18 (2004): 3–29.

Marckwardt, Albert H. "The Sources of Laurence Nowell's 'Vocabularium Saxonicum.'" *Studies in Philology* 45 (1948): 21–36.

Marx, Karl. *Capital: A Critique of Political Economy*. Vol. 1, translated by Ben Fowkes. London: Penguin, 1990.

Marx, Karl. *Capital: A Critique of Political Economy*. Vol. 3, translated by David Fernbach. London: Penguin, 1991.

Mate, Mavis. "Medieval Agrarian Practices: Determining Factors?" *Agricultural History Review* 33, no. 1 (1985): 22–31.

Mau, Søren. *Mute Compulsion: A Marxist Theory of the Economic Power of Capital*. London: Verso, 2023.

McCabe, Richard A. "Edmund Spenser, Poet of Exile." *Proceedings of the British Academy* 80 (1993): 73–103.

McCabe, Richard A. *Spenser's Monstrous Regiment: Elizabethan Ireland and the Poetics of Difference*. Oxford: Oxford University Press, 2002.

McLane, Paul E. "Skelton's *Colyn Cloute* and Spenser's *Shepheardes Calender*." *Studies in Philology* 70, no. 2 (1973): 141–59.

McRae, Andrew. *God Speed the Plough: The Representation of Agrarian England, 1500–1660*. Cambridge: Cambridge University Press, 1996.

McRae, Andrew. "Husbandry Manuals and the Language of Agrarian Improvement." In *Culture and Cultivation in Early Modern England: Writing the Land*, edited by Michael Leslie and Timothy Raylor, 35–62. Leicester: Leicester University Press, 1992.

McRae, Andrew. "To Know One's Own: Estate Surveying and the Representation of Land in Early Modern England." *Huntington Library Quarterly* 56, no. 4 (1993): 333–57.

Medovoi, Leerom. "The Biopolitical Unconscious: Toward an Eco-Marxist Literary Theory." *Mediations* 24, no. 2 (2009): 122–39.

Meyer-Lee, Robert J. "Conception Is a Blessing: Marian Devotion, Heresy, and the Literary in Skelton's *A Replycacion*." In *Form and Reform: Reading across the Fifteenth Century*, edited by Shannon Gayk and Kathleen Tonry, 133–58. Columbus: Ohio State University Press, 2011.

Middleton, Anne. "Narration and the Invention of Experience: Episodic Form in *Piers Plowman*." In *The Wisdom of Poetry: Essays in Early English Literature in Honor of Morton W. Bloomfield*, edited by Larry D. Benson and Siegried Wenzel, 91–122. Kalamazoo, MI: Medieval Institute Publications, 1982.

Mileson, S. A. *Parks in Medieval England*. Oxford: Oxford University Press, 2009.

Miller, David Lee. *The Poem's Two Bodies: The Poetics of the 1590 "Faerie Queene."* Princeton, NJ: Princeton University Press, 1988.

Miller, David Lee. "Spenser's Vocation, Spenser's Career." *ELH* 50, no. 2 (1983): 197-231.

Mohl, Ruth. "Theories of Monarchy in *Mum and the Sothsegger*." *PMLA* 59, no. 1 (1944): 26-44.

Montaño, John Patrick. *The Roots of English Colonialism in Ireland.* Cambridge: Cambridge University Press, 2011.

Moore, Jason W. *Capitalism in the Web of Life: Ecology and the Accumulation of Capital.* London: Verso, 2015.

Muldavin, Joshua. "The Time and Place for Political Ecology: An Introduction to the Articles Honoring the Life-Work of Piers Blaikie." *Geoforum* 39 (2008): 687-97.

Müller, Anne. "Presenting Identity in the Cloister: Remarks on Benedictine and Mendicant Concepts of Space." In *Self-Representation of Medieval Religious Communities: The British Isles in Context,* edited by Anne Müller and Karen Stöber, 167-88. Berlin: Lit Verlag, 2009.

Musson, Anthony. "Reconstructing English Labor Laws: A Medieval Perspective." In *The Middle Ages at Work: Practicing Labor in Late Medieval England,* edited by Kelllie Robertson and Michael Uebel, 113-32. New York: Palgrave Macmillan, 2004.

Myers, Benjamin P. "The Green and Golden World: Spenser's Rewriting of the Munster Plantation." *ELH* 76, no. 2 (2009): 473-90.

Norbrook, David. *Poetry and Politics in the English Renaissance.* Oxford: Oxford University Press, 2002.

Northrop, Douglas A. "The Uncertainty of Courtesy in Book VI of *The Faerie Queene*." *Spenser Studies* 14 (2000): 215-32.

O'Brien, Robert Viking. "Cannibalism in Edmund Spenser's *Faerie Queene,* Ireland, and the Americas." In *Eating Their Words: Cannibalism and the Boundaries of Cultural Identity,* edited by Kristen Guest, 35-56. Albany: State University of New York Press, 2001.

O'Keeffe, Tadhg. "Kilcolman Castle, Co. Cork: A New Interpretation of Edmund Spenser's Residence in Plantation Munster." *International Journal of Historical Archaeology* 21, no. 1 (2017): 223-39.

Orlemanski, Julie. "Langland's Poetics of Animation: Body, Soul, Personification." *Yearbook of Langland Studies* 33 (2019): 159-83.

Ormrod, W. Mark. *"Winner and Waster" and Its Contexts: Chivalry, Law and Economics in Fourteenth-Century England.* Cambridge: Brewer, 2021.

Oschinsky, Dorothea. "Introduction," in *Walter of Henley and Other Treatises on Estate Management and Accounting,* edited by Dorothea Oschinsky, 1-257. Oxford: Clarendon, 1971.

Palmer, Patricia. *Language and Culture in Early Modern Ireland: English Renaissance Literature and Elizabethan Imperial Expansion.* Cambridge: Cambridge University Press, 2001.

Parker, Douglas H. "Introduction," in *Rede Me and Be Nott Wroth,* by Jerome Barlowe and William Roye, edited by Douglas H. Parker, 1-47. Toronto: University of Toronto Press, 1992.

Parris, Ben. *Vital Strife: Sleep, Insomnia, and the Early Modern Ethics of Care*. Ithaca, NY: Cornell University Press, 2022.

Patterson, Annabel. "Re-Opening the Green Cabinet: Clément Marot and Edmund Spenser." *English Literary Renaissance* 16, no. 1 (1986): 44-70.

Perry, R. D. *Coterie Poetics and the Beginnings of the English Literary Tradition from Chaucer to Spenser*. Philadelphia: University of Pennsylvania Press, 2024.

Peters, Jason. "The Trouble with Authority in Skelton's *Replycacion*." *Philological Quarterly* 101, no. 1-2 (2022): 23-45.

Pineas, Rainer. *Thomas More and Tudor Polemics*. Bloomington: Indiana University Press, 1968.

Pluymers, Keith. *No Wood, No Kingdom: Political Ecology in the English Atlantic*. Philadelphia: University of Pennsylvania Press, 2021.

Prendergast, Thomas A. "The Work of Robert Langland." In *Renaissance Retrospections: Tudor Views of the Middle Ages*, edited by Sarah A. Kelen, 70-93. Kalamazoo, MI: Medieval Institute Publications, 2013.

Prescott, Anne Lake. "Spenser's Chivalric Restoration: From Bateman's *Travayled Pylgrime* to the Redcrosse Knight." *Studies in Philology* 86, no. 2 (1989): 166-97.

Quilligan, Maureen. "On the Renaissance Epic: Spenser and Slavery." *South Atlantic Quarterly* 100, no. 1 (2001): 15-39.

Rentz, Ellen K. *Imagining the Parish in Late Medieval England*. Columbus: Ohio State University Press, 2015.

Rhodes, William. "Personification, Power, and the Body in Late Medieval and Early Modern English Poetry." In *Personification: Embodying Meaning and Emotion*, edited by B. A. M. Ramakers and Walter S. Melion, 95-120. Leiden: Brill, 2016.

Robertson, Kellie. *The Laborer's Two Bodies: Literary and Legal Productions in Britain, 1350–1500*. New York: Palgrave Macmillan, 2006.

Robertson, Kellie, and Michael Uebel, eds. *The Middle Ages at Work: Practicing Labor in Late Medieval England*. New York: Palgrave Macmillan, 2004.

Robinson, Cedric. *Black Marxism: The Making of the Black Radical Tradition*. Chapel Hill: University of North Carolina Press, 2000.

Rocha, Gabriel de Avilez. "Maroons in the *Montes*: Toward a Political Ecology of Marronage in the Sixteenth-Century Caribbean." In *Early Modern Black Diaspora Studies: A Critical Anthology*, edited by Cassander L. Smith, Nicholas R. Jones, and Miles P. Grier, 15-36. Cham: Palgrave Macmillan, 2018.

Röhrkasten, Jens. *The Mendicant Houses of Medieval London, 1221–1539*. Münster: Lit Verlag, 2004.

Rozumalski, Jason Ross. "Lords of All They Survey: The Social and Economic Origins of the English State, c. 1520-1620." PhD diss., University of California, Berkeley, 2017.

Saito, Kohei. *Karl Marx's Ecosocialism: Capital, Nature, and the Unfinished Critique of Political Economy*. New York: Monthly Review Press, 2017.

Scanlon, Larry. "Langland, Apocalypse, and the Early Modern Editor." In *Reading the Medieval in Early Modern England*, edited by David Matthews and Gordon McMullan, 51-73. Cambridge: Cambridge University Press, 2007.

Scanlon, Larry. "Penance and Personification." *Yearbook of Langland Studies* 21 (2007): 1–29.

Scase, Wendy. "*Dauy Dycars Dreame* and Robert Crowley's Prints of *Piers Plowman*." *Yearbook of Langland Studies* 21 (2007): 171–98.

Scase, Wendy. *Literature and Complaint in England, 1272–1553*. Oxford: Oxford University Press, 2007.

Scase, Wendy. *"Piers Plowman" and the New Anticlericalism*. Cambridge: Cambridge University Press, 1989.

Scattergood, John. *John Skelton: The Career of an Early Tudor Poet*. Dublin: Four Courts Press, 2014.

Scattergood, John. *The Lost Tradition: Essays on Middle English Alliterative Poetry*. Dublin: Four Courts Press, 2000.

Schiff, Randy P., and Joseph Taylor. "Introduction," in *The Politics of Ecology: Land, Life, and Law in Medieval Britain*, edited by Randy P. Schiff and Joseph Taylor, 1–30. Columbus: Ohio State University Press, 2016.

Schiff, Randy P., and Joseph Taylor, eds. *The Politics of Ecology: Land, Life, and Law in Medieval Britain*. Columbus: Ohio State University Press, 2016.

Schwyzer, Philip. "Exhumation and Ethnic Conflict: From *St. Erkenwald* to Spenser in Ireland." *Representations* 95, no. 1 (2006): 1–26.

Segall, Kreg. "The Precarious Poet in *Colin Clouts Come Home Againe*." *Studies in English Literature 1500–1900* 53, no. 1 (2013): 31–51.

Segall, Kreg. "Skeltonic Anxiety and Rumination in *The Shepherds Calender*." *Studies in English Literature 1500–1900* 47, no. 1 (2007): 29–56.

Shortslef, Emily, and Bryan Lowrance. "Renaissance Political Ecologies." *Journal for Early Modern Cultural Studies* 13, no. 3 (2013): 1–6.

Simpson, James. *Reform and Cultural Revolution*. Oxford: Oxford University Press, 2002.

Simpson, James. "Trans-Reformation English Literary History," in *Early Modern Histories of Time: The Periodizations of Sixteenth- and Seventeenth-Century England*, edited by Kristen Poole and Owen Williams, 88–101. Philadelphia: University of Pennsylvania Press, 2019.

Simpson, James, and Eva von Contzen, eds. *Enlistment: Lists in Medieval and Early Modern Literature*. Columbus: Ohio State University Press, 2022.

Smith, D. Vance. "*Piers Plowman* and the National Noetic of Edward III." In *Imagining a Medieval English Nation*, edited by Kathy Lavezzo, 234–58. Minneapolis: University of Minnesota Press, 2004.

Smith, Scott T. *Land and Book: Literature and Land Tenure in Anglo-Saxon England*. Toronto: University of Toronto Press, 2012.

Smyth, William J. *Map-Making, Landscapes and Memory: A Geography of Colonial and Early Modern Ireland c. 1530–1750*. Notre Dame, IN: University of Notre Dame Press, 2006.

Sobecki, Sebastian. "Hares, Rabbits, Pheasants: *Piers Plowman* and William Longewille, a Norfolk Rebel in 1381." *Review of English Studies* 69, no. 289 (2018): 216–36.

Spearing, A. C. *Medieval to Renaissance in English Poetry*. Cambridge: Cambridge University Press, 1985.

Specht, Henrik. *Chaucer's Franklin in the Canterbury Tales: The Social and Literary Background of a Chaucerian Character.* Copenhagen: Akademisk Forlag, 1981.
Staley, Lynn. *The Island Garden: England's Language of Nation from Gildas to Marvell.* Notre Dame, IN: University of Notre Dame Press, 2012.
Staley, Lynn. *Languages of Power in the Age of Richard II.* University Park: Pennsylvania State University Press, 2005.
Starke, Sue Petitt. "British Knight or Irish Bard? Spenser's Pastoral Persona and the Epic Project in *A View of the Present State of Ireland* and *Colin Clouts Come Home Againe.*" *Spenser Studies* 12 (1998): 133-50.
Steel, Karl. "Biopolitics in the Forest." In *The Politics of Ecology: Land, Life, and Law in Medieval Britain*, edited by Randy P. Schiff and Joseph Taylor, 33-55. Columbus: Ohio State University Press, 2016.
Steel, Karl. "The Rules of the Game: Wolf-Hunting and the Usefulness of Knights in *Piers Plowman*." *Yearbook of Langland Studies* 36 (2022): 123-36.
Steiner, Emily. *Documentary Culture and the Making of Medieval English Literature.* Cambridge: Cambridge University Press, 2003.
Strakhov, Elizaveta. "Political Animals: Form and the Animal Fable in Langland's Rodent Parliament and Chaucer's *Nun's Priest's Tale.*" *Yearbook of Langland Studies* 32 (2018): 289-313.
Sweeney, Del. "Introduction," in *Agriculture in the Middle Ages: Technology, Practice, and Representation*, edited by Del Sweeney, 1-17. Philadelphia: University of Pennsylvania Press, 1995.
Szittya, Penn R. *The Antifraternal Tradition in Medieval Literature.* Princeton, NJ: Princeton University Press, 1986.
Tawney, R. H. *The Agrarian Problem in the Sixteenth Century.* New York: Harper Torchbooks, 1967.
Tawney, R. H. *Religion and the Rise of Capitalism.* London: Verso, 2015.
Thirsk, Joan. "Enclosing and Engrossing." In *The Agrarian History of England and Wales*, vol. 4, *1500-1640*, edited by John Thirsk, 200-255. Cambridge: Cambridge University Press, 1967.
Tonry, Kathleen. *Agency and Intention in English Print, 1476-1526.* Turnhout: Brepols, 2016.
Trigg, Stephanie. "The Traffic in Medieval Women: Alice Perrers, Feminist Criticism, and *Piers Plowman.*" *Yearbook of Langland Studies* 12 (1998): 5-29.
van Es, Bart. "Discourses of Conquest: *The Faerie Queene*, the Society of Antiquaries, and *A View of the Present State of Ireland.*" *English Literary Renaissance* 32, no. 1 (2002): 118-51.
von Nolcken, Christina. "*Piers Plowman*, the Wycliffites, and *Pierce the Plowman's Crede.*" *Yearbook of Langland Studies* 2 (1988): 71-102.
Walker, Greg. *John Heywood: Comedy and Survival in Tudor England.* Oxford: Oxford University Press, 2020.
Walker, Greg. *John Skelton and the Politics of the 1520s.* Cambridge: Cambridge University Press, 1988.
Warley, Christopher. "Reforming the Reformers: Robert Crowley and Nicholas Udall." In *The Oxford Handbook of Tudor Literature: 1485-1603*, edited by

Mike Pincombe and Cathy Shrank, 273–90. Oxford: Oxford University Press, 2012.

Warner, Lawrence. *The Myth of "Piers Plowman": Constructing a Medieval Literary Archive*. Cambridge: Cambridge University Press, 2014.

Warner, Lawrence. "Owen Rogers and *Piers Plowman's Crede*, 1561: A Census of STC 19908." In *Later Middle English Literature, Materiality, and Culture: Essays in Honor of James M. Dean*, edited by Brian Gastle and Erick Kelemen, 189–218. Newark: University of Delaware Press, 2018.

Warren, Nancy Bradly. *Chaucer and Religious Controversies in the Medieval and Early Modern Eras*. Notre Dame, IN: Notre Dame University Press, 2019.

Wawn, Andrew. "Truth-Telling and the Tradition of *Mum and the Sothsegger*." *Yearbook of English Studies* 13 (1983): 27–87.

Weber, Max. *The Protestant Ethic and the Spirit of Capitalism*. Translated by Talcott Parsons. London: Unwin, 1985.

Weiskott, Eric. *English Alliterative Verse: Poetic Tradition and Literary History*. Cambridge: Cambridge University Press, 2016.

Weiskott, Eric. *Meter and Modernity in English Verse, 1350–1650*. Philadelphia: University of Pennsylvania Press, 2021.

Weiskott, Eric. "More Prophetic *Piers Plowman*." *ANQ* 30, no. 3 (2017): 133–36.

Weiskott, Eric. "Political Prophecy and the Form of *Piers Plowman*." *Viator* 50, no. 1 (2019): 207–47.

Weiskott, Eric. "Prophetic *Piers Plowman*: New Sixteenth-Century Excerpts." *Review of English Studies* 67, no. 278 (2016): 21–41.

Weiskott, Eric. "A Sixteenth-Century Political Prophecy Inspired by *Piers Plowman*." *Notes and Queries* 66, no. 2 (2019): 217–19.

Werlin, Julianne. *Writing at the Origin of Capitalism: Literary Circulation and Social Change in Early Modern England*. Oxford: Oxford University Press, 2021.

White, Helen C. *Social Criticism in the Popular Religious Literature of the Sixteenth Century*. New York: Macmillan, 1944.

Whiting, Bartlett Jere. *Proverbs, Sentences, and Proverbial Phrases from English Writings Mainly before 1500*. Cambridge, MA: Harvard University Press, 1968.

Wilmott, Hugh. *The Dissolution of the Monasteries in England and Wales*. Studies in the Archaeology of Medieval Europe. Sheffield: Equinox, 2020.

Wilson-Okamura, David Scott. "Problems in the Virgilian Career." *Spenser Studies* 26 (2011): 1–30.

Wolf, Eric. "Ownership and Political Ecology." *Anthropological Quarterly* 45, no. 3 (1972): 201–5.

Wood, Ellen Meiksins. *The Origin of Capitalism: A Longer View*. London: Verso, 2002.

Wood, Sarah. *"Piers Plowman" and Its Manuscript Tradition*. York: York Medieval Press, 2022.

Yeager, Stephen. *From Lawmen to Plowmen: Anglo-Saxon Legal Tradition and the School of Langland*. Toronto: University of Toronto Press, 2014.

Zurcher, Andrew. *Spenser's Legal Language: Law and Poetry in Early Modern England*. Cambridge: Brewer, 2007.

Index

"Acte Agaynst the Pullynge Doun of Tounes" (1489), 94
Acts and Monuments (Foxe), 92
Aers, David, 38, 40
Anderson, Judith, 10, 138
antifraternalism, 48–67
apocalypticism, 16
Aston, Margaret, 49
Augustine, 194n25
Augustinians, 49, 51, 53, 54
Avery, Bruce, 153

Badcoe, Tamsin, 207n14
bailiffs
  duties of, 29–30
  Piers and, 35
  role of, 34, 190n60
Ball, John, 171
Barlowe, Jerome, 92–93, 108–12, 116, 129, 159
Barr, Helen, 9–10, 52, 58, 65, 80, 194n24
Bartholomaeus Anglicus, 80
Bataille, George, 71
Batman, Stephen, 11
Bede, 200–201n59
bees/beehive, 19, 63, 72, 78–79, 80–86
Bellow, John, 117–18
Bennett, Jane, 3
Betteridge, Thomas, 196–97n5
Bevington, David, 131
biopolitics, 4, 5–6, 25, 126
Blatant Beast, 137–38, 139, 145, 146
Boke of Husbandry (Fitzherbert), 7, 13–15, 20, 91, 93–97, 99, 102, 169
"Boke of Moralities of Chess," 95
booleys, 158–62, 163–66
Bowge of Court (Skelton), 195n1
Boxholme, John, 118
Brackmann, Rebecca, 163, 207n15
Braddyll, John, 117
Breen, Katharine, 85, 185n46

"Brief Note of Ireland, A," 170
Brigants, 137, 139, 141–45, 154

Cain (Caim), 49, 62
Calepine, 137
Calidore, 136–37, 139–45, 150, 154
Camden, William, 207n15
Campbell, Bruce M. S., 187–88n10
Capital (Marx), 4, 98–99
Carew, Richard, 117
Carlson, David R., 195–96n1
Carmelites, 49, 51, 52, 53–54, 55, 61
cattle herding, 159–61, 164–66
caves, 137, 142–43
charity, 42, 43
Charles V of France, 78
Chaucer, Geoffrey, 1, 10, 63, 65, 100, 194n16
church
  disendowment of, 99–100
  dissolution of monasteries and, 116–18, 124, 127, 135–36
  ecclesiastical corruption and, 109–11
  Roman, 114–15
  wealth of, 20
  See also antifraternalism
Churchyard, Thomas, 9
Clanchy, M. T., 190n60
Cole, Andrew, 38
Colin Clout (Spenser's), 130, 137, 139–41, 145–46
Colin Clouts Come Home Againe (Spenser), 20, 134, 135, 140, 146–54
collective reform, 18–19
collective salvation, 46–47
Collyn Clout (Skelton), 9, 18, 20, 92–93, 100–109, 134–35, 141, 144, 146
colonial reform, 155–56
colonialism, 130, 131–33, 135–36, 138–39, 140
colonization, 114–15, 138–39, 155

227

228 INDEX

consumption
    profit motive for, 111
    useless, 73–74, 83–84
    wasteful, 104–5
    See also waste
Cooper, Lisa H., 193n6, 194n20
courtesy, 136–37, 138, 140–41
Crassons, Kate, 51, 52
Cronon, William, 175
Crowley, Robert, 8–11, 18, 20, 91–93, 100–101, 116–29, 135, 162, 176, 184n40
Crowned King, The, 68, 70
Cynthia, 151–53

Dauy Dycars Dreame (Churchyard), 9
Davis, Rebecca, 43
Day, Iyko, 204n20
De opere monachorum (Augustine), 194n25
De proprietatibus rerum (Bartholmaeus), 80
De re rustica (Palladius), 78
de Worde, Wynken, 14
demesne/demesne farming, 6, 14–15, 25–28
Desmond, Earl of, 135
Desmond rebellion, second, 17, 134, 156, 170
documentary records in *Mum and the Sothsegger*, 86–89
Dominicans (Jacobins), 49, 51–54
Donne, John, 130
Dream of John Ball, The (Morris), 172
dream world in *Mum and the Sothsegger*, 74–86
drones, 63–64, 79–80, 83–85
Druzak, Courtney, 205–6n41
Duffy, Maureen, 172, 176
Dyer, Christopher, 25, 34–35, 38

ecclesiastical corruption, 109–11
eco-Marxism, 5
ecosystemic, as term, 180n5
Egerton, Thomas, 163
Elizabeth I, 146, 147, 151, 152
Ellis, Steven, 151
enclosure, 5, 93–94, 99, 116, 144
engrossing, 93–94, 111
estate management texts
    context for, 2
    ideal audience of, 77
    overview of, 13–16
    political ecology and, 24–33
    See also individual texts

Eudoxus, 156–60, 166
exchange-value, 54–57
Extenta Manerii, 14, 27, 30, 96, 98

Faerie Queene, The (Spenser), 10–11, 20, 134–47, 150, 154
famine, 26, 44–46, 166–67, 170
Federici, Silvia, 17
Fenian mythology, 205–6n41
Ferguson, Arthur, 69, 89
Ferster, Judith, 71
fines, 37–38
Fish, Simon, 91–93, 109, 112–16, 119, 127, 129, 131, 162, 174, 176
FitzGerald family, 156
Fitzherbert, John, 7, 13–15, 20, 91–99, 102, 112, 127, 129, 158, 169
Flower, Robin, 208n18
Foster, John Bellamy, 5, 58, 99
Foucault, Michel, 3–6, 25, 161, 195n30
Four Elements (Rastell), 130–33, 173
Fowler, Elizabeth, 195n1
Fowre Hymns (Spenser), 147
Foxe, John, 92
Franciscans (Minors), 49, 51, 53–54, 56, 61
Frank, Robert Worth, Jr., 44
fraud/fraudulent management, 26–27, 30
friars, 48–49, 57, 73, 104. *See also* antifraternalism

gender, division of labor and, 35–36
"General Prologue, The" (Chaucer), 194n16
Genesis, 43, 49, 115
Gentleness and Nobility (Rastell), 130–31, 132, 133, 173
Ghengis Khan, 88, 89
Giancarlo, Matthew, 77, 85, 88, 89
gold, 122–24, 127
Gower, John, 100
great transition, 1
Green, Richard Firth, 88
Grey, Arthur, 136, 156
Griffiths, Jane, 107
Grosseteste, Robert, 25–26

Hadfield, Andrew, 135, 170, 204n25, 208n27
Halpern, Richard, 3
Hamilton, A. C., 10
Harvey, Gabriel, 182n26
Harvey, Richard, 182n26
Harwood, Britton, 40
Henry II, 135, 156, 157–58

INDEX

Henry VIII, 92, 113–16, 117, 127, 133, 136
Herron, Thomas, 205n33, 207n12
Hewett-Smith, Kathleen, 190n56
Heywood, John, 130
Hogan, Sarah, 172
Holdych, Richard, 183n29
Holsinger, Bruce, 65
Humfrey, Duke of Gloucester, 78
Hunger, 8–9, 18, 23–24, 40–46, 64, 74, 116, 123, 166–67, 171
hunting, 36–37, 38

idlers/idleness, 39–41, 45, 64, 79–82, 159, 173–76. *See also* labor
Indigenous people, 172–73, 175
Irenius, 137–38, 149, 153, 156–62, 164–68

Jacobins (Dominicans), 49, 51–54
Jahner, Jennifer, 173
Joachim of Fiore, 185–86n60
Job, 94
Job, Book of, 7
Johnson, Eleanor, 13, 38, 46, 188n21
Jones, Mike Rodman, 171
Joseph, Chief, 175
Jusserand, J. J., 174–75
Justice, Stephen, 171

Kao, Wan-Chuan, 175
Kett's Rebellion, 184n40
King, John, 201n62, 204n17
kings/kingship, 70–71, 72–73, 80–81, 83–85, 87–88, 127–28. *See also* sovereignty
Kinsman, Robert S., 108
knights, role of, 36–38

labor
    avoidance of, 142
    clergy's avoidance of, 104–7, 115
    dream world in *Mum and the Sothsegger* and, 74–77
    The Faerie Queene and, 137
    human purpose and, 94
    postplague legislation of, 24–25, 38
    See also antifraternalism; idlers/idleness
Lambarde, William, 14, 162–63, 188n19, 207n15
Lancastrians, 68
Langland, William, 1, 25, 166–67, 172. *See also Piers Plowman* (Langland)
Latour, Bruno, 3
Lent, 104–5

literacy, 64–65
literary self-consciousness, 65–66
Little, Katherine, 142, 171
Lochrie, Karma, 171–72
London Blackfriars, 52

Maginn, Christopher, 151, 195n36
Maley, Willy, 156
manorial system/estate, 1–2, 4, 6–7
Marx, Karl
    on ecological changes, 17
    exchange-value and, 54–55
    Foucault and, 3–4
    metabolic rift and, 58, 98–99
    on primitive accumulation, 4–5, 98, 99, 135, 155
    silent compulsion and, 195n30
    social metabolism and, 55
Mary I, 117, 124
Mau, Søren, 195n30
McCabe, Richard, 138
McRae, Andrew, 96
medievalism, 175
metabolic rift, 5, 58, 98–100, 116–29
Minors (Franciscans), 49, 51, 53–54, 56, 61
mobility
    cattle herding and, 161
    Collyn Clout (Skelton) and, 103
    friars and, 57
    lack of, 28–29
    problems caused by, 31–32
    restrictions on, 152–53
monasteries, dissolution of, 116–18, 124, 127, 135–36
monetary circulation, 54–57
Montaño, John Patrick, 164
Moore, Jason W., 17, 98
More, Thomas, 92, 114, 130, 131, 172
Morris, William, 172, 176
Mount Acidale, 139–41, 146
Müller, Anne, 55
Mum and the Sothsegger, 9, 11, 19–20, 47–48, 63, 66–67, 68–90, 102–4, 172, 195n1
Munster plantation, 2, 17, 134, 135–36, 156, 160, 166–67, 170
Myers, Benjamin, 205n33

New Boke of Purgatory, A (Rastell), 131
New English, 135
Nez Percé Native Americans, 175
Nowell, Laurence, 162–63

INDEX

On Husbondrie, 37, 78, 194n20
Oschinsky, Dorothea, 26, 32, 35

Palladius, 78
Paul, 22–23, 94
Paul, Epistle of, 7
Perambulation of Kent, 162
Perrot, John, 163–64
personification in *Piers Plowman* tradition, 11, 13, 20
pests and parasites, 37
Philargyrie of Greate Britayne (Crowley), 9, 11, 18, 20, 92, 93, 100, 101, 116–29, 176
Philippine-American War, 173, 175
Pierce the Ploughman's Crede, 9, 19–20, 47, 48–67, 80, 103, 161, 172, 176, 195n1
Piers Plowman (Langland)
  Crowley and, 116, 135
  as focus, 1
  Pierce the Ploughman's Crede as addendum to, 50
  Pierce the Ploughman's Crede compared to, 64
  plowing of the half acre in, 8–9, 10, 18, 23–24, 33–47, 116, 174–76
  Roosevelt on, 173–76
  Skelton and, 100, 195n1
  surviving versions of, 8
Piers Plowman tradition
  establishment of, 9–10
  overview of, 6–13, 48
  personification and prophecy in, 11–13
  See also individual authors and texts
Piers Plowman Tradition, The (Barr), 10
Pineas, Rainer, 113
plague pandemic, 1, 26
plowing of the half acre, 8–9, 10, 18, 23–24, 33–47, 116, 174–75, 176
Plowman's Tale (Chaucer), 200n42
Pluymers, Keith, 136, 156, 160
poachers, 183n29
poetry
  role of, 47
  vatic power of, 141
political counsel, effective, 86–87
political ecology, use of term, 3
power-knowledge relations, 195n30
primitive accumulation, 4–5, 20, 93–100, 135–36, 155
prophets/prophecy, 11–12, 45–46
purgatory, doctrine of, 112–13

Quilligan, Maureen, 143

rack-renting, 127
Raleigh, Walter, 146, 147, 150, 163
Rastell, John, 17–18, 114, 130–33, 172–73
Rede Me and Be Nott Wroth (Barlowe and Roye), 92, 109–12, 116
reeve, Piers and, 33–35
regimentation, 161
Richard II, 68, 69
Richard the Redeless, 68
Roberts, James, 102
Robinson, Cedric, 17
Robinson, Marilynne, 172, 176
Rogers, Owen, 8, 50
Roman church, 114–15
Roosevelt, Theodore, 173–76
Roye, William, 92–93, 108–12, 116, 129, 159
Rules (Grosseteste), 25–26
rural depopulation, 99, 111, 143–44, 145
Ryce, Enid Baxter, 173

Salvage Man, 137–38, 142
Scanlon, Larry, 117
Scase, Wendy, 182n28
Scattergood, John, 65, 102, 195n1
Schott, John, 109
Scots, 162
Scythians, 162
Seneschaucy, 13–14, 23, 25–28, 30–31, 34, 37
septency, 163–64
Serena, 137–38
Shepheardes Calender, The (Spenser), 9, 10, 134, 136
Skelton, John, 9–11, 18, 20, 91–93, 100–109, 113, 129–31, 134–35. *See also* individual works of
slavery, 143
Smyth, William, 136
Sobecki, Sebastian, 8
social metabolism, 55
Society of Antiquaries, 162–63
Society of the Sons of the American Revolution, 173
sovereignty
  Bataille on, 71
  control and, 89
  Foucault's approach to, 4, 5–6
  husbandry and, 81
  in *Mum and the Sothsegger*, 87–88
  See also kings/kingship

Spanish-American War, 173, 175
Specht, Henrik, 194n16
speculum principium genre, 73, 193n6
Speke Parott (Skelton), 101
Spenser, Edmund
   Churchyard and, 9
   Colin Clout and, 130, 134–36
   Colin Clouts Come Home Againe, 20, 134, 135, 140, 146–54
   The Faerie Queene, 10–11, 20, 134–47, 150, 154
   as focus, 1
   influences on, 10–11
   Ireland and, 133–36, 138–39
   Munster plantation and, 17
   Piers Plowman tradition and, 170–77
   Piers Plowman version read by, 8
   Skelton and, 92
   A View of the Present State of Ireland, 17, 20–21, 111, 137–38, 140–41, 144, 148–49, 151–69, 173
Staley, Lynn, 78, 194n22, 200–201n59
standardization, 96
Statute of Laborers (1349), 5
Statute of Westminster II (1285), 14, 26, 32, 96
Steel, Karl, 193–94n10
stewards, role of, 27–28
"Summoner's Prologue, The" (Chaucer), 63, 65
Supplicacyon for the Beggars, A (Fish), 92, 112–16, 174, 176
Surveying (Fitzherbert), 13–15, 20, 91, 93–96, 158
Sutherland, Keston, 172, 176
systematic colonization, 155
Szittya, Penn, 48–49

tanistry, 163–64
taxes/taxation, 52
Thessalonians, 7, 22–23, 80, 94
three-estates model, 38, 40
trade, controversies over, 117, 124
Travayled Pylgrime (Batman), 11
trespass trial, 13
Trevisa, John, 84
"Trouble with Wilderness, The" (Cronon), 175
Truth, 8, 23–24, 33–35, 39–40, 42–43, 46, 81, 118, 128
Tyndale, William, 109

Utopia (More), 172

van Es, Bart, 207n15
vassalage, 158
Vastator (Waster), 46
vates/vatic poets, 101, 102, 108, 146
View of the Present State of Ireland, A (Spenser), 17, 20–21, 111, 137–38, 140–41, 144, 148–49, 151–69, 173
Vocabularium saxonicum (Nowell), 162
von Nolcken, Christina, 50, 190–91n2

Wakefield, E. G., 155
Wallerstein, Immanuel, 98
Walter of Henley, 13–15, 18, 23, 25–27, 29–31, 34–35, 42, 91, 100
wandering mendicants, 55. *See also* antifraternalism
wandering narrators, 47
wandering social critic, 28
Warley, Christopher, 119
waste, 26, 31–33, 37, 51–53, 80–81, 104–5, 109, 188n21. *See also* consumption
Waster, 46, 116, 166
Wastour, 8, 23, 39–41, 45, 61, 81
Wawn, Andrew, 89
wealth creation/expropriation, 118–27, 136
Weiskott, Eric, 100
Werlin, Julianne, 181n12
White, Helen, 171, 172
white supremacists groups, 175
Why Come Ye Nat to Courte? (Skelton), 101
William of Saint-Amour, 194n25
William the Conqueror, 95
Wolfe, Reyner, 50
Wolsey, Cardinal, 100–101, 104–6, 109, 113
women, role of, 35–36
world systems theory, 98
writing, function of, 47
Wycliffite writing, 49, 50
Wynnere and Wastoure, 12–13, 177, 195n1

Yeager, Stephen, 77

Zurcher, Andrew, 137, 150

www.ingramcontent.com/pod-product-compliance
Lightning Source LLC
Chambersburg PA
CBHW030646230426
43665CB00011B/975